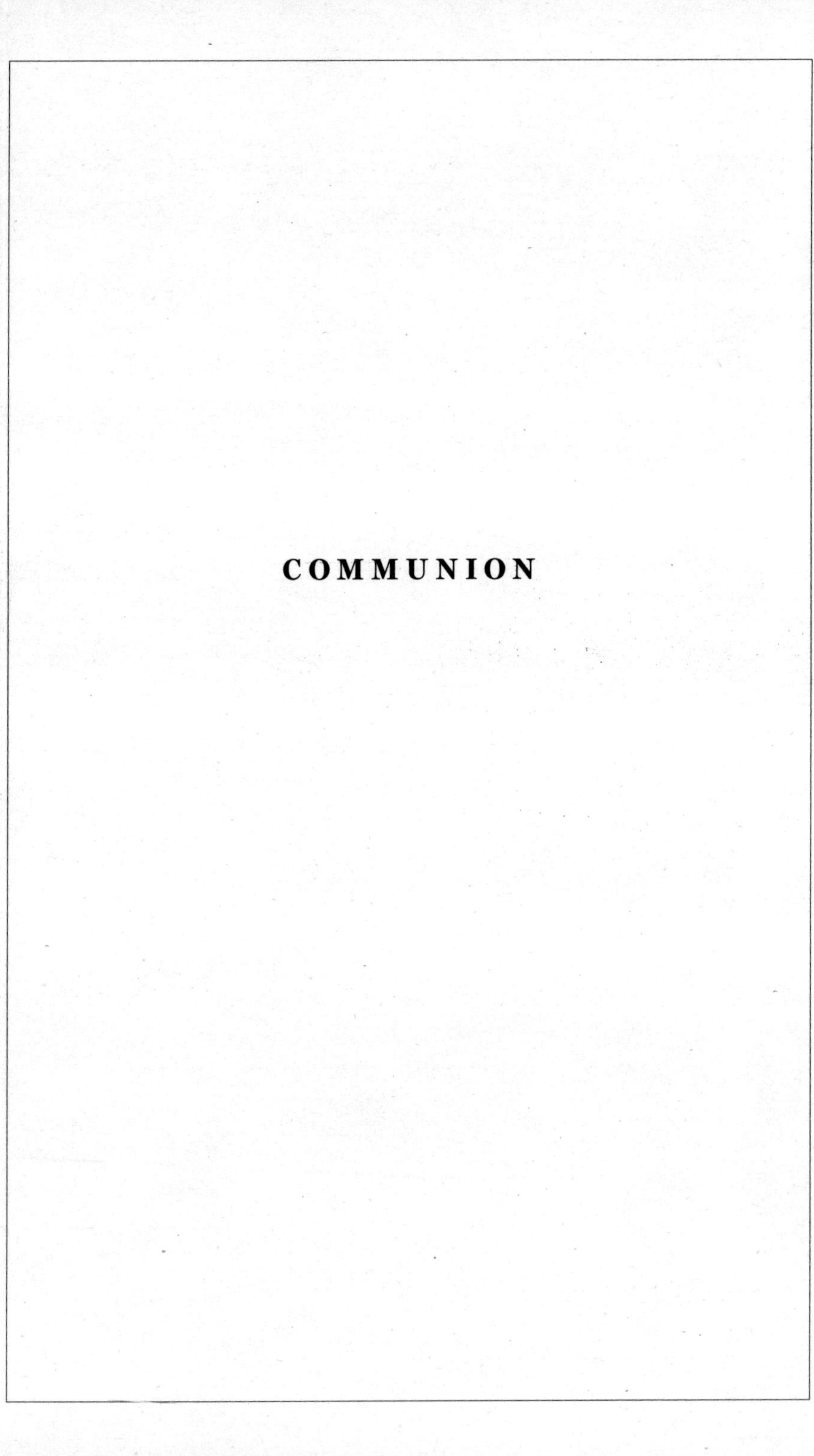

COMMUNION

ALSO BY JD VANCE

Hillbilly Elegy

COMMUNION

Finding
My Way
Back to Faith

JD VANCE

William Collins
An imprint of HarperCollins*Publishers*
1 London Bridge Street
London SE1 9GF

WilliamCollinsBooks.com

HarperCollins*Publishers*
Macken House, 39/40 Mayor Street Upper
Dublin 1, D01 C9W8

First published in Great Britain in 2026 by William Collins
First published in the United States by Harper in 2026

1

A catalogue record for this book is
available from the British Library

HB ISBN 978-0-00-884663-3
TPB ISBN 978-0-00-884664-0

All scripture quotations, unless otherwise indicated, are taken from
the King James Version, used under public domain.

The names and identifying details of some of the individuals
mentioned in this book have been changed to protect their privacy.

Set in Adobe Caslon Pro
Printed and bound in the UK using 100%
renewable electricity at CPI Group (UK) Ltd

For my darling Usha,

who taught me to think on those things

that are honest, just, pure, and lovely.

CONTENTS

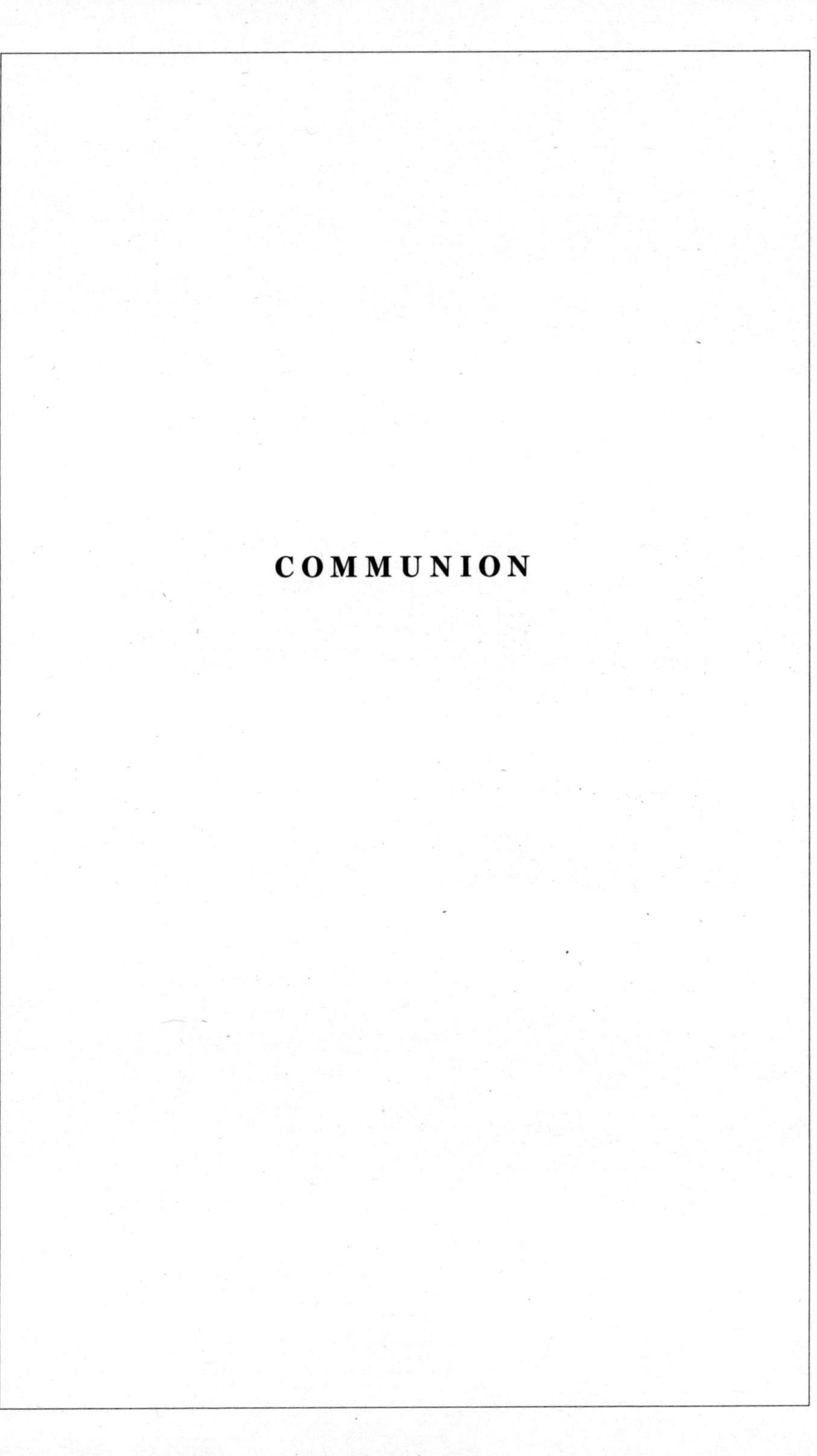

COMMUNION

INTRODUCTION

True Witness

I take my kids to church every week—well, usually. Sometimes less, sometimes more. While I hope that they will one day come to appreciate this family ritual, they are still at an age—nine, six, and four, respectively—where they complain. Bitterly. About half the time these days, we attend Mass at home, in the three-story historic mansion where we are living during my term as vice president. But on the Sundays we leave the house, it's sheer chaos: Ewan unable to find his shoes, Vivek yelling, "Why do we even have to go to church?" and Mirabel demanding that we delay departure until after she's had her second breakfast. In this, as in all things, Usha is the anchor, managing the mayhem and packing our kids off to the car. She gives me a look as if to say, *I'm not even Catholic, I just do this because I love you.* Sometimes we arrive late, trailed by an army of Secret Service agents, and heads turn away from the service to stare at us. I quietly apologize, wondering if the other parishioners can tell that we didn't brush our daughter's hair.

Still, this is one of my favorite family rituals. Although the kids do wriggle, talk, and occasionally punch each other in the pews, I treasure the more reverent moments: Mirabel passing out couch pillows to spare our knees while we kneel (when we celebrate Mass at home); Vivek clasping his hands angelically as we pray for peace or for those afflicted by disease; Ewan bowing his head and reciting the Lord's Prayer: "Our Father, who art in heaven, hallowed be thy name. . . ."

An uncomfortable reality for any devout Christian is that so many people raised in the faith later fall away from it. As a father, I am acutely aware that my kids may cast religion away as adults. So many Christians I know are substantially less devout than their parents. Some no longer even call themselves Christians. In fact, that was once true of me.

There is much to say about this. But there's another story I want to tell, too: how a guy like me, who was raised Christian but considered himself an atheist for a time, came back to the faith.

We are all searching for something in our lives. We search for truth. For meaning. For a job that gives us a sense of purpose. For prestige or status. For enough money to support a comfortable life—or sometimes, for too much money.

In my case, one of the vices that animated me—looking back, probably since the earliest days of my life—was the arrogant desire to rise above others. In college I was obsessed with the question of social mobility. What were the odds that a person born in the bottom fifth of the income distribution would rise to the top fifth, or even to the middle? This question lay at the heart of the American Dream: Do poor kids have a chance of making it in our country? But it was also very personal for me: I was a poor kid, and I was desperate to make it.

Well, now I have. I am the Vice President of the United States, among the youngest in history to hold the office. I made money in venture capital. I give my children everything I didn't have and more. They want for nothing. They have every advantage. Yet, as I progressed through life, winning every prize society told me to win, I began to feel that, as an adult, I had lost something important that had, for all my outward disadvantages, enriched me as a kid.

A single phrase kept returning to my mind: *By their fruits ye shall know them.* It comes from a parable from Jesus recounted in Matthew 7:16–20:

> Ye shall know them by their fruits. Do men gather grapes of thorns, or figs of thistles? Even so every good tree bringeth forth good fruit; but a corrupt tree bringeth forth evil fruit. A good tree cannot bring forth evil fruit, neither can a corrupt tree bring forth good fruit. Every tree that bringeth not forth good fruit is hewn down, and cast into the fire. Wherefore by their fruits ye shall know them.

What I saw around me, and what started my journey back to my faith, was that Christianity bore the best fruit. It was the set of ideas and practices that generated the most good, the most truth, and the most beauty of anything I'd encountered. Nothing else came close.

I don't mean to undervalue the core of the Christian faith, that Jesus Christ is the only begotten son of God, was born of the Virgin Mary, was crucified for our sins, and rose from the dead. And along my own faith journey, I also came to realize that salvation is impossible if man fails to reconcile himself to, and find peace with, God. In 2024, I gave an interview on this topic and got some pushback from fellow Christians for talking too little about Jesus. Here's what I said:

> Look, I think there were a couple of things that really appealed about [Christianity] to me. . . . I was thinking about the big questions. . . . And when I started to think about the big things, like, what do I actually care about in my life? I really want to be a good husband. I really want to be a good father. I really want to be a good member of the community. I wanted to be a virtuous human being, in other words. That was sort of the thing that I kept on coming back to was how to be virtuous. And I thought the Christianity that I had discarded as a young man answered the questions about being a virtuous person better than the logic of the American meritocracy.[1]

My critics were half right; there are undoubtedly better answers out there. But the truth is the truth. I eventually came to believe that Jesus Christ is in fact the only begotten son of God, but that's not where I started. I didn't meet Jesus on my way to Damascus. I didn't see Him cure a blind man. But I did witness faint echoes of His teachings refracted in the world around me. I saw my dad and stepmom welcoming drug addicts into their home to detox when local hospitals had turned them away. I saw grandmothers taking

1 Lulu Garcia-Navarro, "The Interview: A Conversation with JD Vance," *New York Times Magazine*, October 12, 2024, https://www.nytimes.com/2024/10/12/magazine/jd-vance-interview.html.

care of their grandkids with divinely inspired patience. I saw normal people who—unconcerned with whether they'd ever be rich or powerful—were more content and less restless than friends in my Ivy League circles. I looked into my son's big brown eyes and realized he didn't need me to be rich or powerful, he just needed me to be a good dad.

In becoming a husband and a father, my world simultaneously narrowed and expanded. I began to think about virtue and vice and sin without having the vocabulary to understand them. And I began to see that the fruits I had reaped since discarding my faith were rotten. I had become, without realizing it, a striver—so focused on winning the game of life that I had neglected the deeper truths. Despite the material comforts of the life I'd built, my own shortcomings—my own sins—weighed on me as never before. It was a surprise in some respects, but it shouldn't have been. Across my life, it was often the people of faith—the people I had once derided as simpletons—who seemed to have their act together. They weren't chasing credentials. They didn't care which college anyone went to. But they had something I didn't. Their trees were bearing much better fruit.

Around this time, a friend who happened to be a priest wrote me a thoughtful email in which he shared the idea of a true witness:

> Maybe you find the idea of a dead man rising from the dead insane, but consider this: If you believe the church's teachings on virtue and sin, if you think Christians—however imperfectly—are on the right path, if you think the moral teachings of Jesus are both profound and true, then consider that all of these people are right about the

> divinity of Christ. The church doesn't ask you to accept everything uncritically—it will accept faith the size of a mustard seed—but you must consider that a true witness won't lead you astray.

This book is, in the end, not a work of Christian apologetics. I know that many won't find my witness sufficient to guide their own paths to faith. I missed or misunderstood signs from God along my way, and there are many reasons to become a Christian that I won't cover.

Instead, this is one man's story. No more, no less. But I do hope that if you're interested in Christianity, my search for a relevant faith will hold some value.

The story of how I regained my faith, of course, only happened because I had lost it to begin with. The interesting question that hangs over this book, and over my mind, is why I ever strayed from the path. Why the Christian faith of my youth failed to properly take root. I'm glad I found my way back to the Church. I learned much along the way. But if you believe as I do, you know I've been fortunate and touched by God's grace. Many people like me, once lost, never return. This is what worries me and so many other Christians, and it's why I will spend so much time on what led me to discard my faith.

I'm not a particularly sectarian person, and this is not a particularly sectarian book. As I'll describe later, I chose to become Catholic for what I believe are good reasons. But I'm not sure I would have ever found my way back to God without the spiritual foundation I developed in a variety of Protestant churches growing up. To this day, I'm grateful for those roots and for the ferocious love of God I saw and continue to see from countless evangelical friends and family members. Some of the most rewarding conversations I've had about faith have been across denominational lines, and that tradition of Christian ecumenism is part of what makes our nation so great.

More broadly, I have an open spirit about specific questions of doctrine and faith. For example, some Protestant friends really don't like the Catholic practice of praying to saints. They're fine with asking a living person to say a prayer—"Please pray for my mother, she's sick and needs all the help she can get"—but they draw the line at consulting dead people—"Holy Mary, Mother of God, pray for us sinners, now and at the hour of our death."

Fair enough. Maybe they're right. I think they're wrong. But I'm not here to settle this argument.

Likewise, some Catholics feel that the Reformation weakened Christianity. I do think it's a tragedy that the Christian Church is so divided in modern times. But one of the mysteries of our faith is that God works on His time, not ours. You can believe God will unify His children when the time is right, and we know not the day nor the hour.

I hope that there are things each group of Christians can learn from the other. One of the things I admire about my own church is that fundamental questions of doctrine change very rarely, and then only after a long and arduous process involving many ecclesiastical authorities. This makes Catholicism feel more stable, which appeals to a number of young converts I've spoken to who are overwhelmed by the chaos of modern life and who crave a deeper sense of communion with others—but also with the traditions of their faith.

By the same token, I've never felt more welcomed in my life than

I did when I walked into a Southern Baptist or Pentecostal church as a kid. I have encouraged priests I know to go to an evangelical service to see what I mean. Besides the amazing music, I promise you'll find people who invite you to coffee or to their house for a meal, or encourage you to come back next Sunday. Evangelicals are extraordinarily good at fostering the kind of community that sustains believers.

For me—and for all of us Christians—it's about Jesus. If you believe Jesus is the son of God and rose from the dead on the third day, you're on the right track.

To summarize this book: I'm a Christian, and I became a Christian because I believe that Jesus Christ's teachings are true. But I didn't always think that, and by sharing my journey I might be helpful to others—Catholic, Protestant, or otherwise—who are seeking reconciliation with God.

I hope and pray that I'm right. With a spirit of humility, I ask that you pin the shortcomings of this book on the man who wrote it, not the faith that inspired it.

CHAPTER 1

What's the Matter with JD Vance?

Some years ago, I was driving through rural Indiana with a teenaged family friend, Wesley, when he shared that his mom had recently tried to commit suicide. Or at least that's what he feared had happened. He wondered whether she had *actually meant* to finish the deed.

"I don't even think you can overdose on that kind of drug," he said, more to himself than to me.

I knew, from personal experience, exactly the type of internal deliberation he was having—the hope that someone he loved wasn't so sick that she had tried to end her life versus the unsettling suspicion that she was. It is impossible in those moments to separate fact from feeling, to accept reality when that reality strikes at the heart of your life.

Our conversation eventually turned to God and religion. Wesley, like me and so many of his generation, had grown up in a church with few institutional roots. His pastor was articulate and caring, and the services had a certain evangelical thrill: modern music, thunderous sermons, and the occasional speaking in tongues. His church had no formal affiliation with any defined theology, proudly declaring itself "nondenominational." It was entirely the creation of its pastor. By the time Wesley hit adolescence, its superficial appeal had waned. Church became a chore, something he attended only when other people made him. And now, at this moment of personal crisis, as he grasped for meaning and understanding, he found nothing useful in the faith he'd grown up around.

"My grandma tells me that this is all part of God's plan and that He'll take care of everything," he said sarcastically. "And when I tell her that God hasn't done anything, that if He could fix everything, why put us in this mess in the first place, she doesn't have a good answer. 'Humans mess things up, and God makes them right again,' she says. I'm sorry, that's the stupidest thing I've ever heard. I get that bad things happen to everyone, I'm fine with that. But the idea that God never messes anything up, that humans mess things up and then He comes in and fixes them, doesn't make any sense."

As Wesley talked, I heard echoes of my own deliberations over God when I was about his age. He was dealing with pain and sorrow, and he had no patience for the idea that God had nothing to do with his hardships. To pin everything on humans was a cop-out.

He then said something that might have come from my own mouth back then: "I still believe in God," Wesley told me. "But I just don't think He has any relevance to my life right now."

I felt compelled to respond. Yet every thought that came into my head seemed inadequate, and I worried that yet another trite reassurance from an adult would merely confirm Wesley's worst suspicions about his faith.

So I kept my mouth shut.

* * *

My own crisis of faith began, ironically enough, with the death of the woman whose life had taught me the most about Christian love and virtue. My Mamaw loved Jesus. She read the Bible every day. She scribbled daily prayers—often requests that God see her family through crisis—on napkins and stored them near her bedside. Whenever I screwed up in school or mistreated my sister, Lindsay, she reminded me that the Lord demanded better of me. But Mamaw hardly fit the stereotype of a sweater-knitting, kindly old grandmother, and her faith wasn't always, well, perfectly consistent with her own religious upbringing. She loved to say the f-word, and when she died she owned nineteen loaded handguns. Mamaw's God suited her: loving and forgiving, but tough, demanding, and possibly packing.

Thanks to the chaos of my home and my parents' absenteeism, I spent much of my childhood with Mamaw. We spoke often about theology. Our conversations escalated in complexity and sophistication as I grew, but she willingly engaged me even when I was very young. When I was about seven, after my great-uncle's funeral, I asked Mamaw about the concept of a soul and how a person could possibly go to heaven when his lifeless body was trapped underground in a coffin. After some back-and-forth, I settled on an analogy that betrayed our mutual love of firearms.

"So the soul is like the bullet, and the body is like the casing? And God shoots off the bullet to heaven but the casing gets trapped here on earth?" I asked.

She considered the question for a bit, not wanting to lead me astray. "Well, goddamnit, I guess it is like that."

Mamaw was many things, but she was not especially patient. Yet when I asked about the Lord, she had all the time in the world.

Our family attended church very rarely. Our faith was amorphous, tied to family and oral traditions and not to institutional orthodoxy. Mamaw loved Billy Graham but hated most other televangelists, whom she saw as little more than faith profiteers. Yet we watched their broadcasts regularly. She had special contempt for the faith healers, who allegedly cured their congregants with a kiss or a touch or even a hard exhale. One in particular—a man named Benny Hinn—would wave his hand flamboyantly, often making a guttural noise or screaming, and entire rows of his followers would fall over as if they'd been hit by an especially potent dose of the Holy Spirit.

We'd watch this in amazement, me wondering whether it was real and Mamaw wondering how the hell anyone fell for it. "They're all crazy," she'd say, a little stunned by the spectacle. "And he's an effing crook."

Mamaw had good instincts. We'd later learn that Hinn had made millions off his followers, despite scant evidence of healing caused by his intercession. One woman, for instance, was so certain that he had cured her lung cancer that she ceased visiting her oncologist. She later succumbed to her illness. (Interestingly, Hinn recanted some of his teachings years later.)

Occasionally, when Mom decided we needed to "get religion," we'd find ourselves at church. Or sometimes I was the catalyst: I had internalized Mamaw's religious teaching, but I hungered for something a little more communal than watching people on TV or discussing the Bible through ballistics analogies.

Mamaw rarely joined me. "I'm too old and sick," she'd protest.

But she seemed to enjoy herself when she did go. She really liked one pastor in particular, an older man who had recently started a church not far from our house in Middletown, Ohio. Mamaw thought he was a good man, and she rarely missed the mark on character judgments. But we only went a few times, and the pews were mostly empty.

When I was growing up, the churches we attended seemed closely aligned with the Republican Party's social conservatism. I heard a fair amount about the evils of abortion and homosexuality. President Bill Clinton's extramarital conduct hadn't yet reached crisis proportions, but his rumored moral failings concerned us. We shared the sense that the country had become less moral, or at least less ashamed. "Kennedy was a man whore," my grandmother told me. "But at least he didn't flaunt it like modern politicians do."

This was my first introduction to the fusion between Republican politics and the Christianity of my youth, a trend long in the making. Scholars differ on how this relationship became such an important part of American society. In the 1970s, a war broke out in the Southern Baptist Convention—the country's largest Protestant denomination—between theological moderates and conservatives. The conservatives eventually gained the upper hand, forcing the moderates from major positions of leadership. Around the same time, conservative evangelicals of all stripes explicitly changed their approach to politics and formed movements like Jerry Falwell's Moral Majority to actively infuse Christian beliefs into politics. In the Reagan years of my early childhood and beyond, leaders like Falwell and James Dobson came to define the religious right, pulling social conservatism into the center of national life and driving a generational realignment in our politics.

Yet most of what I encountered at church during these years had a decidedly apolitical flavor. In 2024, nearly 90 percent of weekly churchgoing white evangelicals voted for Donald J. Trump over Kamala Harris.[1] The congregations of my youth were far more politically diverse.

During one Sunday school class—at Miltonville Baptist Church, which my mother and I briefly joined—we analyzed part of the Book of Exodus, which narrates the plight of Hebrew slaves in Egypt. When Pharaoh threatens to murder the Hebrew children, God instead takes the lives of Egypt's firstborn sons. The lesson—and the lively debate that followed—centered on the defensibility of God's conduct. Eventually, our teacher settled the matter (at least for himself) by telling us that the dead Egyptian children had surely gone immediately to heaven.

Another week, the sermon discussed different versions of the Bible and why good Christians ought to stick with the King James Version—not the watered-down New King James Version or the much-loathed New International Version. I never quite

1 Public Religion Research Institute, "Analyzing the 2024 Presidential Vote: PRRI's Post-Election Survey," December 13, 2024, https://prri.org/research/analyzing-the-2024-presidential-vote-prris-post-election-survey.

understood why our church found these more modern versions wanting.

Over the years, we spent some time in a "nondenominational" church. We spent some time in a Pentecostal church. And we spent most of our time in different Baptist churches—generally affiliated with the Southern Baptist Convention. All the churches we attended fit broadly within the conservative Protestant tradition. I didn't know then about the various theological differences between these churches. Nor did I know of the host of mainline Protestant denominations whose teachings aligned more closely with the American Left than the Right. I knew Catholics existed, mostly because my aunt—Mom's sister—had married one. But I didn't appreciate that anything besides worship style distinguished one church from another. Different denominations seemed generally to believe the same things, but the Catholics kneeled more and the Pentecostals had better music.

Though I lived with Mamaw for much of my youth, and consequently spent long stretches back in Eastern Kentucky with her, I rarely saw the inside of a church there. Sometimes Mamaw's younger sister Rose took me to her church, but Mamaw never went. Even the full gospel church she had attended as a child—which stood just a few steps from her childhood home—she now refused to enter. But it wasn't because she felt it was corrupt or too obsessed with money, like the televangelists she loathed. "I think the man who runs it now is a pervert," she told me.

I hadn't quite picked up on the fact that Mamaw's views deviated from the teachings of the churches we occasionally attended. When she disagreed with a pastor or congregant at one of these churches, it usually rested on some difference in emphasis or tone.

Mamaw thought the theory of evolution was bogus because it contradicted the most literal reading of Genesis, but she didn't mind that people disagreed with her. Unlike most Christians I knew, Mamaw believed that abortion was an individual moral matter and should remain legal. She felt that the government had no business involving itself in such a personal decision.

"I don't care much for drinking, either," she'd tell me when I pushed back. "But I don't think it ought to be illegal."

Her views rested on a type of pragmatic social libertarianism, not on theological or moral grounds.

Mamaw seemed much more interested in questions of personal morality than in church attendance. To her, God was deeply concerned with my individual conduct. To slack off at school was to squander my God-given abilities. To mistreat my sister was a failure of both family loyalty and Christian duty.

She walked me through her thoughts as the people she loved struggled with alcohol and gambling addictions. The Book of Numbers says that God punishes children for the sins of the fathers. Our pastors often treated this as an abstract concept about the nature of cosmic punishment and divine justice. For Mamaw, the passage had much more immediate implications: Drunks and cheats didn't just ruin their own lives, they corrupted their families. She had seen this in her community, her neighborhood, and her own family.

Mamaw's husband, my Papaw, had much less influence on how I thought about God. I can't recall him ever mentioning his faith. When I took it upon myself at age eleven to read the Bible cover to cover, he congratulated me. It was a largely unintelligible exercise for a child with little formal religious training—much of the Old

Testament simply recites genealogy—and I couldn't tell whether his pride owed more to my perseverance or to his own religious sentiment.

Shortly before Papaw died, Mom welcomed my biological father back into my life. Her timing was perfect, as Papaw had been my only real male role model up to that point. I hadn't spent much time with my dad before then, but his religious faith figured prominently in my imagination. I knew he was a "Holy Roller," as Mamaw said, which I took to mean that his church resembled what we saw on TV. But I knew little else about his faith, or about the man himself, for that matter.

I soon learned that despite the awful things I'd heard about him, my dad was more complex than Mom and Mamaw gave him credit for. He was a man of deep faith, attending church at least once per week with his wife and my stepsiblings. He worked hard in construction. He swore that he had never wanted to abandon me but was forced to by our family dynamics. Years of separation complicated our new relationship, but I wanted to know my father and he felt the same way about me, so we began to spend more time together.

With Dad, I had a home church for the first time. I saw him mostly on the weekends, so we spent Sundays together at his church. The rocking music and charismatic displays never matched my style, but I devoured every word from the articulate pastor. I sometimes felt as if I was the only congregant to appreciate the sermons more than the music.

Dad's church offered something I had sorely missed: a real community of believers. When Dad fell on hard times and needed a car, his church collected money to buy him a used van. Mamaw may not have loved everything about my new church, but she seemed to appreciate that it offered something I needed. Instead of asking her my questions, I now had trained pastors to field them.

I learned many good things. I learned that God loved us, that He demanded our best but would forgive our worst. I learned that community was important, both in how we worshiped the divine and in how we supported one another here on earth. And many of the church's best teachings were implicit. It was in Dad's church, for example, where I first saw black and white and brown people worshiping together, all genuinely part of the same faith community.

In Dad's church, religious and political conservatism were more explicitly linked. It was the late 1990s, and President Clinton's scandals and trials had barely dented his popularity. Yet the church's pastor advised against voting for Democrats. Their liberal views on abortion and other social issues remained a third rail, no matter how good the stock market might be.

As politically oriented as Dad's church could be, the politics were complicated in ways that didn't fit the prevailing sociological narrative: that the heartland's predominantly religious middle and working classes voted against their economic interests by sharing a political coalition with the wealthy. This was the thesis of the popular book *What's the Matter with Kansas?*. The reality I encountered on the ground was a little more complex.

For starters, the congregation at Dad's church understood they had a Christian obligation to serve the poor, and they took it to heart. It was the church that put on Christmas toy drives and hosted weekly soup kitchens. For all my later questions and doubts about my faith, I rarely encountered people who didn't care deeply about Christian charity.

Besides that, the Christians I encountered were self-aware about the limits of politics and the complexities of their own coalition. They weren't as distracted by social issues as they were aware that social issues—and liberals' unwillingness to budge on them—forced an uneasy compromise.

Importantly, they recognized that they had landed in a political coalition that didn't always share their interests or values. My stepmother hadn't voted for a Democrat in years, but when I asked her about her politics at breakfast one day, she was clear-eyed: "Republicans don't care about working people, it's that simple. Like my dad always said"—her father was a longtime union man—"Republicans are for the rich. But if you give me a choice between a party that stands for the rich and a party that refuses to stand for the unborn, I know my choice." Her complaints about Republicans echoed Mamaw's, who addressed the tension by simply refusing to vote at all.

I heard similar sentiments whenever I asked others about politics. Most voted against Democrats but had no illusions about their own party.

Over time, however, these coalitions started to unravel. I didn't realize it at the time, but I was starting to witness the beginning of a fissure in the Republican Party: between its business elites and its religious rank and file. This fissure would, decades later, manifest itself powerfully in our politics—and in a roundabout way, eventually lead to my election as vice president.

In the mid-1990s, a wave of prophetic theory was sweeping through American evangelical churches. Tim LaHaye and Jerry B. Jenkins's blockbuster *Left Behind* books told the story of an impending apocalypse and were wildly popular in Dad's church. One old woman told me that I had handsome eyes, which might earn me a beautiful wife if the Lord didn't come before I was old enough to marry.

A family member purchased the popular televangelist John Hagee's *Prophecy Study Bible*, which fused Hagee's prophetic theory with relevant passages from the New King James Bible. I watched telecasts by Hagee and Hal Lindsey, another famous apocalypse theorist. I became convinced that the world would end in 2007, at the latest.

In Dad's church I also encountered a skepticism of modern science that was new to me. If I must believe, as a matter of faith, that God created the Earth six thousand years ago, then I couldn't believe that the universe was billions of years old, or that evolution had produced man in his modern form over hundreds of millions of years. Much of what I learned in science class was not just false, according to this way of thinking, but a direct assault on faith. Dad's church taught me that American culture was waging a war against our faith. The "War on Christmas"—from lawsuits against nativity displays to the familiar abbreviation *Xmas*—figured prominently in sermons and conversations. I once returned to Mamaw's house after a weekend with Dad and confidently informed her that it was offensive to replace *Christ* with an *X*. (Only years later did I learn that the *X* is in fact a stand-in for the Chi-Rho, an early symbol for Jesus, and that Christians have been abbreviating the name of the holiday as *Xmas* for well over a millennium.)

The Christian faith I'd developed by the time I was fifteen was adversarial: disengaged from mainstream culture, even terrified of it. I began to expect assaults on my faith, whether from teachers at school or from the books I read. When the first *Harry Potter* book was published right after my fourteenth birthday, it earned my fellow churchgoers' ire. We hadn't read it, but we were entirely convinced it contained real Satanic rituals and that its popularity was direct evidence of the devil's influence on our culture. I worried whether my own favorite books, the similarly fantastical *Lord of the Rings*, passed Christian muster, but there was enough debate among the congregation that I felt comfortable keeping my copies. I also liked classic rock, but I discarded my most offensive CDs (like Black Sabbath) and hid my Led Zeppelin albums.

During my high school years, I developed new political views. In my family, we had been blue-collar, union Democrats for as long as anyone could recall. We believed Republicans were the party of the rich. Yet I began to worry that the things Democrats had done to help us poor people weren't succeeding. Our neighbor received support from a variety of government programs, but she seemed unhappy and remained in dire circumstances. Like Mamaw, I wasn't ideologically opposed to government help; I just didn't think the help being offered was doing much good. Nor did I think conservatives had all the answers; I just thought their criticisms were fair. In that sense, my political affiliation was oppositional—based in criticism of what hadn't worked, not in a vision of what would.

Though my politics hadn't come from my religion, my religion did offer my politics a nice home. I graduated high school in 2003 and enlisted in the Marines. The Iraq War had just started, and George W. Bush was president, with sky-high approval ratings. Religious conservatives like me felt a certain triumphalism about politics. The *Left Behind* books reflected this moment, replacing an old, immoral fictional president with a new, pious one. Even in this fictional account of Armageddon, our affinity for a president who had once answered "Christ" as his favorite philosopher shone through.

When I left for boot camp, I felt entirely comfortable in my Christianity and my conservative politics, which seemed to meld together.

* * *

And yet: My life had not been easy. I had watched addiction ravage my family and nearly bankrupt my grandparents. I had experienced emotional and physical abuse at home. I had seen my mother arrested. I had lied to Child Services and the local courts to keep our family together. I had lost my beloved Papaw, the most important man in my life.

The future would bring much worse. It would bring more addiction and death. It would bring poverty and a sense of hopelessness. It would bring war and feelings of guilt that I was abandoning my family to fight for our country. It would bring intellectual and scientific challenges to the foundation of my faith. The faith I'd developed in Mamaw's house and my father's church was no match for these challenges. I wasn't prepared for them, and I did not have the spiritual and intellectual tools to negotiate them. The irony of my adversarial faith from that period is that I did, in the years to come, experience a spiritual war. But the battles weren't about bad politicians or modern science or children's books, they were about real people as their lives fell apart.

* * *

The first seeds of doubt appeared in 2005, as I prepared to leave for Iraq, where the war was taking a negative turn. Every time I spoke with Mamaw, I could hear her distress over my impending deployment. She had long been physically frail, but she had never been emotionally needy. And I sensed that the rest of my family felt the same way she did.

The past few years had been tough on us. Mamaw had protected me from the worst of my mom's addiction, but it was impossible to hide entirely. The same was true of Mamaw's deteriorating health and worsening financial situation. I had never felt rich as a child, but real poverty had hit us only briefly during my early years. That changed during high school, as Mamaw went from being my primary to my sole caregiver. And though, as a Marine, I was no longer a financial burden on her, I was certainly still an emotional one.

One day, Mamaw called to tell me that she couldn't afford her health care. She was an incredibly proud woman, so the fact that she had asked me for help meant she was truly desperate. I shouldn't have been surprised, of course. It was inevitable: Mamaw had barely enough money to support herself until she died. Having a teenage boy to clothe and feed had stressed her resources well past the breaking point, even with some help from other members of our family.

I was struck by the contrast between what was happening in our lives and the political issue that most animated church communities at that time: the fate of Terri Schiavo. Schiavo, a beautiful young woman, had survived a heart attack but sustained injuries that left her in a vegetative state. Her husband sought to remove her feeding tube, against her parents' wishes. Conservative Christians sprang into action to prevent the tube's removal. The case raised a host of moral and ethical issues that entangled even the president of the United States and the governor of Florida. Eventually, the feeding tube was pulled and Schiavo died.

I shared the view that we ought to err on the side of life in a case like Schiavo's. But, to my younger self, the passion behind the Schiavo fight, juxtaposed with the problems in my life, laid bare how the church I loved seemed to prioritize faraway controversies over the everyday needs of our community. As tragic as Schiavo's case was, it seemed like a genuinely freak occurrence in a world filled with overlooked tragedy. It felt to me like our pastors spoke in abstractions about family values, while glossing over the divorce and family instability that had wrecked my family and community. They worried about the unborn, but ignored the abuse, neglect, and struggles in homes like mine.

When I look back on this period, I feel ashamed at my lack of charity. The idea that faith leaders cared more about Terri Schiavo than about their congregants is absurd. Chalk it up to the petulance of youth. But emphasis matters, and the church's emphasis didn't speak to me in my moment of crisis.

I had been helping Mamaw with her bills for only a couple of months when my sister called to tell me Mamaw's lung had collapsed and that she was unresponsive. She died a week later, and after her funeral, I drove back to my Marine Corps base in North Carolina. The weight of the world seemed to bear down on me; my mind raced so quickly that I sat in silence throughout the ten-hour drive—no music, no phone calls, no nothing. Instead, I thought about things. About my mother, and whether she'd seek shelter from grief in addiction, as she'd done before. About my sister, and whether she'd survive that storm without Mamaw, our emotional rock, there to steady her. About my sister's three little kids, and whether the past she had worked so hard to shield them from might crash down upon them like a hurricane. About my aunt, now forced by circumstance to become the family matriarch that Mamaw had been.

I felt like I was leaving my family to fight a spiritual war without my help, and I knew that my departure for Iraq would compound the trauma of Mamaw's loss. I felt a strange combination of guilt over abandoning my family and fear of what lay ahead.

I told myself, *JD, you're not an infantryman. The odds that you'll be hurt are slim. Just go over there, do your job, make them proud, and then you can fix this when you come home.*

But as I drove, I still didn't really believe it.

* * *

I was on my way back to the base after the funeral, deep in the heart of Virginia's share of the Appalachian Mountains, when I came around a corner and lost control of my car. It had been raining lightly, and some combination of speed, slickness, and bad luck sent me hurtling toward a guardrail. If a car had been coming in the other direction, I'd have been dead. But my more immediate fear was that I would hit the guardrail and go tumbling over the side of the mountain.

I had no control and no expectation that I'd stop. *Maybe the guardrail will do its job*, I thought. But the speed was too great, and my most realistic hope in that instant was that I'd survive the fall over the mountain.

What happened next is the closest I've ever come to a supernatural experience.

I just stopped.

Right before hitting the guardrail, the car came to a complete, restful halt. Something stopped it—something beyond my comprehension or control. I didn't even feel the jerk of the seat belt. To this day, I have no way of explaining it.

I am suspicious of anyone who's had an experience that defies the laws of physics. And of course it's possible that those same laws explain what happened. Perhaps I wasn't going as fast as it felt in the moment. Maybe some freak gust of wind slowed my car. I don't know.

Regardless, I felt shaken. I had no idea what to make of it at the time, and I don't think I could tell you exactly what it means now. But what I can say is that even during my later years as a strident atheist, the experience sat there inconveniently in the back of my mind. It was as if it existed to annoy me, to challenge the confidence I had in the laws of the universe and the idea that I sat firmly—and alone—in life's driver's seat. To this day, every time I think of that moment and the way the car came to a rest, the hairs on the back of my neck stand up.

* * *

Back on base, Mamaw's death surfaced many issues that had nagged at me before but now seemed to overwhelm me. I remained a conservative Christian, with all the views on the social issues of the day that you'd expect. Yet the political issues that most animated the faithful were tangential to the problems in my community and family. Looking back, I wonder how much my feeling of disconnect came from the loss of my church community when I moved to North Carolina. I had TBN—the Trinity Broadcasting Network—but was otherwise all alone.

In July 2005, just months after Mamaw died, news came that we would deploy to Iraq sooner than expected, in early August. August 2, 2005, would be my twenty-first birthday, and my aunt had made plans for a family trip: a birthday excursion and a send-off. Whenever the thought of Mamaw's death had made me want to crawl into my bed and never leave, the promise of this trip had sustained me. I'd get to see my family, celebrate with them, and share some Mamaw stories before I left for Iraq. But now, because of the call to move up our deployment, it wouldn't happen.

I sat in my barracks room, alone, feeling for the first time in my life that I had nowhere to turn. I was afraid of what might happen in Iraq, but most of all, I felt guilty. Guilty that I was in North Carolina as my family figured out what to do with Mamaw's house. Guilty that Mom had once again descended into addiction without me there to help her. Guilty that my sister had to handle all of this alone. I didn't want to talk to my Marine Corps buddies about how I felt, not because they were bad guys, but because I simply didn't know how to bare my emotions to a group of relative strangers. I had only ever allowed myself to be vulnerable around one person—Mamaw—and now she was gone.

And where was the Church? Just before I left for Iraq, I attended a service at my sister's church. The sermon that Sunday focused on the end times and why every person present must be prepared for the Second Coming of Christ.

I sat there in a silent rage. I looked around at the churchgoers, happy families and elderly couples and children bored out of their minds.

Who are these people? I thought. Did they know any narcotics addicts? Did they labor under the crushing weight of loss and grief and worry? Had they, like me, ever abandoned their families during their time of greatest need?

I hated all of this—the complacency and the irrelevant sermons about the Rapture.

And when my sister asked her pastor to pray for me and my safety, I felt a lot of things: appreciation for his kindness, grief over leaving my family, admiration for my sister's compassion. But I didn't feel the presence of God.

I left for Iraq a few days later.

CHAPTER 2

Semper Why

By the time I landed in Iraq in August 2005, people at home had largely forgotten about Terri Schiavo. But I hadn't, and I continued to stew on it. It's hard to say precisely what about the news coverage of the story so bothered me. It seemed like, essentially, a family dispute. I was sympathetic to the moral worldview of the people who wanted to save her life. But, to my younger self, the grandstanding and media circus seemingly revealed a religious movement divorced from the day-to-day concerns of the faithful. I felt there was something a little off about obsessing over extraordinary circumstances when there was so much ordinary misery in the world.

People discard their faith for all kinds of reasons. Christopher Hitchens, in his atheist manifesto *God Is Not Great*, writes about his own journey away from Anglicanism:

> It was Mrs. Watts's task, when I was a boy of about nine and attending a school on the edge of Dartmoor, in southwestern England, to instruct me in lessons about nature, and also about scripture . . . Seeking ambitiously to fuse her two roles

> as nature instructor and Bible teacher, she said, "So you see, children, how powerful and generous God is. He has made all the trees and grass to be green, which is exactly the color that is most restful to our eyes. Imagine if instead, the vegetation was all purple, or orange, how awful that would be."
>
> And now behold what this pious old trout hath wrought. I liked Mrs. Watts: she was an affectionate and childless widow who had a friendly old sheepdog who really was named Rover, and she would invite us for sweets and treats after hours to her slightly ramshackle old house near the railway line . . .
>
> However, I was frankly appalled by what she said. My little ankle-strap sandals curled with embarrassment for her. At the age of nine I had not even a conception of the argument from design, or of Darwinian evolution as its rival, or of the relationship between photosynthesis and chlorophyll. The secrets of the genome were as hidden from me as they were, at that time, to everyone else. I had not then visited scenes of nature where almost everything was hideously indifferent or hostile to human life, if not life itself. I simply *knew*, almost as if I had privileged access to a higher authority, that my teacher had managed to get everything wrong in just two sentences. The eyes were adjusted to nature, and not the other way about.

Setting aside Hitchens's hilarious lack of humility—What nine-year-old curls his toes in embarrassment at a kindly instructor?—this is a common theme. A teacher makes a religious claim, its absurdity instantly obvious, and that sets a young mind on the path to rejecting faith.

I have one friend, raised Catholic, who realized that scientific reality seemed to conflict with the Church's teachings. Another friend with various Christian influences in his life couldn't accept the story of Holy Communion "becoming" the body and blood of Jesus Christ.

"So," he apparently asked his aunt, "if a patient in a hospital is dying and needs a blood transfusion, could you have a priest bless the wine, and then put that wine in his body, saving the patient?"

Frustrated with the question, his aunt refused to answer, and eventually my friend lost his faith.

This type of disproof is all over the internet. You can find countless posts on Reddit, for example, that smugly assert a lack of evidence for God's existence and mock the faithful by comparing them to toddlers.

In that telling, atheism is the reasoned conclusion of rational judgment. Believing in God is akin to believing in Santa Claus—something that no smart person does after becoming capable of rational thought. There's an implicit assumption that historical progress has made religious claims even less believable. Perhaps religious belief was defensible in the past, but now that we know so much about the universe and the physical world, we should trade faith in for something more modern and elegant, just as we've exchanged horses for cars in daily transport.

These arguments for nonbelief track well with the (largely false) story I would have told about myself in 2007, when I first started college. I claimed that my atheism was purely about the ideas. A college philosophy professor once asked me when I had become an atheist. I responded with a quip about how "usually people don't become atheists in foxholes, but I became an atheist in Iraq, the closest to a foxhole I've ever gotten."

We talked about the theory of evolution and how I'd been an advocate of Young Earth Creationism as a teenager before realizing the superiority of Darwinian theory. We discussed my realization in Iraq that there were Muslims—however small a proportion of them—who believed more stridently than any Christian I'd ever met, but who used their faith to motivate terrible acts of violence.

There was nothing false about these particulars—I really hadn't spoken at length to someone of a different faith until I went to Iraq, I really did doubt that the Earth had only existed for six thousand years—but this missed the most important fact. What paved my path to atheism wasn't books or ideas, it was sadness and a sense of betrayal.

Faith had meant something real to me. I had never cared about Santa Claus. "Screw Santa Claus," Mamaw once told me. "Your presents come from me." But when Mamaw told me that God loved me, I felt meaningfully altered by that fact. When I scribbled Bible verses on letters to my mother, I did so because I believed they contained wisdom directly from God Himself. When I prayed every night—for a better future, for stability, for a permanent address, for my family's happiness—I *knew* someone was listening. Yes, I obsessed over the concepts of Christianity—its ethical demands, the meanings of cryptic prophecies about the end times—but my faith was never just about ideas and intellect. The core of my faith was instead the rituals and emotions of religious practice.

When my great-grandmother lay on her deathbed, her friends and family gathered around and sang church hymns and gospel songs.

Amazing grace, how sweet the sound,
that saved a wretch, like me.
I once was lost, but now am found,
was blind, but now I see.

I still have the tape recordings. And I still can hear the voices of great-aunts and grandparents singing those songs to me as a child. Jesus Christ was very much alive in our minds. Christianity wasn't just a "belief" to us. It wasn't a judgment we arrived at after evaluating the evidence. It was a practice, a way of life. It connected us to our ancestors and our progeny. We listened to our grandparents tell the same stories they had once heard from theirs.

Losing my faith wasn't, consequently, a primarily intellectual act. It was the equivalent of divorce. I was severing myself from my roots as I understood them—from my family, the grandmother I'd just lost, the values I'd been taught. It meant thinking back on the time we sang to my great-grandmother on her deathbed and reframing that religious moment in secular terms—a nice gesture, perhaps, but nothing more.

It meant condescending to those who kept the faith—"Well, they just don't know any better"—or becoming actively hostile to "woo-woo" spirituality.

Why people like me ultimately lose their faith is a hard question to answer confidently. This is especially true given the nature of religious belief, where family pressure, emotional attachment, and rationality intersect in psychologically complicated ways. A

Pew report on people who had abandoned their church found that about half simply stopped believing, without much additional detail; another 20 percent disliked organized religion—an explanation that could cover everyone from my Mamaw to a full-blown atheist; and another 18 percent had retained their faith, or at least their spirituality, but merely stopped going to church.[1] Other surveys have found that young people didn't like their church's worship style or felt the sermons were irrelevant to their lives.[2]

Despite this plethora of justifications, a few broad themes emerge. The first is a simple reality: The share of religiously unaffiliated Americans has grown across my lifetime, and it continues to grow to this day. There are recent statistics about an encouraging uptick in young people, especially young men, attending church, but we American Christians still have our work cut out for us.

Second, the critical inflection point for most people appears to be when they leave the home—often for college.

Third, losing faith is usually a gradual process, even if it's not always characterized this way. One minister described her recognition that she was an atheist as a "eureka moment," despite working through her doubts over a decade-long period of self-reflection.[3]

1 Michael Lipka, "Why America's 'Nones' Left Religion Behind," Pew Research Center, August 24, 2016, https://www.pewresearch.org/fact-tank/2016/08/24/why-americas-nones-left-religion-behind.

2 Griffin Paul Jackson, "The Top Reasons Young People Drop Out of Church," *Christianity Today*, January 15, 2019, https://www.christianitytoday.com/news/2019/january/church-drop-out-college-young-adults-hiatus-lifeway-survey.html.

3 Barbara Bradley Hagerty, "From Minister to Atheist: A Story of Losing Faith," NPR, April 30, 2012, https://www.npr.org/2012/04/30/151681248/from-minister-to-atheist-a-story-of-losing-faith.

Whether people fall away through doubt, work demands, or something else, it usually doesn't happen instantly. As longtime pastor Ryan Bell told *The Christian Post* about losing his religion: "It wasn't that difficult. My beliefs had been shifting for many years. I started out as a very conservative Christian and ended as a very progressive Christian, albeit still in a conservative denomination. I sometimes say it was like whittling a stick—cutting away little bits, shaving off rough edges—and I kept at that project until one day I looked down and there was no stick left."[4]

Not long ago, I was speaking with a friend who described his own transition away from faith. He pointed to a series of common arguments: for example, that God, despite being all-powerful, had chosen to allow a lot of suffering in the world. And he posed an interesting paradox: If all babies go to heaven, why is abortion (or even infanticide) evil? That is, if you allow children to survive to the point where their free will allows them to reject God and the blessings of heaven, haven't you done them a terrible disservice?

I realized during our conversation that this is one reason (among many) that Christian thinkers reject this kind of utilitarian, seemingly logical cost-benefit analysis of salvation. Whether an action is good or bad isn't determined by outcome alone, but by the nature of the act and the intentions behind it. Even if aborted babies receive God's mercy in the end, that fact doesn't negate the tragedy of losing their earthly lives. So I don't think my friend's clever syllogism

4 Leonardo Blair, "Former Pastor Ryan Bell on Why He Abandoned His Christian Faith: I Gave It My Best Shot," *Christian Post*, October 27, 2019, https://www.christianpost.com/news/former-pastor-ryan-bell-on-why-he-abandoned-his-christian-faith-i-gave-it-my-best-shot.html.

defeats the tenets of my Christianity, but it did make me realize how deeply he had actually thought about these questions. He had not lost his faith out of laziness or carelessness. He cared a lot; he just couldn't get there.

"I actually really wanted to believe this stuff," he told me. "I spent a lot of time thinking about things, almost willing myself to think it was true. And I just couldn't do it."

His journey was more intellectual than mine. There was no major falling-out with the faith, no death, trauma, or crisis that started him on the road toward secularism. He slowly began to feel that the only reason he believed in God and the divinity of Jesus Christ was that he had been told to believe it. As he studied the matter himself, he couldn't quite bring himself to believe it was true.

It occurred to me that virtually everything we "know" is heavily mediated through some formal source of knowledge. My six-year-old son believes that crossing the street without my approval is dangerous and could injure him. He's right, of course, but he doesn't know this through independent research. He knows this because he trusts me. And though we may dismiss this as a necessary consequence of age and immaturity, the reality is that this is true for most of the things people know, whether they're three or ninety-three. Our knowledge comes from some source—a book, a newspaper story—that we actually trust and not from independent verification.

Consider most historical and scientific facts: the battles of the Revolutionary War and who won; water boiling at 212 degrees Fahrenheit. Most of the things we "know" are actually rooted in social trust in our education system. I have boiled water thousands of times in my life, but I'm not using the scientific method to check the physics behind the phenomenon. If you're being honest with yourself, most of the facts in your head are things you've never actually verified yourself. Even if you've read them in a book, why trust the author?

(Keep reading . . . there's a point here, I promise . . .)

We "know" most things, then, not through individual study or research, but because we trust what others tell us. There's obviously a critical mass component to this: Some facts, like who won the Battle of Saratoga, are so well accepted that there isn't really a serious reason to contest them.

But even there, it's not so simple. Spend five minutes in the darkest corners of the internet, and you'll find people who deny or downplay the Holocaust. Of course, very few of those Holocaust deniers have done any original research. Their beliefs, too, are twisted by their social networks rather than formed through independent verification.

The point is that no matter how well-read you are, how thoughtful you fancy yourself to be, most of the knowledge in your head is mediated by the people and institutions you trust.

This is especially true when the things about which you're expected to form an opinion are uncertain, or even impossible, to truly "know" in any meaningful sense. Religious beliefs are less like certainties such as the boiling point of water—which can be verified through testing—and more like claims about complex systems.

Take, for example, the following: An increase in the minimum wage would raise the standard of living for low-income people.

That sounds right, and most would agree with this view at first blush.

But it turns out that many economists think increasing the minimum wage could do more harm than good. Some argue that it would actually reduce the number of jobs available to low-income people. The point is: The complexity counsels some humility in the face of difficult questions. If even the people who devote their lives to studying these questions are unsure of the answers, then we should be honest with ourselves about how little we know. Of course, this doesn't excuse us from ignoring basic facts, but it does bear on forming opinions about unprovable or complex topics. It also means that the opinions we form are heavily contingent on which people and institutions we trust. This is true for complicated policy questions. It's true for how we respond to a global pandemic, where dozens of factors shape its transmission and effects. And it's true for the deepest questions about meaning and God.

To bring it back to my friend, and me, and so many of the people whose objections to faith rest on science: The issue wasn't really the incompatibility of my faith with scientific understanding. To believe, as I once claimed, that the theory of evolution disproved the Christian creation story, I had to accept a couple of things on, well, faith. I had to accept that the theory of evolution was true. And I had to believe that the Christian Bible was incompatible with evolution. I did believe these things, but I believed them because of whom I trusted. I trusted that the Christians in my orbit had instructed me well in the tenets of Christianity. And I trusted the many biologists, paleontologists, anthropologists, and geneticists I had read—almost all secular—in their views on evolution.

The problem then, for me (and many others), really isn't science and reason. It's trust—or its absence.

* * *

Many Christian thinkers are troubled by cases like mine. "Why," they wonder, "do our young people abandon the faith?"

I was hardly a perfect Christian, but I had invested in my evangelical faith. I had read the entire Bible twice and the New Testament multiple times. I had taken an early interest in apologetics from reading C. S. Lewis and contemporary defenders of the faith. My good friends included serious Christians who remained active in the Church.

The story I've heard from older Christians is that younger generations drift away from religion because of "brainwashing." They imagine that young Christians go off to college, where professors teach them to reject their faith. The college classroom is, in this telling, a type of hostile Socratic interrogation for students of faith: the cocky university professor, sporting a pipe and tweed jacket, beating down innocent Christians until they finally relent and give up their faith.

As influential conservative commentator Dennis Prager wrote in 2011, "The agenda of Western universities is to produce . . . secularists."[5]

But as Conor Friedersdorf noted in *The Atlantic*, the average professor spends at most a couple of classes with any given student, and college lectures are rarely anti-Christian screeds.[6] For that matter, why would any young Christian abandon their faith based on a few critical words from a professor?

5 Prager, Dennis, "Why God Isn't Doing Well," *National Review*, April 5, 2011, https://www.nationalreview.com/2011/04/why-god-isnt-doing-well-dennis-prager/.

6 Conor Friedersdorf, "Why College Students Are Losing Their Religion," *Atlantic*, April 6, 2011, https://www.theatlantic.com/politics/archive/2011/04/why-college-students-are-losing-their-religion/236874.

Another answer might be that people lose their faith after encountering new ideas and finding them incompatible with their beliefs. In this way, the path to secularization is paved not so much with propaganda, but with exposure to contradictions.

But I find even this explanation inadequate. Most people are aware, especially in our modern age, that other ideas exist out there. This isn't the fourteenth century, when most people couldn't read. It's not even the nineteenth century, when you had to go to a library or deep within an archive for heterodox information. It's safe to say that I rarely encountered an argument about religion in college (or since) that I wasn't already aware of on some level. It was in college, for instance, that I first examined in detail what C. S. Lewis calls "the problem of pain"—effectively, why an all-loving, all-powerful God would allow His creatures to suffer. But I certainly had known of this challenge to Christian faith for many years.

That's true for many disproofs of belief. Maybe I wasn't bothered by them when I was in high school. Maybe I glanced at a book, or read an article, and didn't think of them again. But the path to secularization, for most, isn't paved with epiphanies. We're aware these arguments are out there; we just ignore them or find them wanting.

I'm more persuaded by other explanations, like the inertia of modern life. People leave home and acquire new daily routines, and the habits of old—like reading the Bible and actively participating in a faith community—evaporate. Many young Christians who fall away from the Church do so at this critical juncture between childhood and adulthood.

So prevalent is this problem that a number of Christian organizations have sprung up in its wake. Young Life, founded in 1941, ministers to thousands of high schoolers and young adults, hosting camps and events to create community during this estranging period in their lives.

I attended a few Young Life meetings in high school. We'd sit around in a circle, read a little bit from the Bible, pray, and talk about what was happening in our lives. Not all that different from any other school club meeting, but it did give some Christian flavor to an otherwise normal social function. A few of my friends stayed active in Young Life after they left high school and benefited from its support during the transition to adulthood. But many of them, like most young American Christians, eventually found themselves occupying the uneasy ground between outright secularism and just not caring that much.

However moody they're capable of being, most well-adjusted adolescents don't tend to dwell on existential questions like what awaits them in the afterlife. In my experience, it tends to take having your own kids and caring for elderly loved ones to really get there. And as Western society continues to push back family formation later and later into life, the reality is that most young people won't be forced to reckon with such weighty issues—not by the secular world, anyway.

On top of that, people are fundamentally social animals, and the social lives of modern teenagers and young adults aren't especially compatible with the demands of religious practice. Most of us (including me) tend to fall into the social patterns of the group we're surrounded by. When I was in the Marines and in college, no Christian organization could have counteracted the fact that my friends spent all their free time on two things: finding girls and drinking too much.

I can remember many Sunday mornings when I might have willingly gone to church if it hadn't required going alone, with a hangover from the previous night's festivities. You can call this laziness (it was), but it was also a consequence of my social world.

I think this is part of what motivated my friend Rod Dreher to publish *The Benedict Option*. Rod posits that the constant hum of our modern world—a new iPhone every year, your boss bothering you at all hours of the day, new consumer goods appearing constantly—has made it difficult to form lasting, stable communities. Without those communities, individual Christians find it hard to buttress themselves against consumerism and individualism. So Rod argues, borrowing from medieval monk Saint Benedict, that Christians ought to build their own communities. As he's said, "The best we can do is construct arks within which we can ride it out, and by God's grace make it across the dark sea of time to a future when we do find dry land again, and can start the rebuilding, reseeding, and renewal of the earth."[7]

This is a more subtle version of the theory that kids abandon their faith because of brainwashing. It's not explicit messaging that drives people away from church, but instead the more informal ways in which our social groups make us who we are. It's not hearing an anti-Christian worldview every morning in college lectures; it's having a routine Christian existence replaced by something different. It is the subtle cues from one's environment more than the

7 Zac Davis, "What Might Pope Francis Think About 'The Benedict Option?' A New Talk Gives Clues," *America*, May 5, 2017, https://www.americamagazine.org/faith/2017/05/05/what-might-pope-francis-think-about-benedict-option-new-talk-gives-clues/.

explicit words of secularists. It is the trust you place in the people and ideas that dominate that environment.

If I could go back and give advice to that younger version of myself, it would be to resist that supposedly unavoidable drift into unbelief. It's not inevitable, even if it seems that way sometimes. Be intentional in the social circles you keep; seek out friends who keep you honest and interested in life's great questions. Surround yourself with people and institutions that recognize how flawed we are as human beings yet still insist that you reach for something higher.

Without all that in my life, my anger over the Terri Schiavo controversy crystallized something obvious: Christianity had become completely irrelevant to me. I didn't even know where to find a church near my Marine Corps base in Havelock, North Carolina. I didn't pray regularly. My Bibles were gathering dust in Ohio. My Marine Corps buddies, though nominally Christian, weren't especially devout.

My faith had grown irrelevant to my life long before I realized it. Mamaw had kept me tethered, however imperfectly, to Christianity. With her gone, no one really cared about my faith, and soon I stopped caring, too.

Though I wonder whether "irrelevance" captures entirely what happened to my faith. My belief depended on trust, and through death or the passage of time, I had lost most of the Christians I trusted.

* * *

Having shed my emotional attachment to Christianity, I still scratched at its ideas. Shortly before I deployed, I read most of C. S. Lewis's works. I packed his books to reread in Iraq, even though I knew my friends would tease me for reading *The Lion, the Witch and the Wardrobe* in an active war zone.

A few weeks after we landed, I learned that I'd be decamping to a remote part of our base to train and provide security for Iraqi election workers. This was a break from my usual job of escorting the press and writing articles about the activities of Marines on base. The new role would come with a lot of downtime, so I brought my C. S. Lewis paperbacks along and thought about Jesus Christ.

The Iraqis we worked with were, by and large, nice guys. We didn't interact with the female poll workers because of cultural sensitivities, but every day I'd walk through the camp, inspect the makeshift tent dormitories we'd constructed for the poll workers, and take a night shift at the guard tower. It wasn't totally clear to me what we were doing: protecting the poll workers from the outside world or ensuring that this camp kept some semblance of order. But it was the most time I spent face-to-face with actual Iraqis during my time in the country.

Many Iraqis I encountered, like many American Christians, were only nominally religious. Islam was, for them, more of a cultural identifier than a lived faith. That's true across the Muslim world, of course, but it was truer in Iraq, whose government was more explicitly secular than many of its neighbors.

Nonetheless, there were several devout Muslims among the poll workers. We had fairly shallow and courteous conversations about faith and spirituality, though everyone knew I was Christian. We mostly joked about American pop culture, and they made fun of my blue eyes—rather uncommon in that part of the world. Most Iraqis at the camp spoke at least some English. One who didn't could nonetheless recite on demand an entire catalog of American rap songs. I'm not kidding; this guy couldn't say "Hello, how are you?" in English, but he knew 50 Cent's "In Da Club" by heart.

We were encouraged to avoid deeper topics, but I was curious to know how people felt about the war. It was a biased sample—you wouldn't expect Iraqis who hated America to volunteer in the elections—but I was struck by how apolitical the people I met were. They had no special affection or hatred for America or Americans. Some hated Saddam Hussein but felt that the Americans had no right to intervene in their country. Others seemed happy to have him gone. But even the ones who opposed the American intervention seemed more sad than angry about it. It felt fatalistic, like it was just the way the world worked.

The most common complaint I heard was about security: "You're the most powerful country in the world, but you can't keep a crazy man from blowing up a market? What's wrong with you?" The chaos and disorder bothered them more than the war.

It was among those poll workers where I heard, for the first time, a genuinely compelling critique of American culture—really, Western culture. Oh, I'd heard others complain about stereotypical Americans. We were too fat, too lazy, too dumb. My high school French teacher griped that American kids rarely mastered foreign languages, unlike kids in Europe. And I knew there were regular protests across the world against America's foreign misadventures. I tried to be a smart consumer of news and paid attention to what others thought of my beloved country.

Debates raged back home about whether we could export liberty and democracy successfully—or whether it was foolish to assume that we could force our system on such culturally distinct populations. But the people I spoke to in Iraq had no problem with liberty and democracy. They admired our wealth, our medicine, and even our military might.

What they didn't admire was our culture (besides, apparently, American hip-hop). "I don't want my kids watching MTV," one man told me, which surprised me given that I didn't know anyone still watched MTV.

I encountered a fear among the population that if Iraqi culture grew too "Americanized" it would become too consumerist and hypersexualized. As journalist Brandon McGinley recently recounted, "I think often about a story a friend told years ago about riding a bus in rural Syria. A woman in a niqab was reading the Quran, and a man was rocking while praying, and on the TV was Britney Spears dancing in her underwear."

Meanwhile, I read my C. S. Lewis books and contemplated my own faith. The cleverest was *The Screwtape Letters*, written from the perspective of one demon counseling another demon on how to deceive a young man into abandoning his Christian faith. But my favorite, though written for children, was *The Chronicles of Narnia*. The series recounts the struggle for power in Narnia, a mythical land ruled by Aslan, a Christlike figure in the form of a lion. Lewis would later say that Aslan wasn't merely an allegory for Christ, but was Christ Himself—an attempt to reconstitute Christ in a fictionalized world.

I found myself longing for a Christ more like Aslan than the one I'd encountered in church and scripture. In the Narnian battle between good and evil, Aslan plays a critical role—inspiring the leaders to seek justice or physically taking up the fight himself. The struggle gives purpose to the characters' lives, and I began to envy the idea of fighting with a noble purpose. I had enlisted in the Marines thinking I'd bring Western democracy to faraway lands. But now I was here, and it wasn't clear what George W. Bush had us fighting for. I thought the war on terror would be our generation's World War II, but this was not a galvanizing national struggle—most people back home were more interested in shopping, as President Bush was encouraging them to do. And while they supported the troops, they didn't seem to have much of a stake in the war we were fighting.

I craved Aslan's presence. Just when his followers seem to stray, or begin to lose their faith, he appears. Can you imagine? Your own personal Jesus, appearing when you need Him most?

But most of all I envied his thoughtfulness about the human condition. In *The Magician's Nephew*, Aslan sends a protagonist named Digory to fetch a magic apple, whose seed is destined to grow into a tree that will keep the evil witch Jadis at bay. Digory finds Jadis gorging herself on the apples and promising health and eternal life to anyone who eats of them. Digory is tempted to take an apple for his sick mother, but he obeys Aslan's commands.

This is an obvious allusion to the Book of Genesis, which I'd read dozens of times before. I had heard sermons on the creation story from many pulpits. All I'd ever taken from Genesis was a simple lesson: that everything was perfect before Adam and Eve succumbed to temptation. In Lewis's hands, however, the allegory of the tree of life is much richer: It is about faith, submission, corruption, and natural law. Digory is eventually rewarded—Aslan encourages him to take another apple from the tree to his mother, which cures her.

Another character then challenges Aslan: Given that the witch has eaten the apples, won't she live forever? I suspected that Aslan would reply that he would use his magic to ensure the witch never receives the eternal life she craves. It would have been the simple response, appropriate for a children's book. But he answers differently, more subtly: "Things always work according to their nature," he says of the apple. "She has won her heart's desire; she has unwearying strength and endless days like a goddess. But length of days with an evil heart is only length of misery and already she begins to know it. All get what they want; they do not always like it."

All get what they want; they do not always like it. Lewis's Christianity was richer than the one I'd spent my lifetime trying to understand. For all the brain space I had devoted to the Book of Genesis—arguing with evolutionary biologists in AOL chat rooms, convincing myself that the creation story could be reconciled with science—I had never taken the time to actually learn from it.

You might have expected my reading to lead me to deeper engagement with my faith. Instead, I felt jaded. Years later, a friend of mine would tell me that he found C. S. Lewis boring and stupid, totally unpersuasive. Even though I called myself an atheist at the time, I couldn't agree. I found Lewis thoughtful and compelling. But his books weren't the Christianity I'd been exposed to at home. To adopt Lewis's Christianity would have been no less alien than abandoning my faith altogether. It would have been an act of conversion, without giving it the name.

And what did it say about my faith that the version of Christianity that intellectually resonated most with me was found in a kids' book? Didn't this count against the truth of Christianity? Christ may have implored His followers to "become as little children" (Matt. 18:3) to open their hearts to receive Him, but finding faith this way seemed preposterous to me. Besides, if Lewis's writing, intended for an elementary school reading level, was supposed to reflect divine truth, what did it say that so many readers missed the same point in Genesis?

I recalled the countless times I'd heard people misstate or ignore Christian doctrines. How could something be the Word of God if its followers couldn't even understand it? Was God really that terrible a communicator?

And I was so unrooted. I had no pastor that I could turn to. My best option was Sam Luke, the Pentecostal preacher from Dad's church back home. But he had moved on from that church, and I was too far away to stay in close touch.

Over the remainder of our time in Iraq, I read less and less about religion and more about why our mission in Iraq was in such peril. I was reassigned from protecting poll workers after the Iraqi constitutional referendum, which was hailed as an international success. But the suicide bombings continued, and Americans died at an accelerating rate. We had given Iraq a democracy, but we could not give it peace, or even a respite from the carnage. And so I naturally focused on understanding that intractable problem.

* * *

When I returned home in 2006, I was no longer, in any real sense, a Christian. I didn't attend church and found myself increasingly frustrated with religion in general.

I sat down with the Navy chaplain at Cherry Point a few weeks after I came back. He was late in his career, a captain, and incredibly kind and thoughtful. I was one of three young public affairs

Marines who had gone to Iraq in August 2005 and had just returned home. We were very close to one another, and I was the only one who hadn't seen significant combat action in Iraq. I was young and foolish enough to be bothered by this fact. And the chaplain wanted to talk about how my friends—and I—were doing.

Afterward he asked if I wanted to pray. I answered "yes" reflexively and dutifully bowed my head. There had been moments in my life when prayer felt intensely personal and meaningful. In boot camp, after a particularly grueling week, another Marine put his arm around me while praying at church, and I felt such gratitude and relief that I began crying—the only time I can ever recall crying openly in front of a stranger. When people spoke of having a "personal relationship with Jesus Christ," this is what that meant to me—a feeling of presence so intense it could move a grown man to tears. And yet, as I bowed my head with that kindly chaplain, I felt nothing besides impatience to get it over with.

I had about a year left on my Marine Corps contract, too little time for another deployment (at the time, the standard was at least six months off between deployments) or to get plugged into a long-term project. So my last year on base felt like a case of senioritis.

Our base experienced a fair amount of churn. Our two leaders (a senior enlisted Marine and an officer) left their posts and were replaced by a staff sergeant and a master sergeant ("Top"). Top and the other Marine brought a particular flavor of evangelical Christianity to the office—the same flavor I had known during childhood. They hosted regular Bible studies and encouraged other folks in our unit to join in. We'd drink punch and eat snacks, and at the end of the meetings we'd say a little prayer. It was all very wholesome.

Top led us in the "saving prayer" at each meeting. It was a prayer

I'd said hundreds of times in my life. Though it could take different forms, the basic gist was this: You confess that you are a sinner, and you ask Jesus into your heart to forgive your sins. After saying this transformative prayer, you are "saved"—forever a Christian, guaranteed a spot in heaven, and wrapped in the living presence of God Himself.

Top was a good man, but some Marines found his proselytizing overbearing. One friend—a Catholic who has since left the Church—decided to start a debate about the validity of Church tradition during one of our meetings. If you pay attention to the disputes between Catholics and Protestants, this is a particularly hot topic—whether tradition, as opposed to scripture alone, can inform Christian doctrine. Top called Catholicism "a little culty," and the meeting quickly went downhill from there.

My buddy issued a formal complaint about religious pressure in the unit, and a colonel launched an informal investigation into the matter. At the time, this felt like a very big deal: We all had to speak individually with the colonel, and our commanding officer—forward deployed in Afghanistan—called to chew me out for not preventing this from happening.

How the hell is this my fault? I thought.

But she was right: I should have spoken with my friend before he reached the point of lodging a formal complaint.

In hindsight, this was a tempest in a teapot. Top should have been more careful about how folks would perceive his religious teaching in light of his authority: Were these meetings mandatory? Could I actually speak my mind when a Marine Corps master sergeant was leading the prayers? And my friend probably shouldn't have made a formal complaint.

Still, I started to feel that Top's behavior was a real imposition on my freedom of conscience. Catalyzed by my friend's frustrations, I began to rebel not just against Top but against the faith he represented.

It was the perfect symbolic battle: There were no real stakes. I was due to leave the Marine Corps in a few months, so pissing off a senior Marine carried few consequences.

And watching, for the first time in years, a group of Christians praying together for their salvation, I felt completely alienated from the faith of my childhood.

In one sense, I admired and even envied them, bowing their heads and uttering the saving prayer and thinking their lives would be transformed. I wanted to believe as they did. One "hard charger," as we used to say, had seemed genuinely moved by his first real exposure to Christianity. And for all my cynicism, I really hoped that his faith would take root.

But had any of them ever spent time with people who were truly struggling? Did they realize how many of the worshipers they saw sobbing and praying at the altar then walked out of church and stuck needles in their arms? Had they ever met the kids who dragged their fathers to church, prayed with them, begged them to change, and believed that change had come—only to find themselves beaten and abused when Dad inevitably returned to the bottle?

Sadness and misery and addiction and depression don't just disappear when Jesus enters your heart. *People aren't like this*, I thought to myself. The entire theory of these groups, of these meetings, of the churches I'd grown up with was that God's grace was sudden and complete. It transformed you instantly and irreversibly, as they told it. *Was blind, but now I see.*

In high school I had walked around Middletown's broken neighborhoods with my youth group, finding junkies and other suffering people to pray with and for. We would tell them about the wages of sin (hell) and the promises of heaven, and we'd pray the saving prayer. I'd seen grown men reduced to tears. Men in wheelchairs stand up and dance to revival music. Cancer patients certain their tumors were healed. But I'd seen enough to know that the transformation never lasted.

All the fervor, all the overwrought emotion, infuriated me. I was sick of it and skeptical that it did a bit of good. For all the good intentions of its believers, the religion I'd grown up with felt completely insufficient in that moment. Faith seemed nothing more than sobbing grown men who had deluded themselves into thinking that thoughts and prayers could cure broken human nature.

Eventually, I had my interview with the Marine Corps investigator. I felt conflicted over what I hoped to accomplish. Was I trying to get Top in trouble? Was I snitching on good Christian soldiers?

In the end, I gave an honest assessment of the situation rather than editorializing about my frustrations with Christianity. Yes, these meetings could get a little uncomfortable, especially for people who didn't share Top's faith. But they also built some camaraderie and gave us an excuse to spend time together outside of the office. I thought Top needed to be more careful, but I also made clear that he hadn't meant anything untoward.

The higher-ups advised Top to stop the after-work meetings, and no other action was taken.

For me, God, faith, and understanding felt farther away than ever.

* * *

During my final months in the Marine Corps, a friend introduced me to Ayn Rand, an objectivist philosopher whose main medium was popular novels. Rand's novel *Atlas Shrugged*, published in 1957, is about a group of leading industrialists who, fed up with the government regulation and popular criticism of their work, go on strike. The world, scornful of these great men and the companies they built, soon realizes how much it depends on their goods and services. Without their labor, the world descends into dystopia—railroads stop running, store shelves are bare, and human advancement ceases altogether.

The book, which sold millions of copies worldwide, proved immensely influential on young conservatives. Alan Greenspan, the Federal Reserve's legendary chairman, was a Rand acolyte, and everyone from former Speaker of the House Paul Ryan to current US Supreme Court Justice Clarence Thomas has cited her influence.

At its core, Rand's philosophy celebrates individualism: that people ought to think for themselves, achieve as much as they can, and act in their own self-interest. She even argues that there is virtue in selfishness, in as stark opposition to Christian morality as anything I'd ever read.

Despite this, I found myself admiring Rand's heroes. They were builders of great things—beautiful skyscrapers, great symphonies, innovative metal alloys, and powerful electricity generators.

As Charles Murray put it in a critical reflection on Rand's life and philosophy:

> Rand expressed the glory of human achievement. She tapped into the delight a human being ought to feel at watching another member of our species doing things superbly well. The scenes in *The Fountainhead* in which the hero, Howard Roark, realizes his visions of architectural truth are brilliant evocations of human creativity at work. But I also loved scenes like the one in *Atlas Shrugged* when protagonist Dagny Taggart is in the cab of the locomotive on the first run on the John Galt line, going at record speed, and glances at the engineer:
>
> "He sat slumped forward a little, relaxed, one hand resting lightly on the throttle as if by chance; but his eyes were fixed on the track ahead. He had the ease of an expert, so confident that it seemed casual, but it was the ease of a tremendous concentration, the concentration on one's task that has the ruthlessness of an absolute."[8]

Rand gave everyone this treatment, from the middle-class train operator to the founder of world-changing enterprises. And though she fetishized the artistically and intellectually brilliant, she also glorified the simple act of working hard, and doing a job well, regardless of your station in life. Many of her protagonists came from dysfunctional families, which obviously appealed to me. But they never used their disadvantages or humble beginnings as an excuse. She elevated achievement and self-reliance into paragon virtues.

---

8 Charles Murray, "How Ayn Rand Captured the Magic of American Life," *Federalist*, October 16, 2014, https://thefederalist.com/2014/10/16/ayn-rand-captured-the-magic-of-american-life.

After years of prosperity gospel teaching, I was ready for a sterner lesson. I was tired of the illusion that achievement and wealth came, like magic, to anyone who prayed hard enough for them.

Stop whining, stop praying, and start working your ass off if you want anything out of life, I told myself.

Rand's message reflected why I had joined the Marines in the first place: The Corps was exceptional, and it was hard. Rand's many critics generally missed what made her work so appealing to a young guy like me: I knew that life was a struggle, and I was sick of people pretending it wasn't.

I dismissed Christianity as being too wishy-washy. Pray; hope you get lucky; and if you don't, well, "it's God's will."

I didn't care about God's will. I cared about my own. I cared about winning, never having to worry about money again, and having the type of job that commanded respect.

The great Christian writer G. K. Chesterton said, "When men stop believing in God they don't believe in nothing; they believe in anything."

Rand's philosophy spoke to me in part because it filled a void left by the faith I'd discarded.

Her message—the celebration of aspirations and achievements, the refusal to accept excuses—would reorient my entire life in subtle, and ultimately destructive, ways. It is one thing to celebrate achievement; it is something else to build your life around it. It would take me many years to realize that.

CHAPTER 3

They Probably Don't Serve Beer in Hell, but They Do in Columbus

At the Ohio State University in Columbus, Ohio, two matching high-rises tower over the football stadium. Their names—"Morrill and Lincoln"—are campus shorthand.

"I'll find you on the Morrill side of the stadium," you might say to someone you're meeting.

But I never thought about their names until I got into politics.

In 1862, a Vermont congressman named Justin Smith Morrill sponsored the legislation that created land-grant institutions. States received grants of thousands of acres of land for the purpose of establishing new colleges. The goal of the Morrill Act was "to teach such branches of learning as are related to agriculture and the mechanic arts, in such manner as the legislatures of the States may respectively prescribe, in order to promote the liberal and practical education of the industrial classes in the several pursuits and professions in life."

In other words, A&Ms were designed to power the American economy. President Lincoln signed the law. And Ohio State, one of those land-grant institutions, dedicated its two largest residence halls to the congressman who advanced the legislation and the president who signed it.

Academics debate what land-grant institutions accomplished and whether their intentions were ultimately realized. It's interesting to contrast the statutory purpose of universities like Ohio State with the more academic goals of a liberal arts education. Where the liberal arts were dedicated to developing citizens and statesmen versed in classics and humanities, land-grant institutions were more practical. They trained their students for particular jobs rather than for broad-based intellectual pursuits. Of course, these things aren't mutually exclusive, but my experience at Ohio State suggests that most students—as excited as they were to learn—were there at least in part because they knew it was the pathway to a good job.

When I arrived at Ohio State in late summer 2007, just weeks after being discharged from the Marine Corps, I had never been more excited to be part of an institution. I loved game-day Saturdays, drinking beer with my friends and waking up after 7 a.m.—a real luxury following my time in the Marines. Something I appreciated about OSU was that it was part of the fabric of my home state. Whether you were from Cincinnati or Cleveland or rural Ohio, OSU belonged to you. It was the state's flagship university and one of the few institutions that genuinely cut across class lines. I never noticed any anti-elitism directed at Ohio State.

Everyone—from first-generation students to fourth-generation legacies—was a Buckeye.

Ohio State occupied an almost mythical place in my mind. For four years in the Marines, it was the only place I wanted to be—hanging with my crew of high school friends who had left Middletown for Columbus. When Ohio State beat Michigan in 2006, one of the most storied games of the century-plus rivalry, I flew back to my Marine Corps base in North Carolina dejected that I had to wait another nine months to return to God's country (central Ohio).

I was the first in my family to attend a four-year college, and Ohio State immediately changed me into a college boy. Shortly after matriculating, I drove home for a weekend to visit my family. My nieces and nephew complained about not having anything for breakfast besides cereal. I raised this with my sister like an arrogant jerk.

"You know that stuff is, like, pure sugar, right? They should have other options."

My sister rightly took offense, and we didn't talk for a week.

Whatever the merits of my argument—there is some virtue in not eating Froot Loops every day, though I should have raised this more artfully—it showed how far I was drifting from my roots. Many other things like this popped up, demonstrating the ways in which I had unconsciously absorbed the biases of America's educated class.

There were also the little looks down the nose at my upbringing. People in Columbus were shocked that my mother had been eighteen when she had my sister, and equally astonished that my sister had in turn had three kids before she turned twenty-five.

I was becoming detached from the culture that had made me who I was.

This subtle estrangement is perhaps inevitable when a person travels from one social class to another. For a long time, sociologists have defined "working class" by the absence of a college degree; acquiring that degree would change how the world categorized me. But our separation was exacerbated by my new atheism. Religion was the social glue that had bound me to my family. Even if I might make more money than a friend from back home or have different attitudes from my sister about nutrition, I could still see them both at church or at least share a common spiritual vocabulary. But now I'd lost even that connection.

In the meantime, I was enjoying my life at Ohio State. The careerism that marked me later in life was generally absent at OSU. Yes, there were ambitious people galore. And some of them would brag about their grades or GMAT scores. But despite the stereotypes of OSU as a good-not-great "state school," I have never encountered a place more dedicated to learning, with people more interested in ideas for their own sake. The scale of the university—about sixty thousand students—meant that I could explore almost any interest in a classroom setting. I fell for classical philosophy (Aristotle and Plato especially) and for the early modern political theorists like John Locke and Thomas Hobbes whose ideas influenced the American Revolution. And I could always find professors teaching classes or hosting office hours about what most interested me.

An undercurrent of Christian theology flowed through the work of the thinkers who captivated me. Locke's arguments about religious freedom were rooted in a fundamentally Christian concept of free will: Because we are all endowed with dignity and freedom as individuals, we must be allowed to discover our own pathway to

God. Hobbes's political philosophy was a reaction to the religious and civil wars of seventeenth-century England. Though Aristotle died hundreds of years before the birth of Christ, Thomas Aquinas—a Dominican friar—fused Aristotle's ideas with Christian theology in a blend that still heavily influences Christian thinking on politics, economics, law, and morality.

As I was discarding my personal faith, I was immersing myself in ideas shaped by Christianity. The irony was lost on me.

* * *

After four years in the Marine Corps, the main thing I cared about was my social life. So while I did try to get good grades and take advantage of this once-in-a-lifetime opportunity, I also spent a lot of time getting drunk and trying to meet girls. This was 2007, after political correctness but before the woke era, and before social media and dating apps mediated romance on campus.

As a general rule, relations between the sexes at OSU seemed normal and healthy compared to today's standards. There were, of course, exceptions: regrets, bad setups, worse one-night stands, and some actual heartbreak.

When I talk to young staffers or visit campuses, I feel profoundly sad for today's kids. One friend who profusely criticized the "hookup culture" of the early aughts now looks at it almost nostalgically. She graduated from college the year I started and told me this about her own experience with dating:

> We had our problems in the 2000s. Hookup culture wasn't good in a lot of ways. Girls and boys often had mismatched

> expectations. The girls mostly wanted a relationship, and some of the guys didn't. Some people slept around too much and got hurt in the process. It wasn't exactly a perfect example of Christian sexual ethics. But the mistakes you saw people make were normal mistakes. The kind of things you learned from, talked to your friends about, maybe cried over. But in the end, in 2006, most of the people who wanted to pair off did. Most of the girls I know who wanted marriage and kids ended up getting what they wanted. And most of the social life we lived was in the classroom, at someone's house, or at a bar. People lived their lives in the real world. Now much of it's online, and it's a horror show. The swiping, the text games, the ghosting, and the loneliness. Most of the girls I know who wanted a husband in the early 2020s have either given up or say they don't want a husband anymore at all.

My generation learned about sex and romance the old-fashioned way: through real-life interactions. We all had our own wishes and desires and expectations, of course. In my inner circle at Ohio State, we had guys who wanted to settle down and guys who wanted to meet a new girl every week. Either way, the biggest sin in our dating lives was immaturity.

I was not immune to these primate group behaviors. One of my closest friends, Doug, had recently started dating someone who lived across the state. He was better than most of us at attracting the attention of girls on campus, but despite the temptations and the long distance, he became emphatically monogamous almost immediately.

"Dude," I asked him, as he refused to join me in flirting with the women at a bar, "are you *in love* with this chick?"

It could not have been a more loaded question—dripping in skepticism, right down to the dismissive *chick*.

It was an act of defiance against my crudeness that my friend responded, "Yeah, of course."

And indeed he was: They would later marry and raise a family, and they're still happily married to this day.

If marriage and family were surpassingly important to me as an eighteen-year-old Christian, they scarcely mattered at all as a twenty-three-year-old atheist. I never thought seriously about marrying any of the girls I dated. To me, marriage was what the sociologists call a "capstone achievement": something to be contemplated only after I had checked every other young adult achievement box. If a girl was "too into you," my friends and I took it as a sign of her imperfection—never considering how that reflected on us.

What does it even mean to "not be ready" to settle down? What accomplishment could be more important than finding a person I could spend my life with? Choosing to end a relationship because a woman thought you might be marriage material is, in hindsight, nauseating.

It never occurred to me that disliking someone because she held you in high regard was an implicit acknowledgment that you considered yourself a dirtbag.

Perhaps the most obvious indicator of how our generation saw romance was popular culture. My grandparents grew up on "Can't Help Falling in Love," in which a heartsick Elvis Presley croons about his devotion to a young woman.

When I got to Ohio State, the most popular radio hits were

"Crank That" by Soulja Boy and "Ayo Technology" by 50 Cent. Never have two songs better captured the zeitgeist of their time.

In our bro culture, the very idea of romantic love had become passé. My crew rarely spoke about love, and when we did, it was to mock each other for daring to have real feelings for someone. I was among the worst offenders.

A popular figure at the time was Tucker Max, who blogged online about his sexual and drinking exploits. Max was a funny and engaging writer. Part of his appeal derived from his pure irreverence. In one story from his bestselling book *I Hope They Serve Beer in Hell*, he writes about his displeasure with a summer legal internship: "The law firm and the work bored me. So what did I do? Did I endure the boredom and soldier on? Or better yet, did I find a productive output for my creativity? . . . No. I got drunk and acted like an asshole." In my life, too, getting drunk and acting like a jerk had filled the void left by God.

One of my roommates began dating a girl during my first year of college. She was beautiful and smart. She had a great sense of humor and loved dogs of every size and shape. In a healthier culture, our roommate would have told us how he felt about her and we would have celebrated the fact that he had found someone he wanted to spend his life with. Instead, we teased him mercilessly for being "whipped" and "lame" and having a "ball and chain."

"I care about her, and the rest is none of your business," is as far as he would go. And of course they are now happily married with kids.

It's impossible not to feel embarrassed today at my failures as a friend—at the fact that I joined the crowd in heckling someone for finding the most important thing in life. Predictably, this roommate was the most devoutly Christian of our circle, and consequently the most immune to our weird fusion of Tucker Max bro-ing out and "marriage as a capstone" mentality.

Earlier in my life, my sister had observed that Lynyrd Skynyrd's "Simple Man" reminded her of me. Among its lyrics, a mother's advice to her son: "Take your time, don't live too fast."

But at Ohio State, I took my time with nothing. I had three jobs and was taking twenty-five credit hours at a school where a full-time class load was twelve. One of my favorite professors, a philosopher who taught ethics, asked during office hours what I did with my time. When I walked him through my schedule, he shook his head.

"You can read your assignments and write papers and get good grades, but you have very little time for real education. I don't know anything about your personal situation, but you really ought to spend less time working and more time thinking."

Whatever virtues Lynyrd Skynyrd's simple man had, I was transforming myself at Ohio State into nearly the opposite.

Was this entirely a bad thing? Of course not. Before college, I probably ate more Fruity Pebbles than any grown man or small child should. Thinking about my diet in a new way and immersing myself in fitness changed that. But as my new life revealed ways in which my old life was unfashionable or unhealthy, it drove an invisible cultural wedge between me and my family. To assimilate into this new world would require that I leave the old one behind.

Some of this divide was purely practical. In the late 2000s, before the financial crisis, everyone I knew assumed that if you had a college degree you were set for life financially. So family members would ask for money even though I had a bank account balance approaching zero and was accumulating student loan debt.

On one trip home, I talked with a cousin about my frustrations with a job search: filling out application after application and being disappointed when an interview didn't pan out. "Now that you're a college boy, I doubt you'll ever fill out a job application again," my cousin said. And I protested, but he was half right: I filled out a few job applications during college and in the few months after, but they would be my last.

This divide also expressed itself in deeper ways. One of my college roommates observed that outside of *The Office* and football games, he no longer watched the same TV shows as his parents and sister. They went to church, and none of us did. For many recent Ohio State graduates, the dream neighborhood was Columbus's Short North Arts District: hip and walkable, with modern apartments and trendy coffee shops. My family thought it was a good place to visit, but to live? "The houses are way too small," my mom observed. "Why would you spend all this money and have a bedroom the size of a closet?"

My new life required a new philosophy, and like many young men on the political right, I had absorbed Ayn Rand's hyper-individualism. I gave even love, the most selfless state of mind imaginable, a selfish Randian spin: Love is when we value another person so highly that it's in our selfish interest to be nice to them. Conversely, when we no longer value someone, it's fine to discard past affections.

Seeing romantic love through the prism of individual benefit and value was part of a deeper chauvinism—this was the era of Neil Strauss's *The Game*, where young men were supposed to "neg," or gently insult, the girls they liked. Even the sex scenes in Rand's novels—aggressive men forcefully throwing their female partners around like rag dolls—read like pornography. Rand's followers liked to congratulate themselves online for having recognized hidden, unconventional truths. But Rand's aggressive relationships stripped of romance and characters devoted entirely to their work reflected instead the same selfishness that I was now using as a value system.

In hindsight, my attitude was obviously hogwash. Our bonds of affection—primarily to family but also to community and neighborhood—are so deeply entwined with our sense of self that no reasonable person would throw them away like garbage. It was obvious to me, even then, that the love parents feel for their children is deeply unselfish. The absence of children in Rand's novels is telling: Children exert an incomparable gravitational pull on people, even (or perhaps especially) when the children are at their most "useless."

I never became a true "objectivist," as Rand's followers called themselves. But my encounter with her ideas left two lasting impressions on me: I no longer called myself a Christian, and I saw myself as deserving of everything that came to me. Thanks to Rand, I was a self-professed atheist and meritocrat.

Atlas Shrugged foreshadowed the dominant sentiment of the educated class into which I had been invited: the feeling that people got what they deserved to get. By working hard, elite college achievers earned their social prestige and superior job prospects. Any sense of community attachment—that we owe something to the people from whom we came—gave way to the one-upmanship of modern meritocracy.

In *The New York Times*, Ross Douthat wrote a brilliant column titled "Why We Miss the WASPs" in which he argued, not long after President George H. W. Bush died, that Bush represented something the country needed to recover. Bush, the scion of a wealthy and powerful family, was driven by an overwhelming sense of duty. He volunteered to serve our country in World War II and took on several bureaucratic, often underappreciated, posts before becoming president.

Bush was unquestionably privileged. Yet that privilege imbued him with a sense of duty, Douthat argued, that our modern class of meritocrats lacked. In a world where everything had to be earned through striving, people saw their outcomes in life as the consequence of individual effort. Rand had had the last laugh: Her hyper-individualistic, selfish way of understanding achievement over duty dominated the elite mainstream.

I swam in that mainstream, and I increasingly began to feel as though I was not an especially good person.

CHAPTER 4

More Money, More Problems

Midway through my time at Ohio State, I was fully on the treadmill. I cared far too much about where I went to school, what job I would have, and what kind of money I'd make.

Some of that impulse came from my desire to be a provider for others, like Papaw. We had relied on him: When someone's car broke down, he'd pay for repairs or fix it himself; when we went out to dinner, he always paid; when an unexpected expense hit our family—medical bills, addiction treatment, or a middle school graduation gown—Papaw would pay.

Indeed, it wasn't until Papaw died that our family first tasted real poverty. We were never wealthy. I know now that we would have been classified as working class or working poor. But working class is one thing, and not being able to afford medicine is something quite different. We didn't experience that kind of deprivation until after Papaw died and Mamaw took me under her roof. I wanted to fill his shoes in our family. When I dreamed as a child about the future, I didn't fantasize about the job I would accept, or about where I'd go to college. My dream was a home, a stable family, and enough money that if my family needed something, I could say yes.

At some point in my university career, my desire for stability morphed into a craving for conquest. I didn't just want a nice car, a house, and a decent vacation. I wanted to win for winning's sake.

The benefits of college education are taken for granted, or at least they were. I knew even when I was young that my grandparents wanted me to attend college.

But when I consider how my family discussed education and work, it's clear that we, too, were influenced by the value our culture placed on higher education. Papaw always told me that blue-collar labor was his generation's work and that I would have to make my living with my mind. I never questioned that sentiment as a kid, even though I didn't know what kind of work I wanted to do. There seemed to be a natural generational evolution—Papaw's ancestors worked on farms, he worked in a factory, and I'd work at a desk. But I realize now that this way of thinking devalued people like Papaw. He was one of the smartest people I knew, and he spent more than three decades welding in a complex steel operation. It would be absurd to suggest that he didn't use his mind when he went to work. Of course he did.

So there was maybe a little classism in Papaw's presumption that I would go to college—a recognition that our society valued certain career pathways more than others. He didn't just want me to have more stability. He wanted me to find work that was more valued than his own work. It's heartbreaking that a man who'd worked so hard his entire life saw his contribution as less valuable than what he chose for me.

If you asked me what I wanted to do, going back many years, I might have responded that I wanted to be an attorney. But there was something a bit odd about my supposed passion for the law: I wasn't sure why I wanted to do it. I knew that lawyers made more money. I thought that lawyers had better career security. But I didn't know the first thing about how the average lawyer spent their day. I had no idea whether I would find the job meaningful. I once job shadowed a good friend's father, a local attorney, and my favorite part of the day was when he took me to Skyline Chili for lunch.

David Brooks coined the term *résumé virtues* to describe the things that make us more marketable or successful in the professional world (in contrast to the *eulogy virtues* that people discuss after our deaths). I was obsessed with these résumé virtues and running a race I didn't fully understand. I didn't care; I just wanted to win.

Without any other idea for what I should do after graduating, I tried to get into the best law school I could. But "best" in my mind was not based on the quality of the education or on the cultural fit. "Best" meant the highest-ranked school on the *U.S. News & World Report* list. I applied to the top schools, where my grades and Marine Corps service made me a viable candidate.

Of course, to get into a good school, I had to do well on the LSAT—the law school admissions exam. It was a test not of knowledge but of logical ability and asked you to identify the weakness in an argument or successfully solve a puzzle given a unique set of rules. I couldn't afford the test prep classes, but I found ways of re-creating them with borrowed materials and secondhand books purchased on eBay. Most students took their practice tests in the library; I'd take them in a busy café with lots of distractions and a few minutes cut from the timer.

I don't regret the work I put into college or the time I spent studying for the LSAT, but it is scary to consider how much motivation I had to achieve a goal I didn't understand. I had no idea why I wanted to go to law school or what I wanted to do with my life. In my atheism, I fancied myself enlightened and rational. Yet all of my talents and energies were focused on obtaining, at best, a good option to guarantee financial security and, at worst, the prize in a competition I was unable to comprehend. As much as I thought the ideas in my head were the consequence of reasoned consideration, I made the most important decision in my life thus far almost entirely based on the priorities of my environment.

I wanted to go to a good law school because that's what other people wanted. I wanted to win the race because other people wanted to win the race.

In a sense, I won that race and was admitted to Yale Law School. I've written elsewhere about the sense of relief I felt when I got the call that I would be going to the best of the best. The relief came from knowing that I'd never have to worry about money in the way I had for the first twenty-five years of my life. But it also came from knowing that I had won. Without realizing it, I had become addicted to winning the competitions other people set for me. As a nonbeliever with a chip on my shoulder, I considered myself a young rebel. I was rebelling against God, perhaps, but I had submitted myself instead to the most conventional forces in our society.

Because of the oddities of the quarter system, which then dictated Ohio State's academic calendar, I had about nine months between graduation from Ohio State and my start at Yale. I did some substitute teaching and worked at a tile factory. I felt a certain shame that I couldn't get a better—meaning more prestigious—job, but I lived with my aunt and uncle, and saved some money before starting law school in the summer of 2010.

Yale was a different world from Ohio State. At Yale, the social currency of prestige kicked into overdrive. Ironically, everyone at Yale was sufficiently rich (or at least would be after law school) that having money conveyed little social status. People didn't brag about their net worth or their vacation homes or their boats; that would have been unseemly. Some had perfected the art of the humblebrag: complaining about the remodeling costs on their family's second home or—my personal favorite—how a friend preferred business class to first class when flying. "In first class they just bother you too much."

At Yale, prestige came from a different source. If you learned about someone joining a private equity firm after graduation and making a hefty salary, you might shrug. But hear that someone had a White House job or a federal appeals court clerkship, and you'd be more impressed. In the private sector, working at a tech firm or an elite consultancy had more cachet, despite the fact that those jobs paid less than others on offer.

But prestige, interestingly enough, never flowed from the non-professional parts of life. No one discussed family life with the same level of pride with which they announced their fancy jobs. In other words, prestige could be accumulated through professional choices and accomplishments. But being a good mother or a good husband wasn't valued nearly as highly as achieving a new credential, being admitted to a top school, or getting a great job.

At Yale Law, no job stood higher on the prestige value chain than a Supreme Court clerkship. These jobs are extremely rare: Each year, about forty of the nation's best young lawyers are selected (the nine Justices get four clerks apiece, and retired Justices also hire clerks). To be competitive for these jobs, you have to clerk for a judge on one of the federal courts of appeals (judges who, by and large, clerked for federal judges themselves). Almost all clerks come from the nation's best (there's that word again) law schools, and their grades, recommendations, and legal writing are typically excellent.

Among elite law schools and firms, Supreme Court clerkships have acquired an almost mythical status. David Lat, the founder of the legal website Above the Law, wrote a novel about the hunt for the clerkship called *Supreme Ambitions*. Elsewhere, he has called Supreme Court clerks "the elect." Billionaire investor and venture capitalist Peter Thiel has called his rejection from a clerkship (after two interviews) one of the most devastating moments in his career.

Overtly "gunning" for Supreme Court clerkships was frowned upon at Yale, but when I became a teaching assistant in my third year of law school, I learned just how powerfully this ambition bubbled below the surface. One first-year student asked me how the application process worked. Another asked me how he should structure his law school experience to ensure that he'd get the job. Note that he was barely days into his studies and at least four years away from even *qualifying* for a clerkship at the Supreme Court.

One professor who taught me described this flavor of ambition perfectly: "So many of you are so desperate to get to the river, but you have no idea where it will take you. You don't know why you want what you want. But you're desperate to get it." French philosopher René Girard calls this *mimetic desire*. We are such social creatures that we instinctively want what other people around us want: the same jobs, the same women (or men), the same university degrees.

There's a reason many of the great entrepreneurs of the past thirty years are people who went through this elite pipeline and refused to jump in the proverbial river. The conceit of my atheism was that it sprang from my own rationality. But as a new law student, imbued with ambition but without having much direction for that ambition, I began to realize that I was as susceptible to social pressure as any of the religious simpletons I looked down upon.

It bordered on insane: I had no idea what I wanted out of a Supreme Court clerkship, I knew that it was irrational, yet I desperately wanted to clerk for the Supreme Court anyway. I felt that I had to summit this Everest of prestige simply because it existed. It's hard to overstate how much I wanted it. Such was the power of this social currency.

I pick on the Supreme Court clerkship process not because it's a bad job or because the people who undertake it suffer from some character defect. My favorite person in the world would eventually clerk, though her reasons were remarkably pure. When Usha told me she wanted the job, she said it was an insurance policy: "It's so prestigious that if I do it and then have kids, it won't ruin my career." It wasn't exactly an endorsement of the legal profession, but it was a saintly justification compared to mine. I didn't give up on the dream entirely until I decided I didn't want to be a lawyer at all.

In a brilliant essay in *The Atlantic*, economics writer Derek Thompson describes the phenomenon of what he calls *workism* among the American professional class. He argues that work, for many elites, is not just about surviving or providing for your family. It is also a source of identity and passion, *the* thing that provides both community and purpose for a growing segment of American elites. It's a quasi-religion.

Interestingly, while many Americans are working fewer hours per year than they did a generation ago, one big exception is wealthy men. Thompson writes:

> In 1980, the highest-earning men actually worked fewer hours per week than middle-class and low-income men, according to a survey by the Minneapolis Fed. But that's changed. By 2005, the richest 10 percent of married men had the *longest* average workweek. In that same time, college-educated men reduced their leisure time more than any other group. Today, it is fair to say that elite American men have transformed themselves into the world's premier workaholics, toiling longer hours than both poorer men in the U.S. and rich men in similarly rich countries.[1]

But as Thompson points out, the idea of wealthy men working more than poor men is historically bizarre and economically upside down. People once worked because they had to, but in the new world—where work has supplanted religion as a core source of meaning—people pour themselves into their jobs.

1 Derek Thompson, "Workism Is Making Americans Miserable," *Atlantic*, February 24, 2019, https://commons.princeton.edu/motorcycledesign/wp-content/uploads/sites/70/2019/08/The-Religion-of-Workism-Is-Making-Americans-Miserable-The-Atlantic.pdf.

Why have our elites become so obsessed with their jobs? Thompson articulates one possible explanation, which sounds an awful lot like the credentialism I saw at Yale:

> Perhaps long hours are part of an arms race for status and income among the moneyed elite. Or maybe the logic here isn't economic at all. It's emotional—even spiritual. The best-educated and highest-earning Americans, who can have whatever they want, have chosen the office for the same reason that devout Christians attend church on Sundays: It's where they feel most themselves.

It's worth asking whether this is a healthy way in which to orient one's life. But even if it works out for a few elites, it is not a healthy way to run a society. As Gallup has found, 80 percent of employees are disengaged from their jobs.[2] Most people continue to work because it's necessary to live, and pretending that everyone can fill the void left by community and family and faith with a job is a way of taking the preferences of a small number of rich people and projecting them on everyone else.

During my second year of law school, I cohosted a discussion on work-life balance—a buzzy phrase around campus at the time. One of my cohosts—a good friend and an incredibly smart woman—was interested in the classic question of how a woman could have both a fulfilling family life and a fulfilling work life. The discussion was well attended and featured mid-level associates from elite law firms talking about how they manage the twin demands of work and

2 Gallup, *State of the Global Workplace 2026* (Gallup, 2026), https://www.gallup.com/workplace/349484/state-of-the-global-workplace.aspx.

family. Their firms were more than willing to send those associates to discuss the issue, thinking it might help improve their recruiting.

Something was nagging at me. I felt there was a fundamental tension between the work habits of my chosen profession and the kind of life I thought was most valuable. And it wasn't just about family. What was the point of all this? It's one thing to be a workaholic if you're building a rocket to Mars or saving someone's life on an operating table. Many of my classmates were brilliant people desperately striving for a life where they'd sit at a desk and build Excel models or write deal documents. Is this honorable work? Sure it is. So is welding steel. But where my grandfather had a healthy relationship with his job—he understood that it was a useful thing to do, that people depended on him, and that it put food on the table—my classmates had an almost religious obsession with their work. But most of us were not saving the world.

Though I had helped organize the work-life balance event, I was beginning to doubt that the issues we confronted could be solved by advocating for lawyers to spend more time with their families.

The impacts of professional-class workaholism don't show up in the divorce and abuse statistics. Though well-off married couples may work ninety hours at Goldman Sachs or Sullivan & Cromwell, their divorce rate is still lower than in the community I came from. One possible explanation is the simple stress of poverty: If you don't have much cash in the bank, you're more likely to argue and get divorced. There's some truth to that. But access to money gives elites another advantage: The way they sustain their incredibly demanding professional lives while maintaining a family life that is at least superficially intact is that they outsource everything.

A friend at a private equity firm told me his office would pay to have all his laundry done. Many employers also spring for meals if you work past a certain hour. At first, this sounded like a pretty sweet deal—not doing your laundry, not having to cook for yourself. But I eventually realized that elite professional life demands a disconnection from much of what makes us human. People have house cleaners to clean their houses, cooks to make their meals, dog walkers to walk their dogs, gardeners to do their landscaping, and nannies to care for their kids. This is the logic of the capitalistic division of labor taken to the extreme: Specialize in one area of your life and let other specialists take care of everything else.

Am I a hypocrite about this? Yes, we've sometimes hired people to make our life easier, and in my current role staffers and military aides help me on the home front. But we've also resisted the impulse to outsource the parts of life worth living. I've changed a lot of diapers, not because I can't pay someone else to do it, but because I don't want to give this part of my life away to a stranger.

I started to grasp the devious hidden costs of this system. Work as much as you can. Achieve as much as you can. Make as much money as you can. If that means you don't have time for the kids, fine. If that means you don't even have kids, all the better.

I had thought these people were enlightened—compared to the evangelical Christians I'd left behind. But I began to see they were as screwed up as anyone.

And unlike the many Christians I knew who recognized and were troubled by the fact that they had failed to live up to their creed, the belief system at places like Yale had a way of turning real vice into perceived virtue. People didn't even realize how screwed up they were.

Our event on work-life balance went off without a hitch. The main thing I took away was that to succeed in this world, your entire life would have to be incredibly regimented. There was a remarkable, ruthless efficiency to it. If you were lucky, you'd get a couple of hours in the morning with your kids and a couple in the evening. After your kids went to bed, you'd need to "log back on"—bill a few more hours. On a good day, you'd get six hours of sleep, and if you needed more time to work, you could always just sleep less. It occurred to me that the associates on the panel were perceived as winners in society. And in some obvious ways they were: high salaries, social prestige. But they also had to track their working life in six-minute increments, to the point that lawyers had rules for their bathroom breaks. (As I heard from other associates when I started at a law firm, stop the clock for going number two, but not for number one.) And their children would receive precious moments sandwiched between client calls and legal brief writing.

But there was so much left unsaid at the event. No one mentioned the armies of nannies, maids, dry cleaners, and food service workers needed to make this life function. In private conversations, people debated the relative merits of full-time nannies, elite nursery schools, and au pairs—live-in caregivers, usually from a foreign country, who work for low wages. Yet these people are the proverbial engine grease that makes this hyperefficient life run. Though we fancy ourselves egalitarians, the elites of today depend as much on underpaid servants as Lord Grantham of *Downton Abbey* does.

* * *

Another feature of the professional world is a strident effort to avoid the obvious implications of gender differences. After I got an offer at one firm, I spoke to a male partner who promised that his firm made family life possible—he didn't have to ruin every vacation, and he was even able to coach one of his kids' sports teams. He gave me some hope that I could make this new professional world compatible with the family life I'd always wanted.

But then our conversation turned to a mutual acquaintance—someone who'd achieved an extraordinarily high position in government service. You could detect a bit of regret—almost resentment—in his voice. "Oh yeah, he was a great guy. But he would work a hundred hours a week, and that's how he built such an incredible reputation for himself. I used to tell him, 'Look man, I've got two toddlers, I've got to go eat dinner with my family.' I guess that's why he's there and I'm here."

But if that was true for him, how much harder was it for women? Set to the side the different expectations for men and women in the workplace and the home. The basic biological facts of childbirth, recovery, and breastfeeding mean that for at least the first few months of a child's life, their mother will necessarily carry more of the burden. A standard that rewards spending less time with children (or delaying childbearing) will necessarily fall hardest on women—at least those who decide to have families.

One study showed that when a woman's résumé indicated that she was a parent, she was much less likely to be called back for a follow-up interview.[3] And the "glass ceiling"—the notion that

3 Melissa Locker, "Discrimination Against Working Mothers Is Alive and Well," *Fast Company*, November 15, 2017, https://www.fastcompany.com/40494089/discrimination-against-working-mothers-is-alive-and-well.

working women face a harder path to traditional positions of corporate leadership—is so well accepted that it's become a cultural cliché. Fewer women than men are partners at law firms and investment banks or hold positions on corporate boards. And whatever challenges women face writ large, the path is undoubtedly harder for working moms.

I don't doubt that discrimination plays a role. But these law students who fancied themselves future leaders were reflexively uncomfortable with the idea that men and women might want different things out of life and, on average, show different proficiencies. The refusal to see gender differences as anything besides a consequence of structural forces or the discrimination of powerful men became an article of faith at Yale Law School in the early 2010s. This seemed absurd to me, but few within the institution were willing to question it. *These people*, I thought, *have their own religious zealotry. They just call it something else.*

Take, for instance, a Yale Law School effort called Speak Up, which was unfolding at around the same time as our conversation on work-life balance. A study at the law school showed that women were much less likely than men to participate in classroom discussion. Professors were less likely to call on female students, and female students were less likely to raise their hand to voice an opinion.

I found the Speak Up movement strange on a couple of fronts. First, no one even hinted that men and women might have different preferences in the classroom. Usha didn't want to "speak up" in class because she was there to listen to her professors, not debate what they said.

But there was a more fundamental issue: Telling women to speak up presumed that talkative men were doing things the right way and that everyone else merely needed to follow their lead. Having sat through many an insufferable tirade by above-average guys who think they're brilliant, I can tell you that simply isn't true.

I often wanted to listen to what the professor had to say far more than I wanted to listen to an arrogant classmate drone on about "material dialectics" and the "entropy of justice." I didn't understand how the solution to that problem was to have women talk a lot more. Why shouldn't the men just talk a lot less, if we assumed everyone needed to be equal? Rather than a Speak Up movement directed at the women of Yale Law School, why not a Shut the Hell Up movement directed at everyone?

This attitude informed the entire elite approach to work and life. According to some formulations, working in the home is a drag on women's wages. Some say it can even drag down the entire economy. If women were spending more time at work—"leaning in," as Sheryl Sandberg's bestselling book put it—and less time at home, our economy would have a more productive workforce.[4] As Bloomberg summarized the research: "Women have less time for on-the-job labor because they spend more time doing housework than their male counterparts—so they miss out when they're working in fields that reward long hours."[5]

I find this way of thinking about the world absolutely bonkers. Only a bunch of elite graduates of Yale Law School and Harvard

4 Judith Ohikuare, "Expecting Women to Handle Housework Hurts the Economy," *Refinery29*, August 2, 2017, https://www.refinery29.com/en-us/division-of-household-labor-economy-wage-gap.

5 Jeanna Smialek, "The U.S. Economy Would Be Better Off If Men Did More Housework," Bloomberg, August 1, 2017, https://www.bloomberg.com/news/articles/2017-08-01/the-u-s-economy-would-be-better-off-if-men-did-more-housework.

Business School could read about parents spending more time with their children and think, *But shouldn't they be doing more productive things, like slaving away at an investment banking slide deck?* Again, these people—men or women—aren't exactly saving the world.

Well, as it happens, I do think husbands ought to share the burdens of household labor with their wives—not because it makes their wives more productive workers, but because it's the right thing to do. This isn't a matter of gross domestic product (GDP). We should care about whether men and women have healthy relationships strong enough to withstand the life stressors that can lead to divorce. We should care about whether a man's children spend quality time with him. A corporate culture that tells us to worry more about McKinsey's bottom line than about our families' health is insane. The McKinseys of the world are doing just fine.

Do you know who isn't doing fine?

The American family, which has so taken to heart the message that work and family are incompatible that, for the first time in our history, women are having *fewer* children than they want.

Meanwhile, American children are committing suicide at unprecedented rates. As a child, I learned that the devil perfected the art of deception. And here was an elite institution purposefully forming American leaders distracted from the real problems of our country and focused instead on whether women were spending enough time at their cubicles. Perhaps this institution wasn't so enlightened after all. Perhaps Christianity wasn't all wrong.

During law school, I'd sometimes take the train from New Haven to New York City. It was cheap and easy, and I had never spent much time in New York before, so I made it a priority to get to know the city. On one trip, I sat next to a woman who was, without question, the most stereotypically elitist person I have ever seen. She was white but dressed in all black, wore a beret on her head and a scowl on her face, and looked as if she spent her time mocking Christian conservatives and podcasting about Republicans (I kid). She bore an uncanny resemblance to Sloth's mother in *The Goonies*.

Eventually, another person sat down near us, a young black woman with a baby about a year old. She looked around the age my mother and sister had been when they had their first kids. This kid—as one-year-olds are wont to do—was acting like an absolute terror. I felt awful for the mother. Still, I couldn't help but notice: Despite being obviously overwhelmed, this young woman was so *good* to her baby.

It's not an exaggeration to say our beret-wearing friend was having nearly the opposite reaction, and she wasn't afraid to show it. She reeked of disgust at the screaming child and her overwhelmed mother. She huffed at the screams and made weird guttural noises when the kid inched too close to her. It was an extreme version of something I've seen replayed on airplanes, a self-righteous performance of revulsion when someone else's child has invaded your space.

I'd heard a similar version of that disgust in discussions about unplanned pregnancies. "Teen mothers" were, and are, one of the few remaining groups of people upon whom it is still acceptable to look down. This unhealthy discomfort with children was far more common in the places that fancied themselves enlightened.

I was initially so overcome by the new world I encountered at Yale that I didn't see its shortcomings. And despite my reservations, it still possessed a certain magic. I loved the beautiful architecture. I appreciated that a real thirst for knowledge lurked behind the striving: Any book I had ever wanted was available in the vast libraries. And most of my classmates were fundamentally decent, fun people, who shared my trepidation as we played the same game.

Most of all, I loved New Haven in the cold, walking around the campus when its streets were practically deserted and I could wonder at all the history that had taken place within its ancient walls. Nathan Hale had studied here before he uttered the famous phrase: "I only regret that I have but one life to lose for my country."

I felt that the parts of this institution that were good came from an ancient time, well before the striving and credentialism of the modern era. The bones of this institution were Christian, and its Christian heritage echoed in every corner—from its halls of learning, meant to look like cathedrals, to the famous alumni who counted Christ as an inspiration. I had lost my religion but I could still recognize that faith inspired people to incredible acts of greatness and beauty. Very few of my classmates considered themselves devout Christians. But Nathan Hale had planned to become a minister before he left his studies at Yale and died at the British gallows in the same year the Founders birthed a new nation.

CHAPTER 5

Stranger in a Strange Land

In law school I found myself returning to a written debate between three twentieth-century philosophers—Antony Flew, R. M. Hare, and Basil Mitchell—which I had first encountered at Ohio State. Flew, an atheist (though he later recanted), argues that theological utterances—like "God loves man"—are fundamentally unfalsifiable and thus meaningless. Because a believer won't let facts count against his faith, his views aren't really claims about this world.

Flew's essay mapped well onto so much of what I'd heard people say. In the face of unspeakable tragedy: "The Lord works in mysterious ways." In the face of loneliness and desperation: "God still loves you." If the faithful were simply ignoring real, obvious challenges to these sentiments, then their faith must be pretty hollow.

In my class, we didn't focus on Basil Mitchell's response to Flew, but I have thought about his words constantly in the years since. He begins with a parable about a wartime soldier in occupied territory who meets a "Stranger." The soldier is so taken with the Stranger that he believes he is the leader of the resistance.

> Sometimes the Stranger is seen helping members of the resistance, and the partisan is grateful and says to his friends, "He is on our side." Sometimes he is seen in the uniform of the police handing over patriots to the occupying power. On these occasions his friends murmur against him: but the partisan still says, "He is on our side." He still believes that, in spite of appearances, the Stranger did not deceive him. Sometimes he asks the Stranger for help and receives it. He is then thankful. Sometimes he asks and does not receive it. Then he says, "The Stranger knows best." Sometimes his friends, in exasperation, say, "Well, what would he have to do for you to admit that you were wrong and that he is not on our side?" But the partisan refuses to answer. He will not consent to put the Stranger to the test. And sometimes his friends complain, "Well, if that's what you mean by his being on our side, the sooner he goes over to the other side the better." The partisan of the parable does not allow anything to count decisively against the proposition "The Stranger is on our side." This is because he has committed himself to trust the Stranger. But he of course recognizes that the Stranger's ambiguous behaviour does count against what he believes about him. It is precisely this situation which constitutes the trial of his faith.[1]

1 Anthony Flew, R. M. Hare, and Basil Mitchell, "Theology and Falsification," in *The Philosophy of Religion*, ed. Basil Mitchell (Oxford Univ. Press, 1971), 13–22.

Initially, I tried my best to dismiss Mitchell's response. Flew's argument hit such an emotional nerve—it described so perfectly the bromides of the faith I'd discarded—that I couldn't accept that he had lost the debate.

But Mitchell articulated a version of faith that I had never encountered personally. In my world, doubt was unacceptable. The proper response to a trial of faith was to pretend it had never happened. But here was Mitchell, conceding that the brokenness of the world and our individual tribulations did, in fact, count against the existence of God. Just not definitively.

I eventually stumbled upon this meditation from Saint Augustine on Genesis (emphasis mine):

> In matters that are obscure and far beyond our vision, even in such as we may find treated in Holy Scripture, *different interpretations are sometimes possible without prejudice to the faith we have received. In such a case, we should not rush in headlong and so firmly take our stand on one side that, if further progress in the search of truth justly undermines this position, we too fall with it. That would be to battle not for the teaching of Holy Scripture but for our own, wishing its teaching to conform to ours, whereas we ought to wish ours to conform to that of Sacred Scripture.*
>
> Let us suppose that in explaining the words, "And God said, 'Let there be light,' and light was made," (Gn 1, 3), one man thinks that it was material light that was made, and another that it was spiritual. As to the actual existence of "spiritual light" in a spiritual creature, our faith leaves no doubt; as to the existence of material light, celestial or supercelestial,

even existing before the heavens, a light which could have been followed by night, there will be nothing in such a supposition contrary to the faith until un-erring truth gives the lie to it. And if that should happen, this teaching was never in Holy Scripture but was an opinion proposed by man in his ignorance. . . .

Usually, even a non-Christian knows something about the earth, the heavens, and the other elements of the world, about the motion and orbit of the stars and even their size and relative positions, about the predictable eclipses of the sun and moon, the cycles of the years and the seasons, about the kinds of animals, shrubs, stones, and so forth, and this knowledge he holds to as being certain from reason and experience. *Now, it is a disgraceful and dangerous thing for an infidel to hear a Christian, presumably giving the meaning of Holy Scripture, talking nonsense on these topics*; and we should take all means to prevent such an embarrassing situation, in which people show up vast ignorance in a Christian and laugh it to scorn. The shame is not so much that an ignorant individual is derided, but that people outside the household of faith think our sacred writers held such opinions, and, to the great loss of those for whose salvation we toil, the writers of our Scripture are criticized and rejected as unlearned men. If they find a Christian mistaken in a field which they themselves know well and hear him maintaining his foolish opinions about our books, how are they going to believe those books in matters concerning the resurrection of the dead, the hope of eternal life, and the kingdom of heaven, when they think their pages are full of falsehoods on facts

> which they themselves have learnt from experience and the light of reason?[2]

I couldn't stop thinking about how I would have reacted to this passage when I was a teenager: If someone had made the same argument to me when I was seventeen, I would have called them a heretic. The text represented a partial surrender, the kind of accommodation to science that made a person's faith incomplete. You couldn't be a cafeteria Christian, taking and leaving what you wanted. You had to believe the whole thing. Yet here was Saint Augustine, a person with far more authority and far less interest in surrendering to any secular authority than I, telling us sixteen hundred years ago that my own approach to Genesis was one of arrogance—the kind that might turn a person from his faith. I posted the passage on Facebook and encouraged my friends to engage with it. One older woman from back home—a devout conservative Pentecostal—told me that it made her look at Genesis in a new light. I agreed.

This created the first proverbial crack in my atheist armor. I began circulating the passage among friends—believers and nonbelievers alike—and I thought about it constantly. Above all else, it gave me a certain humility: These debates about science and technology and faith and how to harmonize them hadn't first presented themselves to an arrogant young Christian in Middletown, Ohio, or to an even more arrogant atheist in Columbus. Rather, they were as old as the Church itself. I began to see the world of the Christian faith as richer and more interesting than I realized. There was nothing

2 Saint Augustine, *The Literal Meaning of Genesis*, Ancient Christian Writers, vol. 41, trans. John Hammond Taylor (Paulist Press, 1982).

new under the sun after two thousand years of debate. That didn't make Christianity true, but it did make it more complicated than the twenty-first-century atheists admitted.

As I worked through all of this, I attended a talk with Peter Thiel, a Silicon Valley entrepreneur and investor. He surprised me by speaking not of his business and investment achievements, but instead in personal terms, arguing that we were increasingly tracked into cutthroat professional competitions. We would compete for appellate clerkships and then Supreme Court clerkships. We would compete for jobs at elite law firms and then for partnerships at those same places. At each juncture, he said, our jobs would offer longer hours, social alienation from our peers, and work whose prestige would fail to make up for its meaninglessness.

He also argued that his own Silicon Valley world spent too little time on the technological breakthroughs that made life better—in biology, energy, and transportation, for example—and too much time on things like software and mobile phones. Everyone could now tweet at each other, or post photos on Facebook, but it took us longer to travel to Europe than it used to, we had no cure for cognitive decline and dementia, and our energy production had stagnated. He saw these two trends—elite professionals tracked in hypercompetitive jobs and the technological stagnation of society—as connected. If technological innovation were actually driving real prosperity, our elites wouldn't feel increasingly competitive with one another over a dwindling number of prestigious outcomes. And if our smartest people were building rocket ships and finding cures for cancer instead of financial derivatives, the real economy would experience more dynamism.

Peter gave voice to something I had been feeling, but had not fully understood: that I was obsessed with achievement per se—not to accomplish something meaningful, but to win a social competition. I had prioritized striving over character, and for what was I even striving? I didn't even know why I cared about the things I cared about. I fancied myself educated, enlightened, and especially wise about the ways of the world—at least compared to most people from my hometown. Yet here I was, obsessed with obtaining professional credentials—a clerkship with a federal judge followed by an associate position at a prestigious firm—that I didn't understand. I had hated my experiences in legal practice. I looked to the future and realized that I'd been running a desperate race where the first prize was a job I didn't want.

I immediately began planning for a career outside the law, which is why I spent less than two years after graduation as a practicing attorney.

But Thiel impacted me in another way: Possibly the smartest person I'd ever met, he identified very openly as a Christian. He defied the simple social template I had constructed—that dumb people were religious and smart people were atheists. I began to wonder where his faith came from, which led me to René Girard, the French philosopher under whom Thiel had studied at Stanford.

Girard's thought catalog is rich enough that my summary won't do it justice. His theory of mimetic rivalry—that we tend to compete over the things other people want—spoke directly to some of the competitive pressures I had experienced at Yale. I wanted a Supreme Court clerkship because that's what other people wanted. I wanted a job at a good law firm because that's what other people wanted. Girard gave me a vocabulary to describe the pressures I felt but hadn't been able to articulate. But it was his related theory of the scapegoat—and what it revealed about Christianity—that made me think about the Christian faith in a new light.

One of Girard's central insights is that human civilizations are often (or perhaps always) founded on a "scapegoat myth"—an act of violence committed against someone who has wronged the broader community, retold as a sort of origin story. Importantly, this scapegoat is innocent of what they're accused of.

Take, for example, Remus, whose death at the hands of his brother, Romulus, serves as the foundational myth of Roman civilization. Romulus and Remus were, like Jesus, the children of a god, and, like Moses, were sent downriver in a basket to be saved from a jealous king.

There was a time when I bristled at these mythological comparisons. The New Atheists would point to some creation story—like the flood narrative in the Babylonian epic of Gilgamesh—as evidence that the Bible's authors were plagiarists. How could the Bible be the Word of God if it plagiarized someone else? Couldn't the creator of the universe come up with His own material?

But Girard rejects this inference and leans into the similarities between biblical stories and those from other civilizations. These similarities are evidence not that Christianity plagiarized but merely that the civilizations in question draw from the same place. Girard looked at ideas in the same way that Darwin looked at species: They might have a common ancestor, but the most compelling versions of those ideas tended to dominate their environment in the same way the most well-adapted species did.

To Girard, the Christian story contains a critical difference from other scapegoat myths—a difference that reveals "things hidden since the foundation of the world." In the Christian telling, the scapegoat defeats the judgment of the mob. The victim is infinitely powerful—

able to prevent His own murder—and perfectly innocent, undeserving of the crowd's rage and violence. He submitted Himself to death, and then He conquered it.

In Christ, we see our efforts to shift blame and our own inadequacies onto a victim for what they are: a character flaw in ourselves, projected in violence on someone else. Christ is the scapegoat who reveals our imperfections. There is nothing triumphant about His death or about the crowd who killed Him. The triumph is Christ Himself, who defeats death and reveals to the crowd—including all of us—that *they* are at fault.

As lawyer Frank Devito observed:

> But Jesus Christ turns the scapegoat mechanism on its head, because he is the voluntary scapegoat. He takes all human violence, all unfair hatred, every bit of sin upon himself and willingly dies in order to reconcile man with God. Ordinary scapegoats are insufficient, because they were never the true cause of the violence that plagued the community, nor were they guilty and therefore justly sacrificed. Christ, unlike these scapegoats, is truly innocent, yet takes all human sin, violence, and guilt upon himself. And when Christ rises from the dead, he reveals his innocence. He was not condemned by God as the guilty one; he proves this publicly by defeating death. Thus, those who put Christ to death see him risen, see his sentence and punishment reversed.[3]

3 Frank Devito, "Christ and the End of the Scapegoat," *Public Discourse*, August 26, 2025, https://www.thepublicdiscourse.com/2025/08/98754/.

Girard's work captured so well the psychology of my generation, especially its most privileged members. Mired in the swamp of social media, we would identify a scapegoat and digitally pounce. We were keyboard warriors, unloading on people via Facebook, instant messenger, and Twitter, blind to our own failings. We fought over jobs we didn't actually want while pretending we weren't fighting for them at all. Our prize for winning the meritocratic game was a desk job at an investment bank, preparing pitch decks, or at a law firm, billing hours, making just enough to buy our way into a sense of social superiority.

Besides forcing me to think about scapegoating—about the ways in which we rationalize our own moral failures and project them onto innocent people—Girard also made explicit the social nature of "truth." Our desire to pursue prestige didn't just influence which jobs we sought, it also influenced the thoughts in our heads.

It was in law school that I first became aware that I was susceptible to intense pressure to believe certain things. We talked a lot about diversity of thought in the legal academy, but I ran into the limits of this open-mindedness when I served as an officer of an organization that brought conservative speakers to the law school.

The range of acceptable opinions was very clear at Yale. With Mamaw and my friends back home, people held every kind of outrageous view, and they weren't always internally coherent. Conservatives who wanted universal health care. Liberals who distrusted the push for gay rights. For my entire life, it never occurred to me that a view I held could ruin a relationship or get me fired. If you offended someone over politics, you'd apologize or tell them to get over it.

But at Yale, the groupthink pressure was incredibly powerful. In the early 2010s, we had not yet reached the peak wokeness of

2020, of corporate CEOs or professional athletes groveling before an offended mob. But I should have seen it coming. The Overton window slowly narrowed. As a conservative, you could safely believe in free market economics, but if you actively supported more conservative social views, you were considered backward. You'd often hear people say they were "socially liberal, fiscally conservative"—a rare viewpoint among anyone without a professional degree[4]—which was implicitly a way of signaling that they didn't hold any especially icky views. You could advocate for a lower corporate tax rate, but God forbid you tell anyone that an unborn baby should have greater legal protections.

Of course, being unpopular doesn't mean an idea is correct. Hating black people for the color of their skin is unpopular and also clearly wrong. But I felt that social pressure exerting a powerful force on me in subtler ways. Among a certain type of conservative intellectuals, there's a famous boogeyman: the "Georgetown cocktail party," the sort of party from which DC elites never want to be uninvited. A desire to be part of the clique keeps people in line and ensures they never espouse views that genuinely challenge the left-of-center consensus.

One law school acquaintance, contemplating the possibility of a Mitt Romney administration, worried that he would appoint Supreme Court Justices like Clarence Thomas.

"Great!" said a friend, a devout Catholic, trying to rib our more liberal conversation partner.

---

4 Benjamin Page, Larry M. Bartels, and Jason Seawright, "Democracy and the Policy Preferences of Wealthy Americans," *Perspectives on Politics* 11, no. 1 (March 2013): 51–73, https://faculty.wcas.northwestern.edu/jnd260/cab/CAB2012%20-%20Page1.pdf.

But it wasn't funny, because appointing Clarence Thomas to the federal bench was not a laughing matter. The Clarence Thomas critic took the remark as a personal offense, evidence that his defender was socially undesirable. I never saw the two speak again.

I'd be lying if I said I've ever experienced overt discrimination for my religious views during my four decades on earth. At Yale, however, I really came to realize how disfavored Christianity was among the most well-educated members of our society. They weren't mean about it, usually. They just felt like it was a weird superstition. Even the rare religious persons I encountered at Yale often had sufficiently idiosyncratic views that they avoided any uncomfortable conversations. The conservative Christians I knew were somewhat detached from the mainstream of the law school's social culture. There were also very few of them.

And while this realization didn't exactly make me enthusiastic for Christianity—most people instinctively would prefer not to join a minority of dubious popularity—it did reveal to me how many of my own views were driven by what amounted to popularity. Again, this wasn't exactly conscious. I didn't think to myself, *I am not going to be a Christian because Christians are rubes and I want to plant myself firmly in the meritocratic master class.*

Socialization operates in subtler, but more powerful ways. One of my children, as a toddler, transitioned from jerking our German shepherd's collar to hugging and kissing him gleefully. Part of that shift came from the inherent joy of sharing affection with man's best friend. But part of it came from the fact that I would grimace and complain when he tortured the dog but coo and laugh when he loved on our pet. Our little boy responded to me much as I responded to the educated caste into which I was being acculturated in college and law school. In college, few of my friends and fewer of my professors had any sort of religious faith. At Yale, the numbers were even smaller. Secularism may not have been a prerequisite to join the elites, but it sure made things easier.

I was still not ready to rethink Christianity. If I had discarded my faith in part because of elite pressure, then my faith must have been pretty superficial to begin with. That way of thinking about the world was inadequate but that didn't mean another way was perfect.

But the door was open.

CHAPTER 6

My Favorite Year

Not long before I got to law school, one of my best friends, Mike, went through a particularly tough breakup with a girl. All the standard clichés applied as I did my best to soothe my buddy with a combination of good conversation and copious amounts of Natural Light. During his relationship, he had acknowledged that he and his girlfriend weren't a particularly good match. He had complained that she was jealous. She had demanded too much of his time. Her parents had been intrusive. But all that faded away in the mists of heartache. Now she was perfect, beautiful, the love of his life. She had dumped him, and as I've noticed time after time with my buddies, the only thing worse than heartache is heartache with a bruised ego on top.

Mike and I were home in Middletown over Christmas, so I took him out to our favorite watering hole—Carol's Speakeasy—to play darts and tell stories and drink his troubles away.

It's fresh, but he's in a pretty good place, I thought as we left the bar.

But as I drove him home, the sense of loss—well lubricated by alcohol—came flowing out of him.

There he was in my old Honda Civic (me sober, him not) bawling his eyes out about this girl. I gave him a hug, listened to him in his driveway for about an hour, and told him to just keep putting one foot in front of the other. I reminded him he hadn't been all that crazy about her until she dumped him and that he was a good-looking guy with a lot of options.

"Plus," I told him. "I'm single, and when we get back to Columbus, I can be your wingman. There are plenty of fish in the sea."

"Yeah," he replied half-heartedly. Columbus was nothing if not a target-rich environment for a couple of bachelors.

I hadn't felt the same heartache in my own dating life. For a couple of years during and after college, I'd dated a girl named Mary. She was sweet, and she wanted the same things out of life that I did: a nice house, a decent job, and a couple of kids. My family got along with her fine. No relationship is perfect, but nothing seemed like a deal breaker. Still, I could never escape the feeling that, as much as I liked her, if she were to dump me the next day, I'd get over it quickly. I'd never react the way Mike had reacted to his breakup with Jessica.

"Dude, I don't think I have that gene or something," I told Mike.

"What do you mean?" he asked.

"I've just never fallen head over heels for a girl. Some are better and some are worse. I could rate Mary on all these objective criteria, and she's mostly great. But would I sob if she broke up with me? No way. Isn't that a problem?"

"Maybe she's not the right girl," he suggested.

"Maybe," I said. "But maybe I'm just not that emotional."

* * *

A few months after that conversation, I was still dating Mary—now long distance, from New Haven, Connecticut, where I was a couple of months into my first year of law school. I was walking late at night on an unusually cold and rainy fall day. New Haven is spooky in the fog, and the rain had emptied out the streets. And the whole time I was thinking about another student: Usha Bala Chilukuri.

I called my buddy Mike, who asked about law school, the classmates, the vibe, and the girls.

"Dude, I think I'm obsessed with this chick in my small group. It's unhealthy."

The small group, I explained, was the collection of sixteen students with whom I shared all of my first-year classes.

I told him all about her: That she was smarter than everyone. That her smile could light up a room. That she had the most amazing posture.

"She doesn't even walk like normal people. Normal girls seem kind of unstable in high heels," I told him. "Not her. She glides across the room in whatever shoes she wears. And her laugh, man. Whenever she laughs it's, like, the most wonderful thing. She's super reserved, but she has this chortle that is the best sound I've ever heard."

"JD?" Mike interrupted. "Remember when you told me you don't have the gene where you fall head over heels for a girl? I always thought that was BS. Now I know it is."

He was right, of course. I don't need to belabor the point. A consequence of my current job is that my relationship with the Second

Lady has been written about, analyzed, researched, and dissected more than I ever thought possible. It is strange to read things about the person you love the most that you know are false. For example, a former classmate (and former acquaintance) told some major newspaper that I was initially attracted to Usha because of her "ambition."

Usha and I found this laughable—that I would ever confide in this classmate, but more so that I was attracted to Usha's ambition. There were many things that I thought were unusual about Usha when I first met her. One is that she was intensely competitive, but I saw this as more bizarre than attractive. She was incapable of jealousy, something I assumed came from a supreme inner confidence. But when I asked her—she was more capable than any person I had ever met—what she wanted to do, I was shocked at how uninterested she was in traditional markers of success.

"I just want interesting work," she told me.

Her dream job was to run the Sesame Workshop because she loved kids and the idea of making educational programming that appealed to them. At Yale Law School, every person thinks they're eventually going to run the world. You couldn't throw a rock without hitting a person who thought they'd eventually become a Supreme Court Justice or US senator. But Usha, more capable than any of them, couldn't have cared less about any of that. "There's something a little jacked up about all of this," I told Mike. "The least impressive person at this school is the most ambitious. But the most impressive just wants to have a family and a decent job."

I told Usha something similar: "You have the biggest mismatch between ambition and ability of any person I've ever met. You could be the Chief Justice of the Supreme Court and you have no interest in it."

That complete indifference to what other people wanted to do—or wanted her to do—was just another in a long list of magnetic personality traits.

I once described Usha as a combination of every genetic gift a person would want to have—beauty, intelligence, height. But there was something more: She was intense. I was drawn to her unlike I had ever been drawn to anyone.

I broke up with Mary, in part because of the long distance, but mostly because I couldn't imagine settling for anyone else.

"I will marry this girl," I told my friends. "Or I will be a lifelong bachelor."

Everyone else was like a dim light bulb set against Usha's radiance. My feelings for her overrode every instinct and everything I thought I knew about women. "Play hard to get" was something young men told one another about attracting the opposite sex. But instead, I told Usha before we ever dated that I was in love with her. "Don't come on too strong" was another adage of dating I had learned from the world, but we had been together only a few weeks when I told her I wanted to marry her and would do whatever I needed to do to make that happen.

I had always wanted to move back home to Ohio, and she had fallen in love with New York. So I told her I'd move to New York with her, or California, or Colorado. I didn't care, so long as she was there. I told her everything and I asked her about everything. Her life was the most interesting thing in the world. Politics, technology, business—these were professional interests, things I read about and wanted to work on. But Usha was the only one for whom I'd ever felt real passion.

Amazingly, it worked out. Usha and I began dating in law school, and during our first summer together romantically we were apart physically—me in Washington, DC, at first and then in New Haven, doing research for a professor, and she in New York working for a law firm. We had been together only a few months, and I felt so intensely toward her that she occupied my thoughts nearly every waking moment. This was normal, of course: Two young lovers caught in that early stage of romance, where everything is new and exciting and profound. But I remember thinking that no man had ever felt so strongly about a woman in the history of the world and that I had to hide at least some of my feelings lest I come on too strong. The fact that we spent most of that summer in separate cities—the absence—only compounded it all.

In hindsight, it's a wonder I didn't ruin it. I didn't just come on too strong; I was a lousy boyfriend in many ways. My traumatic childhood had made me resentful and left me with awful conflict management skills. I would overreact or withdraw—fight or flight!—over minor transgressions. If Usha was my soulmate at Yale, I didn't deserve her. But still she stuck around.

She did insist that I deal with my past and that I try to understand my mother, my grandmother, and the alcoholism and addiction that plagued my family. Because of Usha, I attended a few therapy sessions at the Yale student health clinic. The therapist I spoke with was a good guy, but I found therapy too uncomfortable. I didn't like to talk to my own girlfriend about how crazy my homelife was, so why would I talk to a stranger?

But there was a deeper problem with therapy as I encountered it. It was divorced from any sense of responsibility or guilt. In one session, we explored an incident that I've since discussed publicly: Driving with my mother on a relatively rural road, she loses her temper. She accelerates the car, threatening to crash and kill both of us. I hop in the back seat to protect myself, which enrages her further. She pulls over, I get out of the car and run, and the whole ordeal ends up in her arrest. The case is later dismissed, based largely on my refusal to testify against my mother.

The therapist told me that this was an example of *unresolved trauma*, a common focus of modern therapy. Experts tend to describe unresolved trauma as when a person experiences "disruptive physical and emotional reactions in the present as their body and mind continue to defend against" threats they faced in the past.[1]

The gist is that my fight-or-flight response, my temper, and my general resentment about my feelings of insecurity were consequences of trauma I had experienced and hadn't properly "processed." And of course, part of that processing was understanding how trauma across the generations was linked. The trauma I experienced at the hand of my mother was connected to the time my grandfather got drunk and beat her. And of course, my grandfather didn't have it easy growing up in the deep poverty of Kentucky coal country.

I resisted this for a couple of reasons. The first is that the framing turned me into a victim rather than an actor. I'm sure that therapy helps many people, but the thought of being a victim made me want to puke. No matter how bad the things that had happened to

1 Sanjana Gupta, "What Is Unresolved Trauma?," Verywell Mind, November 19, 2025, https://www.verywellmind.com/unresolved-trauma-symptoms-causes-diagnosis-and-treatment-6753365.

me, I didn't want to see myself as a helpless bit character in my own life. A person to whom things happened. I wanted to be the author of my own destiny.

The therapist's framing had another implication. It removed the moral dimension from human conduct. Undoubtedly, I had faced tougher circumstances than most of my classmates. The same went for my mother. But our trauma did not write us a moral blank check. I was searching for a more satisfying accounting of wrongdoing and responsibility. Of temptation and willpower. Of virtue and guilt. There had to be some way of understanding that we are neither beholden to the misdeeds of our ancestors nor wholly independent from them. If it was wrong to bury trauma, pretend it didn't happen, and hope the consequences never reared their head, it was equally wrong to wallow in trauma and pretend it controlled us—or worse, deprived us of our very agency. There had to be a third way.

That third way—a way that could acknowledge the trauma in a child's life without excusing his behavior as an adult—became more and more appealing. But most of all I wanted to be a better person. I wanted to be worthy of this woman I was madly in love with. And I began to fear that the past was a prologue: that whatever happened to my mother, whatever destroyed marriages and friendships in my family, would eventually destroy what I had with Usha.

I began to realize that, of all the influences Usha had on me, the most important was that she always encouraged me to keep searching for deeper truths. We read a lot as law students: casebooks and essays and Supreme Court opinions and legal treatises. But Usha always wanted me to read more fiction. "You can't just fill your brain with facts and data; you need to fill it with interesting thoughts."

She was my guiding light, showing me how to navigate the weird social dynamics of places like Yale and law firms. But she had a far more profound influence on how I thought. She'd send multiple articles a day, often from liberal outlets like *The New York Times*.

"You have to stop reading that garbage," I told her. "Don't you realize it's all biased?"

And she'd roll her eyes and tell me that everything was biased. So, I'd read her essays about the origin of ketchup and obscure corners of the Pacific Ocean because she found them interesting and I did, too.

Usha had an unbelievable capacity to withstand the social and professional pressures of this still-new world. Everyone wanted the same things, the same jobs, the same titles, and the same accolades from professors. She charted her own course and encouraged me to do the same. She had a fascination with the world that made the mundane come to life. And she found beauty everywhere, from the birds in the trees to the shapes of leaves to the way the light fell on Yale's Gothic halls at dusk. She took me to the Yale Center for British Art, and when I made fun of a sculpture or told her that my little niece made better paintings with watercolors, she would encourage me to look deeper for the meaning in someone else's work. She would point out the carvings in the ceilings of beautiful buildings at Yale and ask me what I thought they meant, even though she normally knew the answer and I had no idea.

Usha was raised in a Hindu family. Still, she could tell me when an old church in New Haven or Cincinnati was constructed, and we'd walk around and stare up at the tall steeples and share the awe of the place even though neither of us shared the faith of the people who made it.

To say that I was in love with her would have understated it. Luckily, she was also in love with me. Even though I was something else. She was the tornado in *The Wizard of Oz*: Before her, I existed in black and white. Now, the full color of the world revealed itself.

Child psychologists who study the children of trauma coined the term *resilient child* for those kids who thrive despite their upbringings. One hallmark of resilient children is that they can form strong attachments to one adult, which stabilizes life and allows them to develop normally despite the chaos at home. For me, that was always my grandmother. But now it had become Usha.

That was, of course, unfair to Usha, and our relationship was a roller coaster because I latched on to her pretty tightly. That we'd made it this far was no small miracle.

* * *

During our third year of law school I proposed, and after graduation we spent a year in Cincinnati, where we planned our wedding during our downtime. We had gotten a German shepherd, Casper, before we moved and acquired a floppy-eared hound we called Pippin from a Cincinnati rescue. We lived in a historical neighborhood with a beautiful view of the Ohio River and settled in for our first real experiment of living together—no roommates or law school classmates, just us.

We would look back on our year in Cincinnati and refer to it—only half jokingly—as the best year of our lives. When a study came out recently showing that the optimal salary for a person to be happy was sixty thousand dollars, I didn't buy it.

"Can you believe this crap? This sounds like a study a rich person wrote so the poors don't get too uppity."

Usha laughed, but she pushed back. "Maybe. But we made about sixty thousand each in Cincinnati and it was perfect."

It was a very good year: a young couple, madly in love, planning a wedding with no kids and few responsibilities. We took road trips all over the region. We learned to cook. We discovered our favorite restaurant in downtown Cincinnati and went there all the time because we didn't have anything else to do.

But if this proved to be an amazing year together, it was also an unexpected boon to my faith. In late nights alone (Usha always went to bed before I did) and long walks with the dogs through Cincinnati's beautiful hills and historic neighborhoods, I felt a sense of contentedness I thought existed only in movies. And I had the time and space to focus on the big questions.

Since I had joined the Marine Corps in 2003, my life had been a sprint. In those ten years, I had gone to war and come home, graduated from college in two years, and finished Yale Law School. But it wasn't clear what I was sprinting toward.

Perhaps I was sprinting away from something. Sprinting away from my childhood, from the drama and trauma, from the financial problems and the sense of chaos.

My career was on a rocket ship. I had a prestigious federal clerkship and an offer at a major international law firm. I had an elite law school diploma. I had the promise of financial riches I had only dreamed of as a kid. Prestige . . . elite . . . riches. These were the hollow goals of a person who measured his life by how other people viewed him. I loved the judge I clerked for, but I had no real interest in becoming a lawyer. I had gone to law school because it seemed like a respectable career path, and I had chosen Yale because it was the best school I got into.

The contrast with Usha was striking: She loved the law and was good at its practice. Her drive seemed internal: to build a career she found interesting and challenging. Mine was external: to build a career that others would find prestigious.

I had joined the rat race of modern meritocracy without any finish line in mind. I had gotten all the grades, the credentials, the degrees, and the job offers to impress other people. And man, were they impressed. Family would show me off at social functions and introduce me as the kid who went to Yale. I had all the external validation anyone could want, and yet I found this world unsatisfying.

I found it unsatisfying because it couldn't answer the big questions, and it seemed designed to distract from them or even to replace the normal yearnings of a healthy soul with something else. Many couples I met in this world were at some stage of a long-distance relationship. It always felt a bit bizarre—to give up a year with the person you love to make way for a job. Some couples would spend years apart to pursue their respective careers. *What the hell is wrong with these people?* I thought. *In sixty years, we'll all be dead, and they'll have wasted so much of that time away from the person they apparently loved.*

The obsession with achievement and credentials had left me lost. But if anything made me feel tethered, it was Usha. And she didn't care if I got a Supreme Court clerkship or made a lot of money. She just wanted me to watch old movies with her and take the dogs on walks and read classic novels and send her the interesting articles I found during the day. She wanted me to be a good person, a good husband, and a good father (eventually).

And the truth is that I had a lot of work to do on those fronts. I needed to be more patient. Less hot-tempered. I needed to address my past without wallowing in it. I needed to be able to drive to Middletown and help my family, while still being able to set boundaries on things like how much money we lent them. Usha depended on me now, and my first obligation was to her.

Though I would hardly have described myself as a Christian in 2013, I was now clearly "Christian curious." The meritocracy had made alluring promises but had failed to reckon with the big questions. But the religion of my grandmother was coming back to me and offered something different.

One of Usha's co-clerks was a football player from Massachusetts named Sam. Usha's politics were more moderate than her conservative judge's, but Sam made Judge Amul Thapar seem like a flaming liberal. He was big—an offensive lineman from Amherst—and brash, and we became fast friends.

Raised in a Jewish family in Boston, Sam became an evangelical Christian thanks to influence from fellow students and a professor at Amherst. After a couple of years, he found himself attracted to the tradition and liturgy of the Catholic faith.

He'd go on extended rants about the Reformation and immigration and every other topic. "You think we started to go off the rails with Obama? This all started with John Calvin. He's the real villain of comprehensive immigration reform."

Like me, Sam had climbed to the top of the American meritocracy but had found it wanting. He had striven to get into an elite college, but found that success did not bring many of his classmates happiness.

A few of us took an online university course on the Hebrew Bible, or the Old Testament in Christian parlance. As in law school, Usha did the reading and I mostly listened to the lectures. But we both found it illuminating. I was particularly drawn to the lectures on the creation story in Genesis. For the first time in my life, I encountered Genesis not as a story to be proven or debunked by secular science, but as an ancient text about the origin of man and his relationship with God. Unshackled from the desire to prove its legitimacy, I did something I'd never done before: I absorbed it and learned something from it.

The first thing that struck me was how God stands outside of creation, rather than being part of it. What made the monotheistic account of the Jews so unique was how it understood the world as derivative of God. The God of Abraham is less like the Greek god Zeus—an all-powerful being within the created universe. He's more like the God of the Greek philosophers—the cause of time, motion, and matter, but set outside of it and completely immune to the rules He had created.

In the fairy tale version of the Garden of Eden I had encountered as a child, we learned that everything was perfect until Adam and Eve disobeyed God. Everything, from sin and pain to death itself, entered the world because of their disobedience. I realized that this account was incomplete. For after Adam and Eve eat from the tree of knowledge, God steps in:

> Unto Adam also and to his wife did the Lord God make coats of skins, and clothed them. And the Lord God said, Behold, the man is become as one of us, to know good and evil: and now, lest he put forth his hand, and take also of the tree of life, and eat, and live for ever: Therefore the Lord God sent him forth from the garden of Eden, to till the ground from whence he was taken. (Gen. 3:21–23)

The fairy tale version of my youth had completely eliminated God's role and put it all on us. But the Bible itself makes it clear that all this was God's design. He could have allowed Adam and Eve to live forever, but He chose not to. Now, you might say this is cruel; that's a separate debate. But the biblical account of creation emphasizes God's agency: He could have allowed us to live forever and chose not to. And He doesn't even tell us why. Lying at the heart of our faith is a mystery: why God allows people to suffer, but perhaps more deeply, why only He understands the purpose of our suffering. To a wavering believer, it can seem kind of screwed up: Genesis is not a particularly reassuring piece of scripture. But it is truer to the reality of the world than the fairy tale I once believed.

We also tell ourselves fairy tales about the linear nature of justice: Our sins lead to pain and suffering. Our virtues are rewarded. God is a cosmic father who spanks us when we misbehave and gives us a pat on the head when we do as we're told. But encountering the Bible as a skeptical outsider rather than a devoted insider allowed me to see a richness that had previously been hidden from me: While our sin leads to suffering, sometimes that suffering has nothing to do with us in the long run. When Job demands that God tell him why he, a virtuous man, was allowed to suffer, God refuses to answer directly:

Who is this that darkeneth counsel by
words without knowledge?
Gird up now thy loins like a man; for I will
demand of thee, and answer thou me.
Where wast thou when I laid the foundations of
the earth? declare, if thou hast understanding.
Who hath laid the measures thereof, if thou
knowest? or who hath stretched the line upon it?
Whereupon are the foundations thereof fastened?
or who laid the corner stone thereof;
When the morning stars sang together, and
all the sons of God shouted for joy?
Or who shut up the sea with doors, when it brake
forth, as if it had issued out of the womb?
When I made the cloud the garment thereof,
and thick darkness a swaddlingband for it,
And brake up for it my decreed place,
and set bars and doors,
And said, Hitherto shalt thou come, but no further:
and here shall thy proud waves be stayed?
Hast thou commanded the morning since thy days;
and caused the dayspring to know his place;

That it might take hold of the ends of the earth,
that the wicked might be shaken out of it?
It is turned as clay to the seal; and
they stand as a garment.
And from the wicked their light is withholden,
and the high arm shall be broken.
Hast thou entered into the springs of the sea? or
hast thou walked in the search of the depth?
Have the gates of death been opened unto thee? or
hast thou seen the doors of the shadow of death?
Hast thou perceived the breadth of the earth?
declare if thou knowest it all. (Job 38:2–18)

God's answer to Job is deeply unsatisfying, but unsatisfying in the way that life and death and any honest account of the world must be: *You cannot understand it, but I do. This suffering may not make sense according to your plans, but it makes sense according to mine.*

We are like golden retrievers trying to understand how an iPhone functions. It's not just that we don't get it—it's that we don't have the faculties to fully understand. We must trust in God.

This is, in my view, the inherent contradiction of the human spirit. We have an endowed sense of justice, of right and wrong, that things ought to go a certain way. We're not just sad when a kid dies in a bus crash, or a young father contracts terminal cancer—we sense that this is wrong, that it violates some metaphysical rule given to us by someone much greater than we are. *It's not right that a parent bury a child*, we say to ourselves. But it happens anyway.

In the Book of Exodus, God tells us the sins of the father will be repaid by his children and grandchildren. This, too, seems unfair. We don't believe in collective punishment. But who could look at the wreckages of addiction or crime or a marriage torn apart by cheating and think for a second that the father's sins don't affect his children? We wish they didn't, but we know they do.

The real Old Testament is not a fairy tale. Its account can be brutally evocative of a kind of pathological, cosmic unfairness. But it is a rich description of the world we actually inhabit. Sitting in our small Cincinnati apartment listening to lectures by a Jewish professor, I began to appreciate the truth of this ancient text in a way I never had before.

If the faith of my youth avoided the most vexing questions of our religion—and consequently, the most vexing questions of life itself—the actual Bible threw them in my face. "Yes, God allows good people to suffer," it told me. "Wasn't that obvious?"

I returned over and over to the deeper question: Why? Why did an all-powerful God create human beings burning with a sense of right and wrong to occupy a world where those rules are violated every day? These arguments are as old as religion itself. You can't pick up a book of Christian apologetics without encountering some treatment of the issue. The New Atheists of the early 2000s had used this conundrum to push people away from religious faith. In his bestseller *God Is Not Great*, Christopher Hitchens argues that God is like a cosmic dictator, allowing suffering and punishing people in ways He doesn't have to.

C. S. Lewis, in *The Problem of Pain*, characterizes pain as a wake-up call from God: "God whispers to us in our pleasures, speaks in our conscience, but shouts in our pains: it is His megaphone to rouse a deaf world." However, even Lewis described

God as a "cosmic sadist" in his darkest time, as his wife suffered while dying from cancer. Grief transforms us in ways that defy logic or description, or even understanding. And God doesn't demand that we understand it: Indeed, He cautions against the idea that we can ever understand it. He demands instead that we trust that our suffering is part of a bigger plan. To our demand for answers, He responds, "Hast thou commanded the morning since thy days; and caused the dayspring to know his place?"

The fact that suffering just is—that it cannot be explained or reasoned away—gave me a weird comfort in 2014. If I had achieved a kind of escape velocity from my past—from the chaos, from the lack of money, from the instability—my life, as Michael Corleone said in *The Godfather Part III*, kept "pulling me back in."

I wrote in *Hillbilly Elegy* of getting a call from my mother and driving late at night from Cincinnati to Middletown to help her find a motel. I didn't want to help her, but without me she'd be homeless.

> I stood at a window of one of those sleazy roadside motels, separated from a woman (who certainly hadn't majored in hospitality management) by a thick pane of glass. The light from her office illuminated a few spiderwebs suspended between the building and the makeshift sun blocker that seemed prime to collapse on top of me. On each web was at least one giant spider, and I thought that if I looked away from them for too long, one of those ghastly creatures would jump on my face and suck my blood. I'm not even afraid of spiders, but these things were *big*.
>
> I wasn't supposed to be here. I'd structured my entire life to avoid just these types of places. When I thought of leav-

ing my hometown, of "getting out," it was from this sort of place that I wanted to escape. It was past midnight. The streetlight revealed the silhouette of a man sitting halfway in his truck—the door open, his feet dangling to the side—with the unmistakable form of a hypodermic needle sticking from his arm. . . .

The woman running the hotel that night was the most pitiful sight of all. She might have been forty, but everything about her—from the long, gray, greasy hair, the mouth empty of teeth, and the frown that she wore like a millstone—screamed old age. This woman had lived a hard life. Her voice sounded like a small child's, even a toddler's. It was meek, barely audible, and very sad.

I gave the woman my credit card, and she was clearly unprepared. "Normally, people pay cash," she explained. I told her, "Yeah, but like I said on the phone, I'm going to pay with a credit card. I can run to an ATM if you'd prefer." "Oh, I'm sorry, I guess I forgot. But it's okay, we've got one of those machines around here somewhere." So she retrieved one of those ancient card-swiping machines—the kind that imprints the card's information on a yellow slip of paper. When I handed her the card, her eyes seemed to plead with me, as if she was a prisoner in her own life. "Enjoy your stay," she said, which struck me as an odd instruction. I had told her on the phone not an hour earlier that the room wasn't for me, it was for my homeless mother. "Okay," I said. "Thanks."

I was a recent graduate of Yale Law School, a former editor of the prestigious *Yale Law Journal*, and a member

> of the bar in good standing. . . . I had a nice job, a recently purchased home, a loving relationship, and a happy life in a city that I loved—Cincinnati. . . .
>
> I don't know the precise chain of events that led me to that hotel, but I knew the stuff that mattered. Mom had begun using again. She'd stolen some family heirlooms from her fifth husband to buy drugs (prescription opiates, I think), and he kicked her out of the house in response. They were divorcing, and she had nowhere to go.
>
> I'd sworn to myself that I'd never help Mom again, but the person who made that oath to himself had changed. I was exploring, however uneasily, the Christian faith that I'd discarded years earlier. I had learned, for the first time, the extent of Mom's childhood emotional wounds. And I had realized that those wounds never truly heal, even for me. So when I discovered that Mom was in dire straits, I didn't mutter insults under my breath and hang up the phone. I offered to help her.

But I didn't always help her, and in that moment in 2014, I was certain she wouldn't make it another year or two. When I gave her money, I'd feel guilty that I was roping poor Usha into a life she couldn't possibly understand. When I didn't help her, I'd feel guilty about abandoning her and being a bad son.

This sense of survivor's guilt dominated much of my thinking at the time. My life had taught me that instability is the price we pay for joy. Usha and I were engaged, but I just knew I'd screw up our happy life somehow. When we eventually had kids, I feared that I'd abandon them or abuse them or fail them in some other way. I could win the race against financial or political or business competitors. But with Usha and the kids we didn't even have yet, I felt like I was racing against the ghosts of my past. I couldn't beat them any more than my own mother could beat her addiction.

We all have our crosses to bear, and this was mine. And though I had carried it for my entire life, it was only once I started attending Christian churches again that I found a name for it: the mortal sin of despair.

The irony is that for most of my life, suffering had been my pathway to God. My first real experience of suffering was my great-grandmother's dementia and eventual death, when I was still a little boy. I saw her struggle to remember her grandchildren's names, and I watched my grandmother and other relatives try to care for her body while grieving the loss of her mind. Caring for a person like that is like caring for a newborn: There is no positive feedback, no moment of gratitude, no recognition that they know you are trying your utmost. With an infant, those moments of positive feedback eventually come: You see a first smile, and then a chuckle, and then all the wonderful things that happen as an infant matures into a toddler. With a senile, elderly mother, there is no light at the end of the tunnel. Her condition deteriorates until, eventually, it reaches its natural end.

But my grandmother never doubted her faith in these moments. The grief brought her closer to God, she told me. And even when she was impatient with her ailing mother—or wished for it all to end—the guilt she felt returned her to God. God demanded better of her, and her sense of falling short reminded her of His presence.

By the age of thirty I had been luckier than some and unluckier than others. I had had, objectively, an "underprivileged background" marked by poverty, abuse, and loss. But my suffering had brought me closer to God. From my great-grandmother's dementia to my grandfather's death, from moments of domestic abuse as a kid to the sound of explosions from mortar fire in Iraq as a young man, I prayed to God in times of need. The cliché that suffering brings us closer to God is a cliché for the simple fact that it's true for so many of us.

A voice in my head had been telling me that whatever short-term success I might have with Usha, I'd be unable to break free from the sins of people who'd died long before. That my life was controlled by an invisible hand guided by the alcoholism and addiction and chaos of ancestors.

Saint Paul wrote in his second letter to the Corinthians:

> But we have this treasure in earthen vessels, that the
> excellency of the power may be of God, and not of us.
> We are troubled on every side, yet not distressed;
> we are perplexed, but not in despair;
> Persecuted, but not forsaken; cast down, but not destroyed;
> Always bearing about in the body the dying of
> the Lord Jesus, that the life also of Jesus might be
> made manifest in our body. (2 Cor. 4:7–10)

If my despair threatened to drive me away from God, it was the beauty and truth of this simple passage that drove away that despair. We are neither slaves to the world nor entirely independent from it. We are "troubled on every side, yet not distressed." There were ancestors who had treated their kids like garbage, but there was also Mamaw, who was moved by her unconventional faith to care for her grandchildren in her dying years. And just as it is a sin to assume that we can control everything, so it is a sin to ignore that we can—with the help of grace—defeat the demons of the past and chart our own course. I might never escape my past. But by the grace of God, it would never consume me.

The sociological understanding of my past as "underprivileged," while statistically defensible on a population level, was personally debilitating. I could read studies until I was blue in the face about how kids who were abused were more likely to abuse. Or how married couples with divorced parents were more likely to divorce. These things were obviously true, and the knowledge undoubtedly helped doctors contextualize their patients' problems.

But I yearned for a way of understanding the world that could make room for both the importance of my past and the existence of my own agency. It was one thing to sit in a therapist's chair and talk about what had happened to me and how connected it was to something I did. "Perhaps I lost my temper on the road because I was nearly killed in my mom's road rage incident." Perhaps. But perhaps I lost my temper on the road because I screwed up. One of the ways we allow the ghosts of the past to control us is by scapegoating them for our own misdeeds. The invisible hand is the hand of the devil.

For an evangelical, the weirdest Catholic sacrament may be the rite of confession and reconciliation. The idea of speaking of my sins to a stranger mortified me. Yet our Catholic friend Sam described confession in a way that resonated with me: It's like therapy, but with less whining and more guilt. You can recognize the social aspect of sin—the fact that some people are influenced by the problems and even traumas of their youth. And you can also recognize that even a very damaged person is still responsible for their misdeeds.

I had read atheist writers criticize the concept of Christian guilt as inherently abusive of children. It makes them feel bad for entirely normal and natural things, the argument goes, and it's a form of psychological torture.

But I found liberation in guilt. The recognition that I had screwed up, that I must ask forgiveness—of God and of the people I'd wronged—forced me to think about my own conduct in a profoundly different way. The interconnectedness of wrongdoing served as an antidote to the resentment I held against my mom. "Forgive us our trespasses, as we forgive those who trespass against us." The fact that there was a sacramental ritual around guilt—of publicly confessing something, admitting you did wrong, and performing an act of penance—attracted me to Catholicism.

Running away from the fact that you screwed up or pretending that you didn't is the path to destruction. Believing that you are a slave to your family's past sins is a path to despair. But the Christian concept of guilt and forgiveness existing side by side felt both true and useful.

"By their fruits ye shall know them." (Matt. 7:20) This was one of the faith's best fruits.

I felt anxious about returning to the faith in a formal way. Usha hadn't signed up to be married to a Christian, and I worried that she'd feel alienated from my new interest. But she had the opposite reaction: She joined me at church. Not because she was interested in converting herself, but because she knew that this was good for me.

"Therapy didn't work for you," she admitted. "But church does."

She liked that it anchored me. She appreciated that it connected me to my grandma. It forced me to think about virtue and vice in a productive way.

I found that church focused my mind on the things that mattered. That Usha thought church was "good for me" gave me both permission and inspiration. I wanted more than anything to be worthy of this woman. If church helped me, I'd sit my butt in the pew every Sunday.

I read the Bible regularly, and I found a passage in Philippians that made me feel like God was speaking to me:

> Finally, brethren, whatsoever things are true, whatsoever things are honest, whatsoever things are just, whatsoever things are pure, whatsoever things are lovely, whatsoever things are of good report; if there be any virtue, and if there be any praise, think on these things. (Phil. 4:8)

The meritocracy had focused my mind on the crude and superficial—credentials, careers, money. These things might have been necessary, but they could never form the basis of a truly good life.

And Usha was different. She was truer and purer and more just and lovelier than anyone. Because she inspired me to be better, she forced me to follow a different path. And that, more than anything, is the path that led me back to God.

CHAPTER 7

Like Father, Like Son

After Usha and I married in June 2014, we spent the next couple of years bouncing around the country in the pursuit of various jobs. We lived for a few more months in Cincinnati as we finished our clerkships, and then I started at a law firm in Washington while she clerked for another judge.

Her clerkship lasted a year, and as it neared its end, my desire to get out of the legal profession finally came to a head. Acquiring legal credentials, and not using them, felt almost wasteful. But I had earned them for the wrong reasons, and I began to think more deeply about what it was that I actually wanted to do—not simply to win some elite competition, but because I thought it was interesting. So I headed west for a job in the technology sector as Usha wound down her DC clerkship and joined a law firm in San Francisco. We traveled a lot, worked late hours, and took our dogs on long walks. On the side, I worked on a book slated for publication in the summer of 2016.

When the book was published, I argued with the publisher

(the same publisher of this book!) about whether they had printed enough copies. There was an initial run of ten thousand copies, which seemed low. But a book about the upbringing of a redneck who worked in Silicon Valley didn't generate much prepublication interest. The book came out, I did a few media interviews, and the sales popped a bit. I went to England with Usha for a long-planned post-publication vacation and realized that the publisher was probably right and we'd be lucky to sell that first printing.

While in England, I gave an interview to Rod Dreher in *The American Conservative*. In the summer of 2016, most people didn't give Donald Trump much of a chance of becoming president, but they were trying to understand the man and the passionate following he inspired among the people around whom I had grown up. My interview with Rod touched on politics, on regional pride, and on the sense that the hillbillies had been left behind by the leaders of a country they had helped build with their bare hands. The interview went live right before Usha and I boarded our flight to return home. And by the time I landed, it had blown up. "Oh my gosh," Dreher wrote me. "You crashed the website. We've never seen traffic like this before."

The book's success transformed my life in ways big and small. All of a sudden, I found myself going on TV to talk about politics and the 2016 election. People invited me to fancy conferences with wealthy people to talk about American culture, the "urban-rural" divide, and any number of other topics. Strangers sent me incredibly touching stories and photos from their own families. I became a controversial figure in my own right, and I tasted my first bit of heated public criticism.

One of the first things I realized about my new media platform was that it could be quite lucrative if I wanted it to be. Between TV shows, consulting agreements, further books, columns, and podcasts, being a public intellectual pays incredibly well. I was tempted by the flexibility in particular. If you want to jet off to Europe for a few weeks, you can do that, so long as you get your work done. And it's high profile: How many people my age get to go on TV and talk about the things they're interested in?

But if I was being honest with myself, much of what drew me to this life was its prestige. Shortly after the book was published, I returned to Yale to give a speech and was treated like a conquering hero. Everyone told me how great I was. Conservatives loved the book, and so did liberals. A former professor told me I had more influence than all of his colleagues combined and grew visibly jealous upon learning how many copies my book had sold in the previous week. I had won yet another elite competition, and I was gifted a job and lifestyle that many of my classmates envied. But I didn't want that life any more than I wanted a Supreme Court clerkship, so I decided to lean into the business world.

There were enduring lessons from my brief flirtation with public-commentary fame. "You don't realize how lucky you are," emailed a friend from the tech world. "Most people work their entire lives to get welcomed into these circles. I had to become an actual billionaire before I got invited to these billionaire conferences. For most people it takes thirty or forty years. You went from small town Ohio to dinners with Jeff Bezos in a few years."

God had given me a unique perspective, and I learned a few things. The first is that the social competition I saw at Yale Law

School replays itself all the way to the top. The Hollywood super-agent Ari Emanuel invited me to his pre-Oscars party. It was the best people-watching experience of my life. At one point in the night, someone motioned to a group entering the room and observed, "The p***y patrol"—the name our fellow guest used for Leonardo DiCaprio's crew—"just arrived." They caused a commotion, drank a lot, and departed before I could even catch a glimpse of Leo.

I saw one billionaire, who had nothing to do with the entertainment industry, laughing hysterically with Matt Damon and Denzel Washington. One of the minor celebrities I'd befriended at the bar turned to me and observed: "Look at them, man. It's high school all over again. The awkward kid laughing too hard at the popular kid's jokes. The girls floating around them. The dork paying them too much attention; the cool kid kind of ignoring them." He was right.

The social rituals of the political commentariat were a bit different but were geared toward the same thing: acceptance. In the same way that people were terrified at Yale of saying the wrong thing about the Trayvon Martin shooting or the role of gender in the workplace, there were subtle but very explicit rules about what you were allowed to say. You could be accepted however you identified politically or philosophically so long as you didn't color outside of those proscribed lines.

Though *Hillbilly Elegy* said nothing about the political race between Donald Trump and Hillary Clinton, I was often asked to comment on the election. And I found a comfortable niche as a Trump skeptic: criticizing him from a conservative perspective while defending his voters. If it isn't obvious: I am serving as President Trump's second vice president, so my opinion obviously changed.

I'll explain the reasons for that evolution later, but even at the time I couldn't help but notice that my criticisms made me a "safe conservative." I was rewarded for saying bad things about Donald Trump even though my background and politics made me an odd fit for elite media culture. Trump criticism functioned as social immunity. And this immunity was quite lucrative—it guaranteed better book deals and media appearances. The net result was that I could make excuses for my fellow hillbillies or even empathize with them, so long as I did not commit the unforgivable sin of suggesting that they be given political power through their chosen candidate.

When Usha and I attended a San Francisco wedding in the fall of 2016, all anybody wanted to talk about was Trump and how horrified they were by the way he talked. But when I polled my relatives who were die-hard MAGA supporters, every single one of them laughed, brushing off the constant hyperventilation from the mainstream media. Their reasons ranged from the pragmatic: "He's better than Hillary Clinton, and so I'll vote for the best candidate"; to the defiant: "Are we really not voting for a guy because he tells jokes with offensive language?" So I fired off a tweet to my now significant social media following that made the simple point: Regardless of how you were voting, about half the country would support Donald Trump, and most of his voters were good people.

My tweet caused a mini-firestorm on the internet. Many of my previous media allies—people who'd defended me when I was attacking Donald Trump—could not abide this defense of his voters. Of course, I'd defended his voters before. But doing it now, at the height of Trump derangement, was too much for many of my new "friends."

I recalled my dad's evangelical church and the debates we had had about evolution or abortion or whether a person saved by grace could ever "backslide" away from the faith. In those days, I had established a pretty good barometer for what I was allowed to say. I think most of us have a voice in our head that tells us when we're about to go too far. In my later atheist days, I came to resent that voice, the control it exercised over me, the way it took the views of others and laundered them into my own conscience.

But was this any different? From the professional pipeline I encountered in law school to the social media mob of the 2016 election, the intensity of social control was far greater among our elites than anything I'd seen in a Pentecostal or Southern Baptist church back home. My dad's church had its pieties and its social norms, but people could speak in tongues without ever experiencing the fanaticism I saw in a CNN newsroom in October 2016. The kind of zealotry that turned me from my faith, it just so happened, was far more common among America's wealthy and powerful than in any of the congregations I was a part of growing up.

And that church had something that this new religion didn't: grace and forgiveness. I might have been worried when I was seventeen that if I asked questions I wasn't supposed to, people would judge me. I might have argued with more moderate Christians about their heresy of accepting the theory of evolution. But I knew that above all, we were meant to love one another, and you couldn't do that without a little grace. People might think your views on some theological question made you a heretic, but they would still speak to you with patience and respect. There were, of course, people too willing to dismiss others for doing or thinking the wrong thing. But that was human nature, and whatever excessive zealotry I saw among the Christians of my teenage years, this new, allegedly secular world was much worse.

Trump won, of course. I was invited to an election party, mostly of Trump supporters who expected the now-president to lose. As shock settled over the newsrooms of America, I was offered my biggest media appearance yet: primetime ABC election coverage to explain how it was that Donald Trump and his voters had just stunned the world. I don't remember what I said on air. I vaguely recall being annoyed by then-conservative writer Bill Kristol's pearl-clutching remarks.

But I do recall the sense of grief in the newsroom. As I walked the halls, spoke to producers, and waited for the application of makeup and earpieces, I saw multiple people crying. *Disappointment is one thing*, I thought. *But these people need psychological help.* If Hillary Clinton had won, my evangelical, Trump-loving father would have turned off the TV, prayed, and said, "Well, I hope she ain't as bad as I feared." These people reacted as if a family member had died. For much of my young adult life, I had thought that my father was an irrational religious man, as much as I loved him, and that these newsroom criers were sensible, logical people. I clearly had missed something.

The election results created a second wave of increased interest and sales for *Hillbilly Elegy*. Between my business career and the book, I ended 2016 considerably wealthier than anyone in my family. And I had something else they didn't: an invitation to the White House.

In early 2017, just days before Barack Obama left the White House, I sat with him and a few other conservatives to talk about what was going on in the United States of America. The conversation was interesting but off the record, so I won't repeat it here. But what I remembered most about it was that I couldn't wait to leave the White House and fly back to San Francisco for an ultrasound. No one knew it, but Usha was pregnant, and the next day we would discover we were having a baby boy.

* * *

The first thing I did after finding out our baby's sex was google the "challenges of raising a boy." I had heard boys were higher energy, on average, than girls, and I knew that boys were struggling and falling behind in school. But there was something very personal at work. Having a boy felt like an opportunity to fix something in my past, to give my son the things I hadn't had. And it also forced me to accelerate my religious journey. I knew I wanted to raise my kids in some church, but I didn't know which one. As hypothetical children became a very real child arriving soon, I began thinking about my faith in a far more intentional way.

In my family, we framed men's failures in terms of how they treated women and children: men who abused their wives, who failed to pay child support, who refused to get off the couch and work hard. In the immortal words of TLC, "a scrub is a guy" who talks "about what he wants and just sits on his broke a**." To define failure in this way presumed that a man's role is as a caretaker. Successful men were like Papaw: providers, men who made enough money to put food on the table, who were firm with discipline but in control of their emotions and temper.

By early 2017, the success of men—and boys, in particular—had taken on a broader social significance. In law school we had learned that the patriarchy held women back from breaking the glass ceiling in elite corporate leadership, yet the statistics were telling a different story about younger men. By virtually every metric, boys were doing worse than girls academically, from mathematics grades in elementary school to admissions rates at our nation's best professional schools.

Young men and boys are more likely to drop out of high school than their female peers. "In 2022, the status dropout rate was higher for male 16- to 24-year-olds than for female 16- to 24-year-olds overall (6.3 vs. 4.3 percent)"—a full two-point difference between the sexes.[1]

As a kid, I had been held back for a year in kindergarten. They said that I was immature, but it would have been more accurate to say that I was a holy terror. School was miserable to me. I wanted to watch TV or play video games or run around outside. Sitting silently at a desk while someone talked at me was torture.

I remember the breaking point that led to me being sent home to wait another year. Impatient with my misbehavior, the teacher, Mrs. Morgan, moved my desk next to hers. She meant to shame me into good behavior, but I didn't pick up on the social cues or on the other students staring disapprovingly at me. I found the entire experience hilarious.

My new seat came with a particular temptation: I could see a giant pack of crayons on Mrs. Morgan's desk. This is my first recollection of self-restraint (or my lack thereof). I desperately wanted to snatch those crayons and draw gigantic circles on the classroom wall. I knew

1 National Center for Education Statistics, "Fast Facts: Dropout Rates," accessed April 13, 2026, https://nces.ed.gov/fastfacts/display.asp?id=16.

that Mrs. Morgan would catch me before I made it to the wall—but I didn't care, not even a little. I just had to fresco that wall.

I waited and watched her like a hawk. The minute she was far enough away, I ran to her desk, grabbed a crayon, and began scribbling those gigantic circles.

I have no idea what madness had possessed me, though I recall that it was a particularly chaotic time in my family's life. Sometime after this incident, the school pleaded with my mom to have me diagnosed with ADHD and placed on Ritalin, a comically knee-jerk response: poor kid misbehaves, school officials try to drug him. There's a well-documented connection between socioeconomic status and ADHD diagnosis,[2] with poor kids being much likelier to receive treatment for ADHD. This occurs despite the fact that, as Harvard psychiatrist Nancy Rappaport has noted, we don't really know whether these drugs are safe for young children.[3]

My mother and grandmother's conspiratorial skepticism took over. Mamaw told me she'd kidnap me and hide me away in Kentucky if anyone tried to give me psychiatric drugs, and Mom rejected the school's advice.

"He's just a boy," Mamaw said. "That's all that's happening. He's just a little s***headed boy."

There's something insightful about her diagnosis—that my

2 Abigail Emma Russell, Tamsin Ford, and Ginny Russell, "Socioeconomic Associations with ADHD: Findings from a Mediation Analysis," *PLOS One* 10, no. 6 (June 2015): e0128248, https://www.ncbi.nlm.nih.gov/pmc/articles/PMC4451079.

3 Nancy Rappaport, "We Are Overmedicating America's Poorest Kids," *Washington Post*, June 4, 2014, https://www.washingtonpost.com/posteverything/wp/2014/06/04/we-are-way-too-quick-to-diagnose-poor-children-with-adhd/?noredirect=on&utm_term=.73a74603842f.

problem wasn't that I had a psychiatric disorder, but that I was a boy. Her instinct echoed the research that suggests male development patterns correlate with weak performance in schools. Maybe the problem is male development. Or maybe the problem is with schools and how they negotiate that development. Regardless, while our society obsesses over the gender representation of the partnership track at elite law firms, we've grown comfortable with pathologizing traits that are naturally more common in boys than girls.

I reflected on these memories and the growing body of evidence that boys struggled in unique ways during those early months of Usha's pregnancy. But as I combed through the data about boys falling behind in this and that, I began to feel that something was missing, though I lacked the vocabulary to describe exactly what.

At some point Usha and I found ourselves in conversation about what type of college we wanted our son to attend. In hindsight, this seems absurd: talking about the advanced education prospects of a kid who hadn't even been born. It occurred to me that this illustrated why our society is so terrible at affording opportunities for our poor children to join the upper echelons: We were already preparing to give our future child a head start in the game of meritocracy!

But then it hit me: Why did I care about where this poor kid, still not born, went to college?

I was fixating on the very things I found so inadequate in my own college and law school career: credentials. But I'd met a lot of smart people in the Ivy League who got great grades but weren't curious about the world or the ideas that animated our civilization. My son could achieve in measurable ways, yes, but if he didn't like to read for pleasure or engage with the great ideas of his own and other cultures, would his education have been a success? He could get married, but if he chose—like so many dual-income professional households—to forgo a family to make way for travel and consumption, would he be happy? It was altogether possible, I realized, that we could give our kid every advantage in the meritocracy while saddling him with a huge disadvantage where it counted: character.

This was the vocabulary I was missing. I had lost a way of talking about virtue.

So I began to ask myself: *Does any of this really matter?* Of course, in one sense, we should be terribly worried about the educational prospects of our boys, and how that affects their career paths. I don't mean to diminish this. And while we're at it, we might point out that although boys are struggling in a host of ways that show up in their educational and career outcomes, girls still lag behind in other ways.

Maybe there was something flawed about our ways of measuring the relative positions of men and women: their educational attainment, their career outcomes, their prospects for success in our globalized, hypercompetitive economy.

Around this time, I attended a conference where gender inequities formed a critical part of the conversation. There was much talk about the fact that women are underrepresented on corporate boards, in law firm partnerships, and as corporate CEOs. But I felt there was something pernicious about emphasizing these ways of measuring people in the first place. And there was something wrong with *me* for immediately jumping to questions of educational and professional achievement when contemplating what it would mean to raise a boy.

Maybe my son would be less likely to graduate from Harvard than a hypothetical daughter. But what if he was less likely to be a man of character, virtue, and purpose? What if he got into Harvard, accepted a prestigious job, and was a terrible person? Wouldn't that be a bigger problem than how much he achieved?

I became possessed by the terror that I knew exactly how to help my kid get into a good college but was woefully underprepared to make him a good man.

* * *

In the summer of 2017, weeks before Usha would begin a third clerkship in Washington, Ewan Blaine Vance came into the world. His birth was the first time in many years I could remember praying for anything and meaning it.

> *Dear Lord, protect Usha and the baby. And make me a good dad.*

I said it over and over in the hospital room during Usha's hours of labor.

I know that all parents love their children very much—even those, like mine, who couldn't quite care for them in the traditional ways. And I know it's cliché to say that the birth of a child is among the most important moments of your life. But it was true for me, for all the standard and miraculous reasons. Those twelve hours of labor were exciting and exhausting. Our family was together (save for my sister, who was on vacation at the time) and of course, at the end, there was a little human being—a human being who was a part of us.

The labor was a bit of a blur, so I can't say that I remember everything. Usha did all of the work, shout-out to her. Though I did ensure she had a steady supply of ice chips, which she craved obsessively. I do remember going out to the waiting room to tell everybody that the baby was nearly here. I also remember the tremors Usha experienced as her epidural wore off. And I remember the moment I took our son to be weighed for the first time. The nurse asked, "Dad, would you like to cut the umbilical cord?" It was the first time anyone had uttered the D-word to me directly, and I remember feeling an overwhelming sense of pride.

Becoming a dad was so meaningful for me in part because my own relationship with my various father figures was, well, complicated. My father gave me up for adoption when I was six years old. The stepfather who adopted me walked out on the family well before I was a teenager. Though I was lucky to have my Papaw to fill some of the gaps, by the time I graduated from high school I had learned to know, to love, and to forget a revolving door of father figures. Some of them were good guys and some weren't, but all of them eventually disappeared. I came to resent those men. I resented my mother's choices for bringing them in and out of my life. And I came to resent myself a little, even though I knew all this wasn't my fault.

My son's birth took on extra significance because it was my opportunity to correct the mistakes of the past. It was an opportunity to make real that American Dream I so desperately wanted. It was an opportunity to show my wife that I could be a good father. It was, in a word, an opportunity for redemption.

Before Ewan was born, I read various books about new fatherhood—how to change a diaper, what to expect during the first few weeks of life, how to get babies to sleep, and more. One consistent warning was that you might not immediately feel that strongly connected to your child. The thinking is that your wife has known this baby from conception—she's been carrying him around, felt the first kick, and so on. I had friends with children and knew that, for at least some fathers, this was true. They told me they loved their kids dearly but that it had taken a few months before their feelings matched their wives'.

That ended up being half true for me. It took me a few months to feel that head-over-heels emotional attachment to my son. There were times, especially during those first few weeks, when I didn't especially like him. I couldn't figure out why he cried constantly or why he refused to sleep for more than forty-five minutes at a time. And there were other, more intense feelings. But from the first moment, I had this sense of almost metaphysical obligation, that even if this child annoyed the hell out of me, it was my purpose to keep him alive.

Beyond that, parenting an infant in the age of the internet is a punishment befitting the fallen nature of man. Online, there are entire networks of people—domestic terrorists, really—who encourage you to obsess over a child's microbiome and whether mixing breast milk with formula will ruin a child's metabolism for life.

I felt one emotion above all others: fear. The way that I'd grown up had imparted a sense of fatalism. A despair that the worst parts of my past would define me. I'd known so many people who wanted desperately to be good mothers and fathers only to fail. I'd seen people who loved their children deeply be unable to care for them in the way they knew the kids needed. And so I was terrified that I was going to screw this up.

I began to see grace in a new light. As a kid, I thought Jesus came into your life and transformed everything instantly. But I'd seen so many people healed of a broken back at church who couldn't walk the next day, or drunks transformed by prayer who were back on the bottle just a few moments later. As a new father, I considered that perhaps grace was God making the impossible possible, but on His time, not ours. This God of ours is not particularly concerned with instant gratification.

Ewan was such a big part of my past. That's a strange thing to claim about a baby who had been in the world for only a few weeks. But it's no exaggeration to say that the promise of this baby had gotten me through many hard moments in life. To me, the American Dream wasn't just an abstraction or something a politician said to make himself sound optimistic or forward-thinking or like he cared about the poor. It was a promise for the future. And now that the future was here, I wasn't totally sure what to do with him.

* * *

Ewan was born in Columbus, but we quickly moved to DC for Usha's job. We had long-term plans to return to Ohio, and I had built a niche for myself (along with a few friends) as a guy who invested in technology companies outside of Silicon Valley. Because of that, I split my time between an apartment in Columbus and a town house in DC. I traveled a fair amount for speaking gigs, but so long as I was willing to go to bed late or wake up early (or both), I could usually be home for breakfast or dinner every day. During this year in DC, Usha clerked at the Supreme Court for Chief Justice John Roberts and was the only clerk toting a baby into the chambers for midday nursing and naps.

Despite the travel and the chaos, we had real domestic tranquility. Usha's mom helped a great deal—she took leave from work for a year to care for the baby—and we settled into a nice routine. Like most new parents, we were obsessed with our little guy. I saw in him a perfect mixture of me and Usha: her big, beautiful brown eyes and my chubby cheeks.

I know it's common, when a new baby comes along, for families to magnify the child's similarities with their side. Mamaw was fond of telling the new parents of her grandchildren that the baby "looks just like a Vance." This annoyed my Aunt Donna so much that she finally countered: "All babies have chubby cheeks and flat noses, so by your standard all babies look like Vances."

From the earliest age, Ewan was in love with living things. He would listen to crickets or grunt if we were about to step on a bug. Most of all, he loved his dogs. His second word was *Dada*. His first was *woof-woof*.

As comfortable as I'd become with the routines of fatherhood, I still had the nagging feeling that I didn't know what the hell I was doing. Yes, I could keep Ewan from starving and change his clothes. But there was something missing from my training, something the chaos of my youth hadn't prepared me for.

At one point during the fall, we took him to a pumpkin patch. It was, by all outward appearances, a joyful excursion. My nieces led Ewan through a corn maze. He clapped at the animals and mimicked their sounds. And he picked a pumpkin larger than himself to take home. But as we drove back that night, Usha noticed my intense focus on the road.

"Is everything all right?" she asked. "What are you thinking about?"

I'd grown accustomed in these moments to snapping back to reality and telling her everything was fine. But that day I told her the truth:

"I'm just thinking about all the ways in which you or Ewan might get harmed. I replayed all the faces of the people at the pumpkin patch, because I scanned everyone to make sure they didn't look like kidnappers or mass murderers. I thought about a wild teenage driver running over the stroller during our trip through the parking lot. At the stop sign we just went through, I imagined a semitruck crossing perpendicular to us, the ways he might have careened off the road and T-boned us, and how I would have reacted. Right now, I'm thinking about what would happen if the bridge we're about to go over went out. I think you'd want to roll down the windows—yes, that would let water into the car more quickly. But it would also ensure you had an exit path. You'd also need to press your head hard against the seat on the way down, or we might break our necks or get knocked unconscious—then we'd totally be screwed. The thing I haven't figured out is whether you want to unbuckle your seat belt before you start tumbling down. On the one hand, it's a death trap if you can't unbuckle it, and I don't have a knife in this car to cut it loose; on the other hand, it might increase the odds that you don't slam against the top of the car and get knocked out. In the future, I'll make sure there's a pocketknife in the glove box."

My wife paused for a while, and then she nodded knowingly. She understands my peculiar phobias and neuroses well enough, and there wasn't much to say. I'm sure she thought, *What a psycho I married.*

I simply couldn't help thinking about worst-case scenarios and how to avert them. I now recognize this as a consequence of childhood trauma, at least in part, though I also suspect I'm naturally wired to see the possibility of disaster and prepare for it. But the unfortunate—perhaps tragic—and unavoidable fact of my psychology is that I am permanently terrified that things will unravel. My life quite often feels like a fairy tale, and I am certain that soon the story will end.

Even when I'm in a good frame of mind, the same, deeper worry that plagued me before Ewan's birth remains: *How do I raise a good man?*

It sounds relatively simple, but how to inculcate virtue in a person is the most important question I confront with my son. I don't really care whether he goes to a fancy school (and to the extent I do care, it reveals an obvious character flaw in me). I don't care what profession he chooses. I want him to be happy, of course, but not in the fleeting, superficial ways we so often celebrate in our society. I want him to live a life of meaning and purpose. I want him to do work that fulfills him, even if it's not prestigious or won't make him a multimillionaire. I want him, most of all, to find love, and to be worthy of finding it. In other words, I want him to be virtuous. The question of how to instill this trait in him gnawed at me as Ewan transitioned from baby to toddler, and in some ways, it still does.

A recovering addict once told me that, in jail, he met a preacher whose simple bit of wisdom changed his life: Show me your friends, and I'll show you your future.

I heard that quote during a cynical time, and I dismissed it. But it took on new power as I raised my son: The people we spent our time with, the cultural pond in which we swam, would exert remarkable power over his life. To worry about Ewan's virtue was to worry about his future environment. During infancy, we controlled everything about his life, but our power to shape him would slowly fade over time. Friends, teachers, and so many others would influence ever more of his development. And of course, at some point, something internal would need to click: He would become the master of his own destiny, navigate all of the social cues himself, and make his own choices.

I worried about him in large part because the things Mamaw had taught me to value—those sacred qualities that anchor human beings to one another, like loyalty and a sense of obligation to community, country, and family—took a back seat to credentials and "achievement" in the new world in which we were raising our son.

My Mamaw taught me to distrust people who focus too much on these worldly things. Yet by the time I arrived at Yale Law School, I had largely forgotten that lesson. Perhaps her voice in my head had led me eventually to rethink my path. But Ewan had never heard her voice. He would have only mine.

I wondered whether he would even feel comfortable around a woman like my grandmother. During conferences and speaking gigs and conversations, I enjoyed posing a subversive question: "Would you," I said, "rather have dinner with a former coal miner from West Virginia or a management consultant from Paris or London?"

The point of the thought exercise is this: If you are in the professional class and live in a big city, you realize that America's big cities have more in common with European and Asian cities (and with each other) than they do with small-town America. The jobs, restaurants, and cultural amenities are very similar. Elites in global cities often know more of their peers from around the world than they do rural Americans. At some level, it's hard to blame them. An investment banker in New York will likely have more in common with a strategy consultant in Paris than with a homemaker in Middletown. I'd like my son to get along with both, but if a choice must be made, I'd like him to prefer the middle class of his own country over the rich people of another.

There are irrational, purely emotive reasons behind my preference. But there are also rational reasons, including that my child, thanks to his background, is more likely to become a member of our country's ruling class. And America simply doesn't work if our business leaders don't know the people they hire, if our politicians are ignorant of the people they serve, and if our philanthropists are disconnected from the people they allegedly support.

Usha cared about this divide, too, so we discussed various ways of ensuring our kid didn't become another big-city denizen with no connection to the geographical middle of his own country. Avoiding that would, in part, happen naturally given my family and the relationships we maintained back home. But it would also require intentionality. And it occurred to me that apart from the military no institution of American life successfully brought rich and poor, black and white, working class and college-educated together. Except the Church.

My son's birth fulfilled my dearest hope. And I'd always feared that once that hope was fulfilled, it would be taken in some way. Though I worried that this cosmic thievery could come in the form of a mountain lion snatching my son (I'm sorry, I can't help it sometimes), I was also cognizant of the fact that the men in my family have not lived very long lives for entirely banal reasons. The current life expectancy for American men is seventy-seven, and none of my great-uncles hit that mark. My two grandfathers died, respectively, at twenty-three and sixty-seven. My own father died at sixty-seven. My uncle is the oldest of the bunch, and he's only seventy-five today.

I'd never had an especially powerful fear of death. Even as a Christian, too often my motivation for acting or not acting in a certain way is based on what are essentially earthly calculations, rather than how I'll be judged in the afterlife. But since childhood, I had promised myself, again and again, that I would be a good father to my kids and a good husband to my wife in the eyes of God. It was the only thing I ever really wanted. And I was afraid that having made it this far, nature—it might be a bear attack; it happens—would deprive me of the chance to prove myself.

So sometimes I wrote out little nuggets of wisdom for my kid, in the hopes that he'd find them useful. Sometimes it was things that Mamaw used to tell me.

"When you see an old person trying to do something, get off your butt and help them."

"Too much TV will rot your brain."

"Real men are more than sperm donors."

Other times, it was more practical advice about tying a tie, or making a bed, or using the college library to find textbooks so you don't have to pay for them (this latter trick saved me thousands of dollars at Ohio State, though the digital age has almost certainly made it obsolete).

But the most practical thing I could do to ensure that he was taught the language of virtue and sin was to raise him in the faith in which my grandmother raised me. And the best way to expose him to different people from all walks of life was to take him to church. The only question was which one?

CHAPTER 8

Of New Things

When Usha's clerkship wound down in the summer of 2018, we found ourselves desperate for an end to the transience of our early years together. From 2011 (when we started dating) to 2018, Usha and I had lived in close to a dozen different houses or apartments, sometimes together and sometimes separately. I had driven a half dozen U-Hauls across many different states. We had moved ourselves, begged friends to help us, or paid other people to do it. We were sick of packing and unpacking boxes. "I want to buy a house," Usha told me. "And I don't want to move until we're dead."

I hoped to live in Columbus. Our business had invested in a few companies there, and it was by some metrics the fastest-growing city in the Midwest. Usha thought it was too flat and too new. She wanted mountains (or at least rolling hills) and beautiful architecture. Our compromise was Cincinnati. While scanning listings, we found one house that we promptly dubbed our "dream house" because it combined so much of what we wanted. It was too expensive, but we visited it, fell in love, and bought it anyway.

The question of how to build a culture of virtue, within my own family, within my community, and within our entire society, loomed large in my mind. Now that we were settled in Cincinnati, I found myself worrying over how to fuse a sense of social virtue with a personal one. Humans are so complicated, and sought a moral frame that recognized us as both autonomous and communal creatures. As individuals with free will and the capacity for greatness (and great evil)—but also as members of a community, influenced and formed by what's around us.

At this stage, it was largely an intellectual exercise. Faith was something I read about and thought about, but I didn't really feel much when I sat in the pews. This didn't bother me at the time. Life has taught me to mistrust emotions, though I knew at some level any true faith must be one of both the mind and the heart.

My decade of irreligion had deprived me of the ability to pray. Whether it was because of technology's distractions or getting older, I found that when I closed my eyes to talk to God, I felt uncertain about what to say. The words wouldn't come out, even silently in my own head. So I gravitated toward prayers that had already been written down. There was the Lord's Prayer—"Our Father, who art in heaven . . ." And there were others:

> *Glory be to the father, and to the son, and to the Holy Spirit. As it was in the beginning, is now, and ever shall be, world without end.*

There was also a prayer to Archangel Michael to intervene on our behalf and defeat evil by the power of God:

> *Saint Michael the Archangel, defend us in battle, be our protection against the wickedness and snares of the devil. May God rebuke him we humbly pray; and do thou, O Prince of the Heavenly host, by the power of God, cast into hell Satan and all the evil spirits who prowl about the world seeking the ruin of souls. Amen.*

I really liked that one. It felt medieval despite being written in the nineteenth century. And it felt mystical. You could almost see the angels and demons doing battle when you uttered those words.

Many of these prayers I found on Catholic websites. I was already drawn to Catholicism for intellectual reasons. Catholicism had a rich social tradition, one that tried to understand our Christian commitments not just as belonging to individuals, but to spouses, parents, business leaders, political leaders, and on and on. Catholics understood people as simultaneously occupying different roles, each radiating out from the others. This resonated with me, especially as I contemplated how to be a good husband who could raise a good son.

One of the seminal documents behind this understanding of human beings as social creatures was an encyclical authored by the same pope who wrote the Saint Michael prayer: Pope Leo XIII (not to be confused with the current pope, Leo XIV). *Rerum Novarum* remains one of the foundational Catholic texts about political economy. In this encyclical, the Pope rejects the fundamentalism of socialists and capitalists during a period of rising industrial strife in America and Europe. But it is not a "moderate" argument: It forcefully advocates for the rights of individual workers, for labor unions, and for traditional families—even presaging the "family wage" that would later become a critical part of stable industrial societies.

Yet Pope Leo XIII fits these commitments within a broader theory of how to make human society good for humans—as family members, community occupants, and children of God. It is neither conservative nor progressive; neither liberal nor authoritarian. It is critical of socialism, not for the ideology's concern for working people, but because its "great mistake [is] the notion that class is naturally hostile to class, and that the wealthy and the working men are intended by nature to live in mutual conflict."

Instead, Pope Leo XIII sketches out a compromise between different groups based on mutual cooperation and affection:

> Each needs the other: capital cannot do without labor, nor labor without capital. Mutual agreement results in the beauty of good order, while perpetual conflict necessarily produces confusion and savage barbarity. Now, in preventing such strife as this, and in uprooting it, the efficacy of Christian institutions is marvellous and manifold. First of all, there is no intermediary more powerful than religion (whereof the Church is the interpreter and guardian) in drawing the rich and the working class together, by reminding each of its duties to the other, and especially of the obligations of justice.

The Pope also lays out a vision of society where the state protects the vulnerable, guarantees a just wage for laborers, and ensures that working people have sufficient "rest from labor"—not for "vicious indulgence," but so they can focus on higher matters such as their religious and familial obligations. The first time I read *Rerum Novarum*, I thought of my relatives who were forced to miss Thanksgiving dinners and church services because of their unpredictable retail work schedules.

The Pope rejects child labor, in stark contrast to the economic liberals of his day who defended the practice so long as a child's parents were willing to send them into the industrial workforce. And he repeatedly demands that workers be paid a fair wage:

> Let the working man and the employer make free agreements, and in particular let them agree freely as to the wages; nevertheless, there underlies a dictate of natural justice more imperious and ancient than any bargain between man and man, namely, that wages ought not to be insufficient to support a frugal and well-behaved wage-earner. If through necessity or fear of a worse evil the workman accept harder conditions because an employer or contractor will afford him no better, he is made the victim of force and injustice.

Though in some ways *Rerum Novarum* is a product of its age—focused on the industrial economy and not our own modern, digital one—it sketches out a fully integrated theory of a good human life. People are fundamentally social, so their mediating institutions—unions, churches—ought to be prioritized. This is why the Catholic Church educates millions of American children every year, and why the Church's participation in FDR's New Deal coalition was critical to building the modern middle-class economy of the postwar years. People, Leo explains, are economic creatures who work to earn a living, which means that their employers have a duty to pay a wage sufficient for them to live a good life, with family and children well cared for. They are familial creatures, with obligations and duties that spring from their nature as parents and children. They are individuals, with obvious biological and spiritual needs. And they are members of national communities, whose politics ought to be about protecting people in each of these roles.

This idea that we all exist within particular spheres of family, community, and on and on, building up to a nation, is called subsidiarity. And it recognizes that each sphere of life depends on the others. It is very hard to be a good family man unless you have a decent wage and have support from friends, community, and church.

And it's tough for those institutions to thrive without a functional political system. Churches will struggle to attract working-class people if those people are forced to work on Sundays. Healthy national economies require smart international economic policy, ordered around the production of key goods and vital industries. If you have an economy built around consumption, you ought not be surprised when your workers' skills atrophy and your manufacturing base disappears. Or when the families who depended on the jobs provided by that manufacturing base dissolve, and misery ensues.

Pope Leo XIII's theory of human nature strikes a balance so perfect it seems divinely inspired. It rejects the libertarian view of culture that brackets "personal responsibility" from the political choices that influence how people make decisions. It rejects the liberal view that encourages superficial achievement and meritocratic rise, favoring a more measured emphasis on duty and family. It felt more right than any theory of human nature I'd ever read. I wasn't very good at praying, and I lacked an emotional connection to the faith. But these arguments engaged me at an intellectual level more than anything I'd seen in either the secular or religious worlds I'd previously operated in.

The problem was that Catholicism was, quite literally, a foreign religion to me, rooted in Roman influences that I had very little exposure to. I thought back to the woman who raised me. Mamaw seemed not to have strong views on Catholics. Her younger daughter had married one, and she thought him a good man. She famously told everyone that if Lori (whom I called Aunt Wee) ever divorced Dan, "I'm following him."

She felt the Catholic way of worship was rather formal, but what mattered to her was Jesus. Revelation 18 may have been about the corruption of the Catholic Church, the Whore of Babylon, and all its hocus-pocus, or it may have been about something else. But the Catholic she knew cared about Jesus, so Dan was all right with her.

Still, Mamaw loomed so large in my mind. So many years after her death, she was still the person to whom I felt most indebted and the spirit with whom I argued the most. Without her, I wouldn't be here. And the uncomfortable fact was that the Christ of the Catholic Church seemed a little different from the Jesus I'd grown up with. A little too stodgy, too formal. Warner Sallman's famous portrait of Christ had hung upstairs near my bedroom in Mamaw's house, and that's how I encountered Him: personal and kind, but a little forlorn. Sad, perhaps, about the humans who rejected Him, or about the sin that continued to wreak havoc in the world. But whatever it was, that famous portrait was intimate and deeply personal.

The Christ of Catholicism floated high above you, as a grown man or a baby, wreathed in beams of light and crowned like a king. Mamaw would have felt discomfort with that kind of Christ. He was a majestic deity, and our family had little interest in majestic deities because we weren't a majestic people.

So I continued to flirt with Catholicism without fully committing to it. Usha and I would take little Ewan to church, but not regularly. Sometimes we'd go every other week, and sometimes we'd go every other month.

What felt comfortable at this point was to intellectualize faith. So I read a lot of books. G. K. Chesterton's *The Everlasting Man* had a particularly insightful quote about the nature of mankind:

> The simplest truth about man is that he is a very strange being; almost in the sense of being a stranger on the earth. In all sobriety, he has much more of the external appearance of one bringing alien habits from another land than of a mere growth of this one. . . .
>
> He cannot sleep in his own skin; he cannot trust his own instincts. He is at once a creator moving miraculous hands and fingers and a kind of cripple. He is wrapped in artificial bandages called clothes; he is propped on artificial crutches called furniture. His mind has the same doubtful liberties and the same wild limitations. Alone among the animals, he is shaken with the beautiful madness called laughter; as if he had caught sight of some secret in the very shape of the universe hidden from the universe itself. Alone among the animals he feels the need of averting his thought from the root realities of his own bodily being;

> of hiding them as in the presence of some higher possibility which creates the mystery of shame.

This seemed right to me and still does. Human nature is one of contradictions: of the animal merging with the divine in a complicated, messy biological form. The secular view of man was that consciousness and civilization were a sort of accident of evolution, that we came upon higher mental functions because they were useful for survival. But the creation story tells us that we are both animal and divine on purpose—a purpose, to be fair, we can't fully understand.

Now, I can argue either side of this debate. Were these parts of us called to beauty accidental to Mother Nature and evolution, or were they part of some cosmic design? Both seem plausible. But Chesterton's Catholic view felt truer to me.

I kept reading. I read about Saint Thomas Aquinas and natural law. I read academic treatises on Christian doctrine. I revisited some old Christian apologetics that were popular in my teenage years, and I reread C. S. Lewis's collected works. I can say in good faith that this time I found Christianity more and more intellectually coherent and true.

Our friend Sam talked often about the historical legitimacy of the Catholic Church—the idea that it represented a consistent, unbroken line from Christ to the present day. I'd never thought about it like that, but there was an element of truth to it. Saint Augustine, whose ideas swirled in my mind, was the Bishop of Hippo in the fifth century. I didn't feel rooted in the Christianity I'd experienced as a kid, and I envied Sam's connection to something unbroken and ancient. Catholicism's historical continuity was powerful.

To be fair, my Protestant friends would disagree with this. They'd argue that the Catholic Church underwent such significant transformation in the late sixteenth century, in response to the Reformation, that it was no longer the same Church that had existed in the early centuries of Christianity. And though the Church had maintained some ecclesiastical continuity for much of its first fifteen hundred years, there were periods when popes in France battled with popes in Italy over legitimacy. But even this gave me a strange comfort: The idea that these debates had been going on for two thousand years confirmed for me the Church's continuity and stability.

So many of the Christian thinkers who'd influenced me were Catholics: J. R. R. Tolkien, G. K. Chesterton, Saint Augustine, and Saint Thomas Aquinas. Even C. S. Lewis, an Anglican to his death, has been frequently described as an "Anglo-Catholic"—a tradition within the English Church that shares much in common with Roman Catholicism, without accepting the authority of the Pope in Rome. (To be fair, some Protestant friends also claim Augustine and Aquinas as their own.)

But I was also influenced by people, not just ideas. If there was a single person in my life who most embodied the Christian ideal, it was my Uncle Dan. He did all of the most important things in life, and he did them well: He took care of his family, he was patient and loving with his wife and children, he worked hard without making an idol out of his career. The same was true of the smart, devout friends to whom I spoke the most about Christianity. For whatever reason, they saw something real in the Catholic Church. And through them I began to see it, too.

I was also drawn to the hierarchy and sense of authority in

Catholicism. The Christian tradition was so rich, the Bible so big and difficult to master, that I began to see the structure of Catholicism as a benefit, not a burden. That the Church spoke with literally thousands of years of tradition behind it, that it had long-established processes for evolving doctrine and responding to new realities, made me feel that it was firmly rooted. So many of the churches we had gone to when I was a kid were dependent on—or were the creation of—a charismatic pastor. One scandal, one death, or even just a family move could mean the end of a church, or at least our attachment to it. Catholicism was independent of any particular priest. It was an institution, which meant it had certain faults but also made it feel more enduring. It took a lot for any one priest to fundamentally transform the Church, but a few bad apples couldn't destroy it, either.

A writer friend, knowing of my interest in Catholicism, encouraged me to talk to Father Dominic Legge, a Dominican friar in Washington, DC. Father Dominic's life story mirrored my own. He was once a young Yale Law student, engaged to be married, when he felt the call to become a priest. He gave up his plans and took a vow of poverty, and he now lived in what felt like a monastery with other Dominican priests. Father Dominic's brilliance earned my intellectual respect. As we spoke about doctrinal and theological issues, he encouraged me to talk to a young friar by the name of Henry Stephan in Cincinnati.

Father Henry defied every stereotype I had of a priest. He's an imposing man—six foot five (at least) with a stocky build and a hearty, echoing laugh. My kids have compared him to Friar Tuck, Robin Hood's associate, which embarrassed me but seemed to delight him. He came, like Father Dominic, with excellent academic credentials. A Princeton undergraduate, he had been accepted into multiple PhD programs to study political and moral philosophy. Sometimes God talks to us through little coincidences, and so it was with Father Henry: He was college friends with one of my employees and with Usha's close family friend—more akin to her little brother. Through our backgrounds, we had such a familiarity that we never experienced any personal discomfort or awkwardness, though perhaps that's just how Father Henry treated everyone.

One of the things I loved about evangelicalism was the idea that your relationship with Jesus must be personal—not informal or intellectual, but lived and felt. The problem is that I didn't feel particularly close to Jesus. He was more interesting to me than friendly. Father Henry gave the faith he represented a more personal connection, one based in honest (and sometimes uncomfortable) truths.

I'd known him for only a few months when he offered an observation that was equal parts enraging and perceptive: "You put too much pressure on your marriage because you're too emotionally invested in Usha."

Who the hell is this guy? I thought to myself. But I was a bit more diplomatic out loud: "What do you mean? Isn't it good to be emotionally invested in your spouse?"

"Well, of course," he said. "But you take it too far. I've read your book"—here he was talking of *Hillbilly Elegy*—"and your entire life you have bounced between complete dependence and independence. Your grandmother was your savior. So were your sister and your aunt, to a lesser degree. When they weren't around, you refused to depend on anyone. But you can't be independent from Usha. She's your wife. And you can't treat her like a savior. She isn't your savior. Jesus is."

I didn't know what to say. It was one of those truths that annoys you because it was, in fact, pretty damn accurate. "This is also why you despair about your family life, despite the fact that it's healthier than 99 percent of the marriages I see. You think it's going to fall apart because in your life, marriages always fall apart. Family never lasts. But this is a fundamentally secular view. You may not be able to heal these things. But God can."

"It's a good point," I said. "And it feels true. But here's the problem: I've seen a lot of people who were convinced that God's grace could fix this or that issue, and things still fell apart. I've seen a lot of people ask Jesus into their heart and then go back to the bottle or the needle. I've seen a lot of marriages seemingly centered around faith and the Church before they fell apart."

"Sure," Father Henry said. "And to be fair, I've seen that, too. I've seen it in Catholic and Protestant friends.

"But," he went on, giving voice to something I'd long pondered, "for most of us, grace is not something that happens in a moment. You don't feel God's presence and then change in an instant. Real grace comes through practice. This is why we demand that you live a sacramental life: going to church, taking Communion, doing confession. This is a process. You don't accept Jesus into your heart—or get baptized—and fix everything. That's not the promise of the Church. The promise of the Church is that you are lost, and the Church will provide you a road map to God."

This idea of grace as a process rather than a singular moment was profound to me. I realized that I had misunderstood the promise of the Christian faith. God could save your soul in an instant, but for most people, the transformation of that soul took time. And work.

Father Henry forced me to think about faith as something that was lived, not just thought about. Thankfully, life had thrown plenty of small mysteries before me in recent years—odd little coincidences that kept turning my attention toward God and the mystic in me.

One came at a conference I attended with largely conservative writers and academics. Late at night, at the hotel bar, I questioned a conservative Catholic writer about his criticism of the Pope. (My basic view is that too many American Catholics treat the Pope as a political figure and should instead keep a more respectful distance from Vatican politics.) While he admitted that some Catholics went too far, he was defending his more measured approach when suddenly a wineglass seemed to leap from a stable place behind the bar and crashed on the floor in front of us. We both stared at each other in silence for a bit, startled by what we'd just seen, before ending our conversation and agreeing that maybe God was trying to send a sign.

Another spooky-action-at-a-distance moment took place in Washington, DC, during a particularly grueling week of travel. In moments like this, I sometimes listen to a beautiful psalm sung by an Orthodox choir during Pope Francis's visit to Georgia in 2016. It makes me emotional every time I hear it. This time, I listened to it on the train ride down from New York to Washington.

Father Dominic Legge had invited me to visit his community at the Dominican House of Studies to talk about my growing interest in Catholicism. I stopped by his office and chatted with him for a while about various theological issues, and then we walked down to the chapel together. And there, in a beautiful Gregorian-style chant, the choir sang the exact same psalm. *What are the odds*, I thought, *that God would speak to me in two different languages using the same psalm?*

Now, I know it's easy to make the skeptic's case: "Oh, come on, JD, a group of Christians sang a song and then another group of Christians sang the same song in a different language? Total coincidence!"

But to quote Samuel L. Jackson from *Pulp Fiction*: "You don't judge s*** like this based on merit. Now, whether or not what we experienced was an 'according to Hoyle' miracle is insignificant. What is significant is I felt the touch of God."

So yes, during little moments, I felt the touch of God. I felt pulled to the faith in a way that reading books had never accomplished.

At this point, I was leaning heavily toward being baptized Catholic, but I still had a lot of questions. And just as I sometimes felt the presence of God, the world reminded me that evil still lurked.

During the summer that we moved to Cincinnati, the Church was rocked by sexual abuse allegations against Cardinal Theodore McCarrick, formerly Archbishop of Washington, DC. I knew full well that the victims of abuse by priests had suffered for decades and the Church had covered up this most horrible betrayal of its faithful. Rod Dreher, a conservative writer and friend, had left the Catholic Church in the 2000s after covering the Boston sex abuse scandal as a journalist. I could hear my Mamaw's voice in my head: "If you let these effing perverts abuse that precious little boy, I'll come back from the dead and kill them—and you." A two-year, exhaustive investigation in Pennsylvania of Catholic sexual abuse also concluded that summer while Usha, Ewan, and I were traveling in France. The report was released while we played with our toddler on a Lake Annecy beach.

The report alleged that the Church had taken special pains to avoid calling the abuse what it was: violent, awful rape. That it had failed to investigate allegations of abuse properly, hidden disgusting conduct from parishioners, and—perhaps most appallingly—reassigned known pedophiles to new roles, where they sometimes continued their sexual assault. This suggested not just individual moral failure from certain priests, but deep institutional neglect and culpability from the Catholic Church itself.[1]

If the institutional failures were enraging, the individual victim reports were as horrifying as they were heartbreaking. One fourteen-year-old girl from an abusive home told her school principal (himself a priest) about "inappropriate touching" at the hands of another priest. Incredulous, the principal hauled her father into a meeting, where she repeated the story. Her father, as skeptical as the principal, later beat her.[2]

One serial abuser, a Father Graff, had a more violent side:

> One of [his] victims testified before the Grand Jury and provided a compelling and detailed account of a violent assault by Graff. In particularly graphic testimony, this victim explained how, as Graff prepared to anally penetrate him, he decided that he could either let the rape happen or run. He explained how he fled into the street, mostly nude, rather than allow the assault by the formidable and imposing Graff. He further explained the lasting effect of the assault and its continuing impact on his daily life. This victim's mother testified before the Grand Jury as well. She

1 Fortieth Statewide Investigating Grand Jury, "Report 1: Redacted," in *Pennsylvania Diocese Victims Report*, June 18, 2018, https://www.attorneygeneral.gov/wp-content/uploads/2023/05/INVESTIGATING-GRAND-JURY-REPORT-NO.-1_FINAL_May-2023_Redacted.pdf.

2 *Pennsylvania Diocese Victims Report*, 22.

> stated that her son immediately reported the abuse to her after it occurred in 1984. She reported the abuse to Father John A. Krivak and her son's school principal. In spite of this report, Graff continued in ministry as a priest.[3]

I thought about my precious little boy and wondered how anyone could possibly do such a thing. I felt so angry at the Church. *These people used their authority, direct from Christ Himself, to prey on the most vulnerable.* I hated the Church for letting this happen. Furious, I even lashed out at a bishop on Twitter, after he posted a public message that sounded more defensive than contrite.

Usha brought poor Father Henry in for a good old-fashioned grilling. It was brutal. Usha is so humble and delicate that you don't realize 99 percent of the time that she is a fierce intellect and extremely tough. "I'm going to raise my kids in this church? When it let this happen?" She had seemingly memorized the report. She demanded to know which institutional reforms had been made in order to prevent something like this from happening again. She wasn't angry—Usha didn't really get angry—but it was like watching a star prosecutor badger a key witness. Father Henry later told me it was the toughest conversation he had ever had as a priest.

Father Henry acquitted himself well: "The unfortunate reality is that sexual abuse is an evil that can happen when adults with authority have unsupervised or unquestioned access to children—that includes stepdads, teachers, coaches, and others. But the betrayal of the sacred trust enjoyed by priests, and the ensuing cover-up, was a

3 *Pennsylvania Diocese Victims Report*, 48.

particularly wicked sin. The clergy need to both do penance for this and build more virtuous structures of safeguarding and accountability. The fact that human beings can abuse even the holiest things is a painful lesson from salvation history." It was unsatisfying, but it was also honest. And again, this is another issue where the Bible isn't a fairy tale. It makes two claims very much in tension: that God is real and works divinely through His people, but that those people continue to fail and fail again.

Indeed, it is not just a rationalization to point to the imperfection of the people God has chosen as His intermediaries on earth. You can believe it's absurd that God chose these imperfect people as vessels to reveal Himself. You can also deny the historical legitimacy of scripture, but to believe the Bible is to believe that God has chosen to work His will through imperfect men and women. It is a message the Bible makes explicit.

In a brilliant essay, "The Genealogy of Christ," Dominican priest Herbert McCabe walks through the ancestors of Christ one by one, starting with the father of the world's three monotheistic religions, Abraham himself:

> The faith of Abraham meant that, at an early age, Isaac very nearly had his throat cut by his father. But he survived to be the father of Jacob . . . an entertaining character who won *his* position in the line that leads to Christ by lying and cheating his old blind father. He was cheated himself, however. He slept with the wrong girl by mistake and became the father of Judah.

McCabe later discusses the famous king of Israel, David:

> That first section of the genealogy concentrates on sex. From David onwards the accent is more on violence. David fell in love with a girl he chanced to see bathing naked one evening. He arranged for her husband to be murdered, slept with her and became the father of Solomon, the next in the line of succession towards Christ our savior.[4]

The imperfections of these men are not incidental to our faith: These are the ancestors of Christ Himself, and God chose to put them—and their terrible sins—front and center in Judaism's and Christianity's canonical texts. As *New York Times* columnist Ross Douthat argued:

> Crucially, in claiming the divine is entering the world through this line of "murderers, cheats, cowards, adulterers and liars," Matthew isn't offering some particularly Christian innovation within the larger biblical story. He's simply picking up what his own people, the Jewish people, already said about themselves: We're the chosen people of the one true God, and to prove it to you here's a long story about how awful and promiscuous and murderous and fallible we are, how terrible our leaders often turned out to be, and how we deserved every exile and punishment we received. If you don't find that message credible, well, I understand. But if you find it strangely compelling, then you're close to the case for remaining Catholic at a time when the corruption of the

4 *The McCabe Reader*, eds. Brian Davies and Paul Kucharski (Bloomsbury, 2016), 329.

> church is driving a number of very public defections from the faith.[5]

I found it strangely compelling because it was real. There was a mystery to why God would do this—why He'd introduce Himself through corrupt and corrupted people. But who could look at human history and believe a straightforward tale of good and evil could explain the human condition? It was one thing to believe that God had a bizarre sense of humor; it would be another thing entirely to rest faith on a bunch of fairy tales.

That trip to France was during a period of relative calm: Usha was between jobs and not yet pregnant with our second child, I was able to work remotely, and Ewan was now sleeping through the night. So we landed in Nice, rented a car, and spent a month driving around the country. Before I met Usha, I had left the United States only twice—to go to Iraq and, briefly, to Haiti as a Marine. Now, I was seeing the world with her and our beloved toddler. It felt like a dream come true, but the question of faith weighed on me during the entire trip, as we bounced from ancient church to ancient church in a country once dominated by Catholicism.

We found ourselves at a cathedral in Burgundy, arguably the most famous wine-growing region of the world. Usha had left to find a bathroom, so I pushed Ewan alone in the stroller in the hopes he'd take a nap. It was late, probably six or so in the evening, and the setting sun shone through those giant stained glass windows in such a way that you could actually see the rays of light in the

---

5 Ross Douthat, "Staying Catholic at Christmas," *New York Times*, December 22, 2018, https://www.nytimes.com/2018/12/22/opinion/catholic-christmas-church.html.

dust floating in the air. I couldn't stop thinking about the emptiness of the cathedral and what that said about Europe's cultural decline and Christianity's slow evaporation from the continent. Even here, in one of the most important nations in Christian civilization, this beautiful cathedral sat empty.

Bare ruined choirs. Christianity was on the retreat in Europe, just as it was in the United States.

Ewan had fallen asleep, and I felt overwhelmed by the contrast: the majestic, almost providential beauty of the cathedral and the overwhelming feeling of sadness and disgust at the headlines about the American Church.

This sucks, I thought to myself, *but you belong here.*

My resolve in that moment felt inexplicable.

You can't give up on this institution just because it's going through a tough time, just because it screwed up.

And in that moment I felt a strange sense of possession. This church, in a foreign country, empty but for me and my family, felt like it was mine. I owed something to it, and it owed something to me. *Maybe it's all decay and decline. Maybe I'll raise my kid in this faith and he'll think I'm a simpleton or an imbecile. But if the* Titanic *is going down I'd rather be on board than hop on a lifeboat.*

It would be a lie to claim that every bit of ambivalence I'd ever felt about organized Christianity went away in a moment. But what I do recall was the distinct sense of belonging and presence. This was a sacred space, set aside for divine worship, even if locals were drifting away from the practice. No people were here in this space besides me and my sleeping son. But God was.

It amounted to a moment of genuine epiphany: where I realized that all the reasons I'd come up with over the years for resisting the call—from frustrations about saving prayers and cheap grace, to the political news cycle around the tragedy of Terri Schiavo, to more recent scandals in the Church—were problems ultimately caused by the shortcomings of human beings. And as my eyes progressed down the nave of that old cathedral up toward its impossibly intricate apse, another realization hit me: Man is capable of creating astonishing beauty and real good in this world when he tries, however imperfectly, to reconcile himself with Christ.

I also felt hopeful. The promise of the Christian faith is victory over death. Not physical death, which comes for us all, but spiritual death. Christians have experienced so many crises over our two thousand years, from plagues to civil wars to tyrants dedicated to the eradication of the faith. And yet the church—this physical building, yes, but also the communion of believers—endured.

Eventually, Usha returned to find me sitting in the pews contemplating the nature of God, as Ewan snored away. And from one of the side chapels, a middle-aged woman appeared. She looked to be an African immigrant, and she smiled politely at our toddler before leaving the cathedral. She had been there the whole time, praying quietly in a chapel. I hadn't been alone, after all.

Don't be so melodramatic, God seemed to say to me.

I got back home and told Father Henry I'd like to get baptized.

Typically, adults join the Catholic Church through a process called the Rite of Christian Initiation of Adults (RCIA). You enroll in a class, you attend the sessions, and eventually you meet enough of the standards that you can join the Church. The process is pretty informal—some join a class, some participate primarily through correspondence, I did it through personal study. I really liked that the Church required you to work a little to join. You had to take it seriously, and you had to prove you knew something about the Church, its doctrines, and what the life of a Catholic required.

Father Henry and I nerded out about Catholic doctrine and practice. Most of the "work" was doing the reading necessary for the discussions. Our study stretched from Christian ethics and political philosophy to Lawrence Feingold's *The Eucharist*, a relatively dense (but readable) academic treatise on the Catholic understanding of Holy Communion.

This was always a little weird to me as a Protestant: *You guys actually think this bread converts to the body of Christ?*

As a skeptical friend of mine once asked his aunt, "Doesn't that make you a cannibal?"

No, it turns out, this isn't how it works. Catholics don't believe that the bread takes on the material properties of human flesh, but they do believe in something called "the Real Presence"—that they're receiving the body and blood, together with the soul and divinity, of Christ when they take Communion. It is one of the most powerful means of receiving God's grace.

It also unifies the faithful. The word itself comes from the Latin root *communio*, which means sharing something in common or union or fellowship. For Catholics, Communion means not only to personally encounter Christ but to unite us as a single worshiping body. It turns a congregation into a community, one united across time and space and circumstance. "For we being many are one bread, and one body: for we are all partakers of that one bread" (1 Cor. 10:17).

I was baptized on a beautiful day in mid-August 2019, in a private ceremony not far from my house. It was nearly a year to the day after I took my lonely stroll through that cathedral in France and resolved that, however imperfect the Church or I might be, I was in it for the long haul. I woke up on the day of my reception a little apprehensive, worried I was making a big mistake. For all my doubts about how Mamaw might have reacted, it was one of her favorite phrases that I heard, in her voice, ringing in my ears that morning: "Time to s*** or get off the pot."

I found my baptism very beautiful, though I should admit that I still felt uneasy about something so far removed from my youthful churchgoing experiences. My family and many friends came to support me. Ewan was now two and spent the ceremony chomping on Goldfish crackers. At the end, the Dominican friars hosted us for coffee and doughnuts.

I try to stay humble about how little I know and how inadequate a Christian I really am. I am most comfortable engaging with the intellectual elements of the faith: What do we believe? Were the apostles really martyred? What does the historical record say about Jesus Christ? Reading about and debating ideas has always drawn me in, and that's as true for my faith as anything. But the Church isn't just about ideas passed down by Saint Thomas Aquinas or Saint Augustine.

It's about the heart, as well, and the community of believers. It's about going to Mass and receiving the Sacraments, even when it's difficult to do so. It's about so many things that I'm still ignorant of, though I'm becoming less ignorant over time. This is the process by which grace works on men and women.

And the promise of the Church is not one of linear progress, but of progress, nonetheless. Of taking one step forward, two steps back, and then three steps forward the next month. Of confessing sins, no matter how uncomfortable, to a total stranger. And accepting that the wrongs we commit come both from what we have done and what we "have failed to do, through my fault, through my fault, through my most grievous fault."

Usha has said that the business of converting to Catholicism—studying and thinking about it—was "good" for me.

And I came, eventually, to see that she was right, at least in some cosmic sense. I realized that there was a part of me—the best part—that took its cues from Catholicism. It was the part of me that demanded I treat my son with patience and made me feel terrible when I failed. That demanded I moderate my temper with everyone, but especially my family. That demanded I care more about how I rated as a husband and father than as an income earner. That demanded I let go of grudges and forgive those who've "trespassed against us."

Catholic teachings touched the part of my heart and mind that demanded I focus on the things that actually matter. And if I wanted that part of me to be nurtured and to grow, I needed to do more than read the occasional book of theology or reflect on my own shortcomings. I needed to pray more, to participate in the sacramental life of the Church, to live more fully within the obligations of a communion of believers, to confess and repent publicly.

And I needed grace.

I needed, in other words, to live as a Christian, not merely to think about it. And for me, at least, Catholicism was the right home in which to do that.

CHAPTER 9

Another Munich

Usha and I often refer to our first year together in Cincinnati in 2013 as the best year of our lives. But the years after we actually settled in Cincinnati were a close second, third, and so on. My business was going well, and Usha had a very good arrangement with her California-based firm: She could work out of our home in Cincinnati so long as she made occasional trips to the firm's main offices in Southern California. Because her parents lived in San Diego, we'd head out to California every other month. Usha would check in at the office, Ewan would see his grandparents, and we'd have a weekend with free childcare. I particularly appreciated this arrangement in January and February, when a long weekend away from Cincinnati was necessary to see any sunlight.

We loved our house, built just before the Civil War and set on two beautiful acres only a few minutes' drive from downtown Cincinnati. We could walk to visit many of our close friends. By the time I was baptized in the summer of 2019, Usha was pregnant with our second child, and my most significant concern was the

Bengals roster (they would eventually finish 2–14). Building a life in Cincinnati—rather than New York, DC, or San Francisco—felt oddly countercultural, given that our friends at Yale had mostly settled in larger cities. But some of them would visit and remark on how idyllic our life was (and how inexpensive the houses were).

I first submitted a manuscript for the book you currently hold in your hands during Usha's second pregnancy. It contained many of the same themes, but some of the readers didn't like its politics. In the years since *Hillbilly Elegy*'s publication, my views had become a little less safe and a little more controversial.

Much has been made of my evolution from Trump critic to Trump supporter. To my critics, it was a politically cynical maneuver to gain political power. I doubt I'll ever change their minds. When asked about it, I often spoke of his successful first term—the fact that he had proved me wrong by being an effective president. This was true, but as with any truth, there is a long version and a short version. This is what I told *The New York Times* during one interview:

> I was confronted with the reality that part of the reason the anti-Trump conservatives hated Donald Trump was that he represented a threat to a way of doing things in this country that has been very good for them . . .
>
> The more complete truth is that the country never really litigated the mistakes of the bipartisan consensus until Donald Trump came along, and on the right, nobody had litigated the failures of George W. Bush until Donald Trump came along.
>
> Like a lot of other elite conservatives and elite liberals, I allowed myself to focus so much on the stylistic element of

> Trump that I completely ignored the way in which he substantively was offering something very different on foreign policy, on trade, on immigration.[1]

My political evolution was downstream of the much more fundamental change in how I saw the world. I had looked inside our elite institutions and found them intellectually and spiritually broken. Was it any surprise that I would eventually reject their politics as well?

At the height of my business career, I received an invite to a Business Roundtable event in Detroit. The Business Roundtable is a collection of the most powerful CEOs and financiers in the world—think Jeff Bezos, Bill Gates, etc. The Detroit event focused, naturally, on reinvesting in the heartland, something I believed in and had bet my career on. The event concluded with a glitzy dinner, complete with a private performance by Michigan's own Stevie Wonder.

At dinner, I spoke with the CEO of a major hotel chain who knew me as a Trump critic and who became visibly upset over Donald Trump's immigration policies. I expected something rather conventional about how Donald Trump mistreated immigrants, which had become a fixture of talk show critics during the president's first term. Instead, the CEO delivered a blistering attack on the economics of migration. "Because there are so few illegal immigrants, the labor market is so tight." In his telling, because he couldn't pay illegal immigrants, he had to pay American workers more money to do the same job.

---

1 Ross Douthat, "What J.D. Vance Believes," Opinion, *New York Times*, June 13, 2024, https://www.nytimes.com/2024/06/13/opinion/jd-vance-interview.html.

I didn't point out that many people would see a corporate CEO paying higher wages to poor people as a feature, not a bug. Usha, who had joined me at the event, was shocked by his lack of self-awareness. The irony is that this guy had, in the past, supported Republicans. And he had great compliments for my book. It said something about me that this man saw me as an ally even as he fought efforts to raise the wages of his workers. And whatever it said, it wasn't good.

As happy as my family life was, it felt like so many of our culture's priorities were being turned upside down. We had corporate CEOs angry about paying their workers a decent wage. Law students taught that personal fulfillment would be found in a law firm cubicle at 11 p.m. rather than at home with their loved ones. A country where my friends' and family's life expectancy was actually declining while the media's loudest voices called them racists for being ticked off about it.

I thought back to Girard. To him, ideas and culture were like organisms. The best ideas promoted good outcomes and successful cultures; the bad ones withered and died off like an animal ill-equipped to thrive in a new environment.

"By their fruits ye shall know them." The dominant ideas of American culture were bearing some very rotten fruit. Our politics were no exception.

This became particularly obvious to me in early 2020, as Usha rapidly neared her February due date. Over Christmas and into the new year, a group of investor friends and I had shared alarming stories about a mysterious respiratory illness exploding across China.

With a new kid about to arrive, the news out of China made me paranoid. My investor friends and I decided to take our money out of the markets, as we believed the crash from the pandemic would eventually hit Western economies. I drove to a sporting goods store and bought one thousand rounds of ammunition. Then I went to Walmart and bought enormous bags of rice and flour, twenty pounds of ground beef, and excessive amounts of ketchup. An old woman behind me in the checkout counter looked at my cart suspiciously.

"Do you own a restaurant?"

"No," I replied. "But the China virus is coming." She looked at me like I had an arm growing out of my forehead.

Usha gave birth to our son Vivek Gabriel in February 2020. Before he was a month old, the world shut down. My initial paranoia made me sympathetic to the early reaction from state governments. Back in those days, everyone—from California to Florida—took a cautious approach to the new virus.

As with so many issues in our society, a culture war developed. Usha and I tried as best we could to limit social interactions and observe basic hygiene. But over time the idea that we would need to socially isolate indefinitely began to seem crazy and unsustainable. Many of our leaders seemed unable to make basic trade-offs. Did we really need to keep kids out of school to limit the spread of a respiratory virus? For how long? What about masking toddlers?

Some charity is in order. Everyone responded differently to a strange new disease from a foreign country, and elderly Americans in particular faced great risk from COVID. But at some point, COVID protocols began to feel like their own secular religion. When friends with older kids decided to return to school in the fall of 2020, members of their own families attacked them for being indifferent to the elderly. The lack of grace and zealous enforcement of social rules rivaled any religious tyranny I'd ever encountered. The prevailing orthodoxies of secular America in the twenty-first century felt more and more like a religion without the part about God. This was not a good anchoring philosophy for one's life.

In early 2021, not long after Joe Biden was sworn in as president, Usha and I were in California visiting her family. Because of the time difference, I was asleep when news broke that my home state's junior senator, Rob Portman, would retire. I went back and forth for a while on whether to run before eventually deciding to do it. In some ways, my Senate run was a quirky intellectual project: an effort to make what I thought were more explicitly Christian arguments about the economy.

I focused less on abstractions like the GDP and more on the dignity of workers and the jobs they did. Of course, the culture wars of the early Biden years featured heavily in the race, but my sense was that voters cared most about their personal economic situations. This is conventional wisdom in politics, because it's true.

Much has been written about that Senate race, and I doubt I can offer much original here. But the most important thing to say is that I thought we'd lose but we didn't. And on the way to victory, Usha and I welcomed Mirabel Rose, our first daughter.

When I started in the Senate, Usha and I faced an important personal choice. Many senators get a small apartment in Washington, DC, hoping to spend as much time in their home states as possible. But, in practice, senators spend much more of their time in Washington than in their home states, even in a good year. By my estimate, if Usha and the kids joined me in the nation's capital, I would be able to have dinner with them most nights of the year. If they stayed in Ohio, I'd be lucky to have dinner with them three nights a week.

For most senators, the political costs of moving their families to DC outweighed the benefits. And there are personal costs to transplanting kids with established social lives to a new place. We didn't have the personal issues—our oldest child was in kindergarten—but the political issues remained. To have Usha and the kids in DC would mean less time for fundraising and for networking with DC's political class. It would probably harm my political career.

But the truth is this was an easy choice. Senators have six-year terms, and any potential damage to my political future was abstract. Spending six years away from the kids, however, was a nightmare, and it would probably rank me as a bad and absent father. If I had taken any enduring lesson from my immersion in elite political culture, it was to prioritize family. I took some flak for making the move, but I never once regretted it.

* * *

About a year into my tenure as a senator, I visited Munich as part of a congressional delegation, or CODEL—the junkets on which members of Congress and other American leaders visit some foreign corner of the world to engage in diplomacy. The Munich Security Conference, held every February in Germany, is like the Super Bowl of international defense policy. I arrived on a red-eye, took a quick shower in my hotel room, and wandered around the hotel in search of coffee. A large German man stopped me in a hallway and told me not to move. I thought I was in trouble, that Germans had some rule against stumbling through hotels at 9 a.m. But then Vice President Kamala Harris whooshed by with her Secret Service detail.

Thank God, I thought, relieved I hadn't violated some obscure German protocol.

I'd spent barely a year in the Senate, and I was unusually nervous. The security conference had invited me as a curiosity: a skeptic of the foreign policy consensus of the previous half century. Most of the attendees disagreed with what I said, and more than a few thought I was an evil isolationist who would undo everything they had spent their careers building. My very presence at the conference was viewed as an oddity by the international press.

No one likes being disliked, and I'm no different.

But I was more worried about what was going on at home. I had fallen asleep on the airplane and awakened to a rash of bad news—nothing extraordinary, mind you, just the banal crises that always seem to strike when I'm farthest away from my family. Our elderly dog had lashed out at our puppy, and my wife had nearly broken her hand in the ensuing chaos. Our youngest, barely two, had woken in the middle of the night to vomit all over her siblings, which was bad enough on its own but also guaranteed that whatever had made her insides erupt was now infecting her older brothers.

By Saturday night, I had been in Munich for all of twelve hours, and it felt like my family was falling apart without me. I had slept approximately four hours in the past forty-eight, and I had no clue what I would say to a hostile crowd in the morning. I could dwell on this and prepare something to say, but I decided to take a walk. Though it was about midnight in Munich, my body's internal clock was set to the rhythms of my three kids, who were just sitting down to dinner back in the US. So I walked alone through the chilly Munich night for a couple of hours.

* * *

Aside from a layover during my deployment to Iraq, I had first visited Europe with Usha after we graduated from law school. Before this trip to Munich, I had almost always traveled internationally with her, and only her. I was nervous about the next morning's speech and feeling a little forlorn that my favorite travel companion was home without me, caring for our sick kids with an injured hand.

Usha loved Munich. She was conversant in German, a fact I somehow didn't know until I witnessed her speak to a waiter during a trip to Bavaria. As I walked the streets that night, I began to understand why she was so drawn to the city. It is one of the most beautiful places in the world, with medieval churches and long rows of ancient buildings lining the streets.

Bavaria is a conservative place, at least compared to Germany as a whole. Politics aside, I was struck by how Munich seemed to be designed to make human life more enjoyable.

The people who laid out the city, who designed and built its structures, seemed to have engineered it on a warm, humanizing scale. Simply being in that place lifted my spirits.

I've felt similarly walking in German Village in Columbus or the Garden District in New Orleans. There's something uniquely invigorating about places where everything is beautiful. We have advanced technology, and we are far richer today than the people who built German Village or medieval Munich. Even rural Ohio counties have, as their county seat, ornate courthouses constructed in the nineteenth century. But for some reason, we have chosen to govern ourselves, marry each other, and shop for junk in increasingly soulless public squares and repeating commercial strips. This says something about us, though I'm not sure what.

As I walked, I considered the plight of a friend who had just told me about his impending divorce. It was messy as these things always are, made more so by the fact that the kids were old enough to pick sides and had done that. Two of the kids wouldn't speak to him, and the other wouldn't speak to his wife. His mind was spinning with a combination of existential concerns—Would he ever find love again? Would his daughter ever understand him?—and more practical ones about finances and how to divide property.

"By their fruits ye shall know them." One of the great testaments of the Christian faith is that couples who go to church together are much less likely to divorce. But these are statistics, and for every rule there is an exception like my friend. This challenged my own faith: This guy had done everything right, had even built his marriage on a foundation of faith. There was no cheating or moment of fissure between him and his wife. Things just fell apart, as they sometimes do.

How could a devoutly Christian wife leave her devoutly Christian husband, or vice versa? It is a thorny problem that the Christian faith embraces. Yes, God's grace works miracles in the character of individual men and women; if you're a believer, God is constantly making you a better version of yourself. But many individual believers are terrible spouses regardless. There is King David, a pious man who speaks to God with the ease that most of us call our relatives. Yet King David is terribly unfaithful to his wife and brutally violent in his administration. God's grace is real, the Bible tells us, but it doesn't always fix people, at least not right away.

There's something similar going on with revelation. A college friend, Ethan, once remarked to me how easy it would be to believe in God if, like Peter the Apostle, he saw Christ walk on water and if Christ pulled him out of a lake when he was drowning. I acknowledged that, yes, everyone would believe if they saw a real live miracle. But the Christian argument is a bit more complicated: No matter what we see, we are all tempted by doubt. The Peter whom Jesus pulled out of the sea is the same Peter who denied Christ three times shortly before His crucifixion.

Ethan's view is an easier sell logically. If you see a miracle, you believe; if you don't see a miracle, you don't believe (or maybe you take it on faith). The Bible tells us something different: Even if you see a miracle, you may not believe. Even a man consumed by miraculous grace can act like a barbarian. Even a truly Christian marriage can sometimes fail. Suffering and failure are as much a part of God's plan as redemption and joy. We are asked to believe that there are lessons in this suffering; we are never told that all of us who suffer will understand those lessons in this life.

* * *

I walked the streets pondering these questions. I had no helpful answers for my friend—or for myself. I texted him to tell him I loved him and I was there if he needed me. We made plans to discuss it further over coffee the next time we saw each other.

Of course, I still had no idea what I would say the next morning at the conference. The focus was on NATO, and particularly on whether Congress would support a new foreign aid package to war-torn Ukraine. I was the only skeptic among the dozen or so senators present.

I decided to be honest with the crowd and to make my arguments directly but respectfully. The basic debate seemed pretty straightforward. Most attendees thought it was important to push the Russians back as much as possible and prevent them from gaining an easy victory. If they lost, this would be their last war of aggression, they would never again invade a neighbor, and Eastern Europe would enjoy a lasting peace. But even if Russia was destined to win, we might as well make it as painful as possible.

I certainly agreed that Russia shouldn't have invaded Ukraine, but I felt the United States was far more resource-constrained than my Senate colleagues were willing to acknowledge.

Our limitation was not financial, I argued, but something else. The United States has money, I told them, but the gap between Ukraine's and Russia's abilities to project military power was vast, and we lacked the capacity to enable the Ukrainians to close that gap—and keep it closed—all by ourselves. The United States needed Europe to step up. And so long as that gap remained, there was nothing wrong in promoting a negotiation to end the conflict.

These were the basic contours of the debate, and the summary above is hardly a full account of my view or that of my opponents. I don't want to dwell on this, in part because the calculus of this conflict has changed and changed again in the years that followed, and in part because the Trump administration has since taken serious steps to accelerate defense procurement and revitalize our defense-industrial base.

But I did learn something interesting about the psychology of my colleagues in Munich. Much like my friend going through his divorce, they were mourning the collapse of something they didn't understand.

My Senate colleagues in Munich were all older than me. Most were Baby Boomers—they hadn't fought in World War II, but they'd been raised by men who had. And after the war, their fathers and mothers had laid the foundation for the postwar international order, something my colleagues' generation would build upon.

They were proud of what they'd built, and in some ways justifiably so. For over eighty years, they had avoided a third world war. International trade had created access to cheap consumer goods and lifted billions from poverty. The West had won the Cold War and presided over thirty years of a global order where the United States called the shots, virtually alone. This global order was many of my colleagues' life's work.

My instinct before Munich had been to attack the global order and the people who'd built it. Yes, it undoubtedly had benefits, but it had many drawbacks, too, especially for everyday Americans. Life expectancy had fallen. Deindustrialization had deprived millions of well-paying jobs and had increased our economic dependence on any number of foreign countries. Since 2000, the United States had fought multiple wars that spanned nearly a decade or longer, and each was a disaster of historic proportions. Meanwhile, the opioid epidemic had killed more Americans than the entirety of World War II.

Let's go back to my favorite parable from Matthew 7:16–20:

> Do men gather grapes of thorns, or figs of thistles?
> Even so every good tree bringeth forth good fruit;
> but a corrupt tree bringeth forth evil fruit.
> A good tree cannot bring forth evil fruit, neither
> can a corrupt tree bring forth good fruit. . . .
> By their fruits ye shall know them.

Whatever benefits had accrued, and whatever world wars had been avoided, the fruits of the so-called rules-based international order, especially since the mid-1990s, were rotten. And my original instinct was to throw this in everyone's face: The fruits of your leadership are pointless wars of choice and declining life expectancy in your own country. Perhaps your life's work was for naught.

Did a day in Munich change my mind about the fundamentals? Not at all. If anything, it reinforced my views. For all its pomp, the Munich Security Conference was remarkably conventional. The conversations toed a narrow line. The same kind of thought policing I first encountered at Yale was alive and well, with much greater consequence, among world leaders in Munich. The list of what you weren't allowed to say was a hundred times as long as the list of what you were.

In one of my meetings, with a Russian dissident and opponent of Vladimir Putin, I learned more about the psychology of the Russian state than I had in weeks of reading American coverage. What made it tick? Why was Putin so popular? What might come after he was gone?

But when I pointed out Putin's popularity in another meeting, I was immediately chastised.

"His elections are fake. He's actually very unpopular."

To be fair, there's plenty of fraud in Russian elections. But every independent, objective effort to measure Putin's popularity had found high levels of support among rank-and-file Russians. Munich had become a place where people trafficked in comfortable lies rather than accepting uncomfortable truths. This was psychologically satisfying, but it made wise decision-making hard to come by.

What my day in Munich did change my mind about was the character of the people driving these foreign policy decisions. If the global order of the past thirty years had led to a bad outcome, was it because the leaders of that order were mistaken or evil? Did they mean to hollow out the United States, or did they screw up?

To the conservative movement's base, these people were unmistakably evil globalists. Whether it was Klaus Schwab at the World Economic Forum or NATO's leadership at the Munich Security Conference, they saw elites gathering to impoverish their own people and infringe on their liberties for the vague promises of a one-world government. I understood this attitude but found it self-defeating. The more you learn about our "elites," the harder it is to believe they're infinitely capable.

This truth should inspire some self-confidence: If your nation is controlled by evil genius puppet masters, how do you possibly fix its problems? Correcting the mistakes—even the big ones—of fallible politicians who got it wrong is easier than fighting back against evil genius.

Say what you would about Thom Tillis and Chris Coons, a Republican and a Democrat who had also made the trek to Munich and sat in many of my meetings, they were not evil men. I watched them with the king of Jordan, the chancellor of Germany, and other world leaders. They were smart and accomplished. Though they disagreed politically, they each had played a significant role in building the network of alliances and friendships that constituted the US-led order.

And watching them in their own stomping ground, I couldn't help but feel a certain pity. The one thing we all agreed on was that the world had changed. Others told me that, in years past, Munich had had a self-confident, even self-congratulatory, feel to it. Imagine the Munich Security Conference in the late 1990s. The US was on top. Our politics were stable. The Soviet Union had collapsed.

The Boomer leadership viewed Munich—and the world order created by the people who flock to its gleaming ballrooms—with nostalgia. They were not mere ideologues, they were people who were nostalgic for a moment that, whatever its downsides, had been full of hope and promise.

Many of the people who called the shots back in the 1990s—Hillary Clinton, Mitch McConnell, Joe Biden—still called the shots in 2024. Back then, they didn't yet know about the China shock, or the rise of terrorist threats, or a reinvigorated Russia starting a new European war, or the deindustrialization of the Western world. You could be angry, as I was, about thirty years of failed bipartisan leadership while still recognizing that those leaders were clinging to a disastrous consensus in part because they were mourning its unraveling.

To admit that the United States was limited in its ability to help Ukraine—as even the most fervent supporter of Ukraine does today—to admit that America was unable to bridge the gap between Ukraine's and Russia's firepower alone, to admit that our own country couldn't unilaterally police any conflict of its choosing, would be to admit that their life's work had been a failure.

Before attending Munich, I had called attention to that failure. I had criticized it, even gleefully. But my conversations made me more reflective. The men and women who had built the "US-led order" were, by and large, well-intentioned. Like my friend with his marriage, they had given their effort a lot of love. It just didn't work out.

My friend had said something about his wife that I had initially dismissed as a quirk of grief, but now I wondered whether it revealed a marital dynamic that had contributed to his divorce. His wife, he had told me, was a narcissist so damaged by the trauma of her youth that she liked to torture him. Maybe he was right, but his words lacked Christian humility. And either way, when you go down the path of assigning dysfunctional motives to every behavior, it's hard to see fault in yourself. It's harder still to understand what actually went wrong. Maybe that was the most important Christian lesson to come from my friend's marriage: Reject the temptation to see your partner as evil or yourself as righteous.

That was a lesson I could apply to myself in Munich. Though I hadn't—at thirty-nine years old and in the Senate for barely a year—caused three decades of America's problems, it would be a huge mistake, even for a partisan, to blame the country's problems only on my opponents' evil motives.

The truth was more complex and less satisfying, but it had the virtue of being true.

Following a terrible night of sleep, I woke up and gave my remarks. I was on a panel with some parliamentary leaders from other countries, one of whom would become the Deputy Prime Minister of the United Kingdom. I acquitted myself well enough that nothing I said went viral for its stupidity. I learned through that panel and other meetings that India might be surprisingly receptive to my theory of world affairs.

One Ukrainian parliamentary leader challenged some of my assertions. I responded, and we had a nice chat afterward. The conversation heightened my sense of heartache for my colleagues as they watched our country's position of leadership changing—or even slipping away. This young man's country was fighting a war for survival, and he wanted so desperately for the United States to wave a magic wand and give Ukraine what it needed. I asked him how many artillery shells and missile interceptors his country needed. And when he answered, I told him (truthfully) that even if we gave him everything we had we'd fall short.

My colleagues who wanted to say yes, despite our country's limitations, were misinformed. Naive even. But they weren't bad people.

An irony of Munich is that all of these leaders—American and foreign—were trying to preserve something that had been built by the Christian leaders of a Christian civilization.

In 1959 President Dwight D. Eisenhower closed one of the first NATO meetings by saying: "Those who respect the dignity of man will not flinch before the magnitude of the task. Rather they will prove once again that greatness of spirit and love of liberty will overcome the forces of atheistic materialism and coercion and give to all the nations, under God, the blessings of security, along with a just and durable peace."

Of course, many of the people at that first meeting weren't devout Christians. Some were Jewish, and others only nominally Christian. But Christianity gave them a shared moral language—a foundation on which the entire postwar order was built.

Likewise, in 1963, the host of the first Munich Security Conference was a former German army officer named Ewald-Heinrich von Kleist-Schmenzin. He gathered world leaders in Munich to discuss how to support the cause of liberty in Germany, which was divided at the time between free West Germany and Soviet-controlled East Germany. Von Kleist-Schmenzin was a devout Christian and, like his father, a conservative German politician and lawyer. *The*

Bulwark, the anti-Trump publication, has described the senior von Kleist-Schmenzin as a hero, despite his Christian nationalism.[2]

Why was he a hero? Because he and his son, then barely old enough to drink, had participated in the plot to kill Hitler as World War II drew to a close. Despite Hitler's weakened state, the failed plot amounted to a death sentence for its participants. The son—the founder of the Munich Security Conference—survived the plot's fallout. He was one of just a handful to do so. The Nazis killed his father just a few weeks before the liberation of Berlin in 1945.

These were men who knew what they were defending. It wasn't just ideas—not "liberalism," not "freedom," not even "democracy." It was Western Christian civilization, and the values particular to it: the concept of natural rights, including freedom of speech; a sense of duty to one's neighbors; an obligation of the strong to protect the weak; a belief in free will and individual conscience. That first conference in 1963 was filled with men willing to lay down their lives to defend that way of life from the totalitarian, revisionist forces that sought to abolish it.

But over the decades that followed and especially in the years since the collapse of the Soviet Union, we lost something sacred. Faith receded from public life in both North America and Europe. And as that inheritance weakened, the West did not simply become more "neutral." It forgot what it stood for. In the vacuum, we saw a new creed take form: a secular global liberalism that maintained the vocabulary of rights while shedding the religious foundation that gave them meaning. Free speech came to be treated as

2 Jim Swift, "Just Say No. Not Ever," *Bulwark*, February 10, 2023, https://www.thebulwark.com/p/just-say-no-not-ever.

the dangerous relic of a more self-confident past. Democratic disagreement became something to be managed, especially when the masses voted for a disfavored candidate. And the right of citizens to the value of their own labor—so cherished by Pope Leo XIII in *Rerum Novarum*—was traded away by transnational elites in favor of mass migration.

It shouldn't have been any surprise, then, that the Munich Security Conference in 2024 had about as much Christianity as a 1959 meeting of the Soviet high command. There were no mentions of God. There were, however, lots of appeals to vaguely defined shared values. "Putin is evil," I heard many times. "We are on the side of justice and truth, and our enemies seek to destroy these things," a French parliamentarian told me about the transatlantic alliance.

While I was there, I met the conference's new host, German Chancellor Olaf Scholz. A smart man with a pleasant demeanor, he occupied the same category in my mind as most of my Senate colleagues: a well-intentioned leader who didn't quite understand how the world order he had grown up in had fallen apart.

Just a few years earlier, when Scholz was sworn in as Germany's new chancellor, *The New York Times* hailed his inauguration for making a bit of history. Scholz was the first chancellor, the paper said, who "took God out" of his constitutional oath of office.[3]

So there you have it. These men and women had taken God out of their postwar oaths and alliances, and they wondered why so much else had been lost as well.

3 Katrin Bennhold, "Scholz Takes 'God' Out of His Oath," *New York Times*, December 8, 2021, https://www.nytimes.com/live/2021/12/08/world/germany-scholz-merkel/scholz-takes-god-out-of-his-oath?smid=url-share.

CHAPTER 10

When in Rome

If Munich was a whirlwind, what came after I returned was a category 5 hurricane. Though I had heard that President Trump might be interested in having me join his ticket in the national campaign now underway, I figured it was a long shot. I had only a year of political experience. As a white man from Ohio, I added no diversity to the ticket and didn't deliver a swing state. When his staff told me I was on the short list, I almost thought it was a prank call. But I answered their questions and tried to keep the possibility out of mind.

Usha wasn't looking to upend our lives yet again, but she eventually came to see it as an opportunity to serve the country. However, she insisted that we bring the kids on the road. "Well," the campaign manager told her, "you'll have a 737 to fly around in. I'm pretty sure your kids will fit in that."

The most fascinating part of the process was also the most absurd: the in-person vetting with me, my wife, and a campaign attorney. "You've never cheated on your wife?" he asked.

"I haven't, but I assume that people who have don't just admit it to a stranger."

"Sorry, I have to ask."

"Yeah, I know."

On the morning of the 2024 Republican National Convention, President Trump called me and asked me to join him on the ticket. My family's lives changed instantly, from the media spotlight to the ever-present Secret Service detail. The weekend after I was nominated, I tried to go to the grocery store. But if anyone there didn't already know who I was, they surely noticed the forty armed guards surrounding me.

During one particularly tough patch that summer, the media managed to dredge up every stupid thing I had ever said publicly. But that bothered me far less than the fact that our oldest child was struggling with this new life. I got a call from the conservative radio host and grassroots organizer Charlie Kirk, who had become one of my closest friends over the last few years. "Are you doing okay? They're coming after you hard." I told him I was fine, that I had faced scrutiny before, but that I was worried about my son.

"You're a dad, so maybe you get this," I said. "My seven-year-old is really struggling. I didn't anticipate this at all. I figured he was so young that he wouldn't even realize much had changed. But he hates the cameras and the attention. He told me, 'Dad, I just want everyone to go back to treating us like they used to.' Sometimes I feel like I ruined his life without even asking him."

Charlie was always a good listener. "Don't try to convince your son it's not a sacrifice. It is. Just try to take some solace in the fact that it's a worthy sacrifice. I'll say a prayer for you." I followed his advice, and Ewan slowly adjusted.

The rest, as they say, is history. We traveled around the country. I gave speeches and interviews to the media. Usha found outings in new cities with the kids. The president and I won the election, and I became the Vice President of the United States.

We moved into a giant house at the Naval Observatory in Northwest Washington, DC. We arrived around noon on January 21, 2025, to a delicious meal cooked by our new team of chefs. Father Henry came by to offer a blessing for the new house, and the kids explored their new rooms and playrooms, and told us this place was paradise. "Do we own this house now?" our oldest son asked. "No," I told him, "but we get to live here for a few years."

* * *

In April 2025, the White House sent me to India for a formal diplomatic visit. Despite being married to the daughter of Indian immigrants, I had never visited India. This was partially my fault and partially the fault of circumstances—one-year jobs, a Zika outbreak while Usha was pregnant, and COVID.

Whoever described hell as a "lake of fire" had never ridden on an airplane for eighteen hours with small children. But professional duty called, and the kids were young enough to skip school, so Vice President Clark Griswold brought the whole family on the trip.

We had initially planned on flying straight there, but since we had to make a fuel stop in Rome, we decided to leave two days early and add Italy to the itinerary—for meetings first with Italian Prime Minister Giorgia Meloni and then at the Vatican. That would put us in Rome for Easter.

Rome during Holy Week. What could be more special?

Our meetings with Prime Minister Meloni and her team went well on Good Friday. The war in Ukraine and international trade dominated our discussions. Later that day, we attended the Good Friday liturgy at Saint Peter's Basilica. In defense of our staff, they had told us we'd be on camera for the entire three-hour service, but for some reason I hadn't internalized what that truly meant with three jet-lagged kids.

We walked into the Basilica, and seemingly every camera in the world was immediately trained upon us. It was every parent's worst nightmare. The boys were awake and passably well-behaved (though there were a few hairy moments), but poor Mirabel had fallen asleep in the car en route to the Vatican, so I held her in my arms. She slept for over an hour—which we welcomed, because it bought us an hour of good behavior. Eventually, she began to stir, and I looked at her little face and found her eyes wide open, bigger than I'd ever seen them. She was staring intently over my shoulder. I turned my head and realized she was looking at a Swiss Guard, dressed in purple and yellow stripes, holding a gigantic medieval pike.

I realized how crazy this must have been from her perspective: She gets in a car and falls asleep (a common occurrence in her life). She wakes up in an ancient, massive church. Behind her is a group of robed priests singing in foreign languages. The pews around her are filled with strangers, and immediately at her back is a medieval pikeman with a shiny metal helmet. The absurdity of the moment overcame me. Not wanting the world to see me laughing hysterically during a Mass mourning Christ's passion, I used Mira as a shield while I chuckled silently. Fully awake now, Mira and her brothers alternated between complaining, coloring in their sketchbooks, and occasionally listening to the beautiful Latin chanting. Eventually the Mass ended, and we left in peace without embarrassing ourselves or our nation on international television.

Thanks be to God.

We had planned diplomatic meetings at the Vatican the next day, and it was an open question whether Pope Francis—then in very poor health—would join us. During our visit to Saint Peter's, a priest pulled me aside. "The Pope would really like to meet with you while you're here. But he will decide in the morning whether he is up to it."

The Vatican and American diplomats were clearly worried about whether it would be seen as a snub if the meeting fell through. I felt awful about this. "Please tell Pope Francis that I pray for him every day, and that he should feel under no pressure to see me. I wish him well." I wasn't sure the message took.

Our meeting with Vatican diplomats proved more substantive than I expected. We talked mostly about world conflicts—particularly those in Ukraine and Gaza. But Cardinal Pietro Parolin—at the time considered a favorite to be the next Pope—raised the issue of migration. I had expected this, but I still found our conversation unsettling. Not because the Vatican expressed skepticism of the Trump administration's migration policies but because of how generic its position was. The diplomats acknowledged that the United States had the right to control its borders, but they also encouraged us to treat migrants humanely.

What did they take issue with, exactly? The diplomats never specified. Did they object to deportations? Just to deportations of certain populations? Were they entirely fine with deportations so long as we didn't say mean things about illegal immigrants? Here I was, the most senior Catholic in the United States government, and the Vatican seemed unwilling to move its moral guidance past the point of trite platitudes.

I'm sure they avoided specifics out of a desire to be, well, diplomatic, but what they said was too abstract to be helpful. Obviously I'm not going to always agree with them. And if our country's interests conflict with their views, I've got an obligation to the American people. But I was struck that one of the few institutions with the moral authority and global perspective to address the migration question seemed so afraid of saying something controversial that it chose, effectively, to say nothing at all.

The next day was Easter Sunday. We would leave that evening for India, but first the Vatican had kindly offered us a private Easter service at one of the grand basilicas of Rome, Saint Paul Outside the Walls.

Early Sunday morning, I received a text message telling me that the Pope would like to see me. The kids were still asleep when I hopped in a car and made the fifteen-minute trip to the Vatican. Rome had already come to life on a beautiful Easter morning, and I felt unusually nervous about this final, unexpected diplomatic meeting.

Pope Francis planned to preside over Easter Mass and wanted to say hello beforehand. The visit was maybe ten minutes at most. I saw, for the first time, the emotional power that the Bishop of Rome held for lifelong Catholics. A young staffer of mine named Patrick, a warm but not particularly emotional kid, began to cry while shaking Pope Francis's hand.

Pope Francis was more fragile than I realized, and I felt even worse that he had forced himself out of bed early to meet with me.

Our visit was brief and informal. He gave the kids Easter gifts, and I told him we prayed for him regularly. After exchanging a few more pleasantries, we said our goodbyes. I got back in my car, called Usha, and said, "It's sad. He's in very bad shape. But he was very kind."

In the United States, conservative Catholics and other Christians viewed Francis with great skepticism. I never shared this view, even when Francis disagreed with me directly—as he did on the question of immigration. Even where his views were different from ours, I thought the media exaggerated the conflict for clicks and ratings. He was the Pope, Donald Trump the President, and I the Vice President. We had different jobs, and I preferred his specific exhortations to the vagueness I had encountered during our Vatican meeting. Better to have an honest conversation than one masked by clichés.

* * *

We left that night for India, slept on the plane, and arrived to pomp, circumstance, and intense humidity. Usha and I greeted the welcome delegation in Delhi. As we decamped for our hotel, I spotted a message from one of my Catholic staffers: "Pope Francis died."

I told my kids the news and said a prayer for the Pope. I was one of the last people to see him alive. To the media, I said that I admired his obvious concern for the poor, the sick, and everyone suffering at the margins of society. I meant that, and more. Whatever our disagreements on policy, he had helped keep me focused on the Church's social teachings.

This moment reminded me that Christianity is not merely a private faith. It imposes individual obligations on us to attend church, tithe, pray, and follow certain moral dictates—don't lie, don't steal, honor thy father and mother. But it is also a faith through action, modeled on the life of Christ, that requires good deeds, love, and service. We are each a child of God, but we are also friends, spouses, children, and parents. We are members of neighborhoods, communities, cities, and countries.

Pope Francis was attacked by many American Christians—Catholic and non-Catholic alike—as a communist, a supporter of open borders, a Latin American revolutionary, or at least a liberal. As Sohrab Ahmari, the conservative Catholic writer, argued in a eulogy, this criticism of Francis glossed over the countless ways in which he upheld the traditional order.[1]

Even his skepticism of free market theory was less about socialism than about the Catholic Church's ancient social doctrine. Ironically, Francis's predecessor Benedict XVI—something of a right-wing icon—faced similar, if more muted, criticisms. George Weigel, a prominent Catholic social conservative and writer, practically accused Benedict of allowing the progressives on the Pontifical Council for Justice and Peace to write one of his encyclicals, because it nodded too much to traditional Catholic teaching on economics. And before him, John Paul II declared in 1991 that man had a "right" to a just wage and to join a labor union.

None of these popes were communists. They were just Christians.

Of course, the Catholic Church also condemns communism and defends the right to private property. The point is not that the Church is a left-wing institution, but instead that it doesn't fit neatly into twenty-first-century political debates. That was true of

1 Sohrab Ahmari, "Pope Francis, Trad Icon," *First Things*, April 24, 2025, https://firstthings.com/pope-francis-trad-icon/.

Pope Francis, it was true of his predecessors, and it will be true in the future.

Francis's life—and death—showed how easy it is to allow politics to lead our faith, rather than the other way around. This is not just relevant to Catholicism. Protestant commentators, including my late friend Charlie Kirk, have spoken increasingly of the way contemporary Christian leaders completely ignored questions of economic policy and material well-being. We are very comfortable saying we must protect the life of the unborn or that adultery is sinful. We're fine telling a businessman he must go to church and tithe but not that he must pay his people a fair wage. If it is sinful to abort a perfectly healthy human baby before birth, so, too, is it sinful to depress that baby's chance of living a good life afterward.

We confine Christianity to the most private of questions—relations between husbands and wives, reproductive decisions—and are then surprised when kids like me grow up in the faith and then discard it. We have to do better. If Christianity is true, it must be true for the whole human person at all times of life. To quote the famous Reformed theologian Abraham Kuyper: "There is not a square inch in the whole domain of our human existence over which Christ, who is Sovereign over all, does not cry: 'Mine!'"[2] We are not merely private moral actors but also public ones. We are spouses and parents and workers and community members and neighbors. The Christian faith must speak to all parts of the human experience, but some of the reaction to Francis shows us that when it does, we recoil.

The idea that faith had relevance outside of culture war debates

---

2 Abraham Kuyper, "Sphere Sovereignty," in *Abraham Kuyper: A Centennial Reader*, ed. Jame D. Bratt (Eerdmans, 1998), 488.

was once foreign to me. Sometimes it's easier to keep our faith in a box. It's less inconvenient that way. But the Gospel is inherently an inconvenient message. It demands much of us—so much, in fact, that it tells us up front that every single living person will fail in some profound way. The fact that it is demanding makes it more relevant and is a big part of why I'm a practicing Christian today.

In modern American politics, it's become passé to talk about God. To hear a speech from a politician of the mid-twentieth century is to walk into a different religious world. Roosevelt asked for God's help in his first inaugural address and on the day after the Japanese bombed Pearl Harbor. Eisenhower started his first speech as president of the United States with a prayer:

> *Almighty God, as we stand here at this moment my future associates in the Executive branch of Government join me in beseeching that Thou will make full and complete our dedication to the service of the people in this throng, and their fellow citizens everywhere.*
>
> *Give us, we pray, the power to discern clearly right from wrong, and allow all our words and actions to be governed thereby, and by the laws of this land. Especially we pray that our concern shall be for all the people regardless of station, race or calling.*
>
> *May cooperation be permitted and be the mutual aim of those who, under the concepts of our Constitution, hold*

> *to differing political faiths; so that all may work for the good of our beloved country and Thy glory. Amen.*[3]

Eisenhower saw a shared commitment to "Thy glory" as the principle that united Americans of different political persuasions. God glued together the country's political divisions. Ike's successor, John F. Kennedy, invoked God three times in his own inaugural address and many other times during his brief presidency. When national politicians invoke God that much today, we're warned that *The Handmaid's Tale* has come to life.

* * *

In late 2025, the US Conference of Catholic Bishops issued a rare special message—the first in twelve years—after their annual meeting. Widely viewed as a critique of our administration's immigration policies, the message was considerably more complicated than the media reported. It recognized the right of nations to control their own borders, even acknowledging that failed border enforcement encourages "immigrants [to] face the risk of trafficking and other forms of exploitation." It criticized "dehumanizing" rhetoric against not just immigrants, but also immigration enforcement officers.[4] Overall, the document was admirably measured.

---

3 Dwight D. Eisenhower, 1953 Inauguration Prayer, in "Inaugurations," Dwight D. Eisenhower Presidential Library, revised January 12, 2026, https://www.eisenhowerlibrary.gov/eisenhowers-presidential-years/inaugurations.

4 Office of Public Affairs, "U.S. Bishops Issue a 'Special Message' on Immigration from Plenary Assembly in Baltimore," November 12, 2025, https://www.usccb.org/news/2025/us-bishops-issue-special-message-immigration-plenary-assembly-baltimore.

Or almost too measured. Pope Francis's approach on immigration—whether intentionally or not—had forced difficult conversations. Very often, I'd find myself initially annoyed by a comment he had made, but then I'd read more and learn something that added to my understanding. Did I often disagree with him? Sure. I disagree with a lot of people who still make me think.

The immigration question, like so much of our politics and our public life, calls out for engagement from the bishops and clergy. If you look at majority-Christian societies in the advanced world, every single one has been set on fire by the immigration issue. And it's easy to understand why: Immigration raises deep questions of identity and charity that require moral leadership.

It's why I'd hoped for more out of the conversation with the Vatican diplomats. Immigration is a particularly thorny version of a challenge I encounter every day in my job: how to take an accepted moral principle and apply it in the real world as a Christian leader.

Real engagement with the immigration issue requires real engagement with the trade-offs. Law enforcement is an inherently difficult business. If you arrest a person illegally in the United States, that person will sometimes resist arrest. Even if they don't, and even if everyone agrees their deportation is lawful and moral, there will still be some measure of separation and heartache. To say that a country can control its borders or that immigration officers must treat people humanely is easy because everyone agrees with it. The difficulty is applying these principles in a messy world with competing values. I'm one Christian statesman who would welcome an institutional faith less focused on platitudes and more focused on reality.

One obvious question is: What is the right number of immigrants for a nation to accept? This, it turns out, is a hotly contested topic. I learned in high school about the evils of "nativism," but never about the social forces that caused "nativism" to arrive in the first place. We didn't learn poor immigrant networks led anarchist bombing campaigns against the federal government in the 1910s. We didn't learn about the ethnic violence between Know Nothings and European immigrants, the conflict that would inspire Hollywood movies like *Gangs of New York*. And we didn't learn about the new forms of organized crime—like La Cosa Nostra—that sprang up as new European arrivals clashed with an Anglo-American legal system. One can believe that some nativists have bad motivations—and that many new immigrants are good people—while acknowledging the social instability inherent in assimilating one population into another.

One of the best institutions at taking people of different ethnicities and customs and forming bonds between them is church (the military is another). Yet churchgoing kept declining just as Biden-era immigration policy caused a skyrocketing increase in the foreign-born share of the population. This makes assimilating newcomers even harder.

One of the jobs of a Christian statesman is to preserve the very social cohesion that makes charity and generosity possible. In *Rerum Novarum*, Pope Leo XIII defended private property, but with significant limits. No man has the right to deny another a living wage, he wrote, and this is one reason that Catholics (along with many Protestants) have historically supported the right of workers to form labor unions.

But these economic questions bleed easily into the migration issue: Too much immigration actually destroys the social cohesion necessary to form labor unions. Alex Nowrasteh, an analyst at the

Cato Institute, a free market think tank, has argued that the decline of American labor unions is traceable directly to the relaxation of immigration restrictions in the 1960s. Nowrasteh thinks this is a good thing because he doesn't like the idea of giving workers bargaining power over massive corporations. For those of us who disagree, Christians inadvertently serve a pernicious master when they sign up for large-scale immigration.

The same social cohesion that encourages people to form labor unions also brings other benefits. We want our country's citizens to share some things in common—language, values, an understanding of our history in the past and our purpose in the future.

Achieving these things is hard in any society. But too much immigration, too quickly, makes it much harder.

Of course, if one goal is promoting social cohesion in our own country, there are other considerations. There are genuinely good people suffering all over the world, and nations—like people—have duties of charity to the needy. As much as I believe our asylum system has been abused—and as much as helping doesn't necessarily mean permanent settlement within our borders—there are people out there we should help.

And it is true that immigration can bring benefits to the host country in its own right. Just think of Elon Musk and the hundreds of thousands of jobs that trace directly to his decision to come to the United States.

There are innumerable prudential considerations at work. And even if we agree on the right levels of immigration, that's just the tip of the iceberg. Some populations assimilate more easily than others. Certain economic skill sets are in higher demand. As you can probably tell, I tend to favor a low level of immigration, in the hope that a period of assimilation and integration will lessen the social divisions of modern America. But regardless of where you set the level, you might expect a resident of Guatemala City who speaks fluent English to contribute more quickly to the United States than a resident of rural Guatemala who can't even read or write in Spanish.

Then there's the question of how you enforce the immigration system you choose. As we learned during the Biden administration, if you're too loose on enforcement you encourage people to break the law—and you even promote human trafficking along our border.

Of course, critics of the Trump administration say we're too tough. The point is not to litigate this issue on these pages but to highlight that any application of moral principles in the real world requires a constant evaluation of trade-offs. Undoubtedly, that's what the Christian faith demands of us.

I can believe (as I do) that I owe a given immigrant—even an illegal one—duties of charity and grace, while accepting that in a world of limited resources those duties necessarily come up against other responsibilities. If I am so generous to illegal immigration that it facilitates a system of human trafficking, I have failed a moral test.

The Church's invocation of the dignity of migrants forces deliberation over the moral trade-offs. And one can believe those trade-offs result in favoring a strict migration policy without dehumanizing anyone.

* * *

One of the most challenging issues for Christians is abortion. *Roe v. Wade*'s demise has revealed the political unpopularity of our position. In 2023, I worked hard to defeat a ballot issue in Ohio that would have created a constitutional right to abortion late into the second term. The political problem for the pro-life side was that the state of Ohio had an extremely restrictive abortion law on the books. Polls showed that most voters thought current Ohio law went too far, and given a choice between one extreme and another, the pro-life side got blown out: About 60 percent of Ohio—a relatively Republican-leaning state—voted for the ballot initiative.

Some people argue we should give up on the idea of protecting the unborn. I take a different view: Prudence is the better part of virtue. If your political argument on the abortion question—or any other—fails to persuade your fellow Americans, you have to make a better argument.

Most of the women I know who've ended pregnancies did so out of a fear that they had no other choice. To have a baby they didn't expect, they felt, would ruin careers, relationships, and educational opportunities. Some were pressured by parents or threatened by partners. To these women—some of whom regret their choice—so much of the pro-life movement is about eliminating the last option they thought they had left.

That's why we lost the Ohio referendum, but it's also how we'll start winning people over: by reflecting Christian charity in the way we champion the unborn.

Examples are everywhere. All over the country, pregnancy resource centers help young women afford food and diapers, and support young mothers through the inevitable chaos of an unexpected pregnancy.

To actually protect the unborn, we'll need to elevate these Christian charities and the spirit of the people who fund and operate them. And we'll need to make a better Christian argument, about building the kind of culture and economy that can actually sustain young families and the life they bring into the world.

It's possible to shift public opinion in the right direction. Across US history, there's no shortage of examples of moral arguments that went from minority positions to winning over public approval. But persuasion requires patience, humility, and a willingness to meet people where they are. Politicians have a role to play in guiding that effort.

It will also require our politicians to be more respectful of those on the other side of family policy debates. And when I say "politicians," I very much mean myself . . .

And that brings me to another lesson of the faith for Christian statesmen: It's okay to admit error.

One of the dumbest things I ever said came when I argued that "childless cat ladies" across the Democrat Party were running our country into the ground. The comment caused two firestorms: the first when I made it, the second years later during a political campaign. It was a boneheaded comment, intentionally (and successfully) provocative rather than illuminating.

Aside from enraging a great number of people, it had the added benefit of distracting from the actual point I wanted to make, which was that our society is becoming pathologically hostile to having kids. If you couldn't tell, it's one of the qualities of striver culture I most resent: the idea that raising a family will prevent you from realizing your utmost potential in your professional life, and thus, you shouldn't have kids.

But I could have made that point much more effectively, and with the benefit of showing a little charity to the many Americans who—some for reasons beyond their control—don't have children. When I consider the Church's admonition to respect the dignity of every life, this was a clear moment where I failed.

It would be convenient for someone in my shoes to just say, "The Christian faith deals with moral issues and I deal with political ones; never the twain shall meet." And of course, to an extent this is true. It's not my job to weigh in on what the Catholic Church says about a particular liturgical question or on whether Baptists agree with Pentecostals on the question of backsliding sinners and their status as Christians. And I wouldn't expect the Pope or a Lutheran minister to tell me who I should hire as chief of staff or police my tone.

But to divorce political judgments from morality is to make yourself less human. The Christian faith is not a weird little compartment of my life, something I appeal to for an hour or two on Sundays or when a relative gets sick. It is the lens through which I see the world. When the Church offers its insights on abortion I sometimes hear people on the left say, "The Church should stay out of politics." I hear the same thing when conservatives backbite a Christian pastor for talking about taking care of the poor or treating immigrants with dignity. This attitude makes the Church irrelevant. It takes a faith that should inform the whole of a person, cuts it off, and isolates it in a box.

The Church demands more of us, and it certainly demands more of me.

One thing it demands is a more fulsome understanding of the role of faith in public life. If you remember the Terri Schiavo case that so frustrated me as a young Christian, part of what I was reacting to was my own limited understanding of Christian social teaching. To me, Christians cared about abortion (bad) and marriage (good), but their politics seemed so disconnected from the real lives of most people. But if what brought me back to my faith was the sense that the Church answered life's big questions, then I must resist the effort to confine Christ's moral teachings to a few social issues.

What would a Christian approach not just to marriage and family, but to economics in the modern era look like?

CHAPTER 11

A Dismal Science

The first (and only) time I ever visited Japan, I read a bunch of articles by economists about Japan's stagnant economy. Japanese economic growth had stalled and living standards had flatlined. Economists broadly agreed that something had gone terribly wrong with Japanese economic policy, though they disagreed about what should be done.

After about two hours in Tokyo, I realized that the dire predictions of the expert class had nothing in common with the actual Japan I saw. Children seemingly no more than five years old rode the subway without fear, and the public bathrooms in the subway stations were cleaner than the member bathrooms in the United States Senate. Public transportation ran perfectly on time—if a bus or a train arrived two minutes late, the public employees acted ashamed.

Meanwhile, the Japanese had apparently perfected the art of cuisine. Have you ever gone to a grocery store and gotten an excellent batch of strawberries or blueberries? In Japan, every fruit tasted like the best strawberry you've ever eaten, even the almost expired pack in a small convenience store. You could walk into a random hole-in-the-wall restaurant and order a delicious, healthy meal at barely the cost of a McDonald's cheeseburger.

Now, I'm not saying Japan doesn't have problems. Its own leaders worry a great deal about the demographic crisis in the country—the fact that so few children are born in the island nation that the population is declining. But in their focus on the quantitative metrics of society, the economists had missed something important about Japan.

If you're focused on GDP, a $6 pint of Japanese strawberries is no different from a $6 pint of American strawberries. If you're focused on dollars and cents, each contributes equally to the economic indicators. But if everyone in Japan eats better strawberries than everyone in America, the economic indicators have failed to measure something meaningful.

When I got back home, a friend asked me if I learned anything on my trip to Japan. "Yes," I replied snidely. "Maybe economics is just fake."

* * *

One of the things I've picked up during my two jobs in government is that the economics profession dominates many of the background debates in our politics. This is because politics fundamentally tries to answer two questions. The first is a question of values: What are we trying to accomplish here? The second is a question of practicality: How do we accomplish this thing?

Say you want to reduce carbon emissions for environmental reasons. Should you tax carbon? Or subsidize non-carbon-based forms of energy, like nuclear power? Should you apply an import tax on foreign goods that depend heavily on carbon emissions, or should you ban those products altogether? What are the unintended consequences of these policies? Enter the economics profession to provide answers to practical questions.

But as the decline of Christianity has left us without a shared moral language, economics has stepped into the vacuum. We pretend there are scientific answers to questions of values. Take one of the major issues of the 2024 campaign and a significant focus of our time in the White House: Should our trade policy be oriented around protecting domestic industries and jobs or around ensuring a short-term supply of cheap consumer goods? This is a tough thing to quantify, but the rise of economic thinking and rhetoric in our public life is striking. Economist and *New York Times* columnist Justin Wolfers analyzed how mentions of the economics profession evolved over time in our country's paper of record. He found that economists have gone from getting the occasional mention to being the most discussed of all social scientists. There are also about twice as many mentions of economists as there are of the next-most-discussed academics (historians) in the *Congressional Record.*

There are less quantifiable ways of observing the trend. As Wolfers said, "Today, the profession is so ubiquitous that if you are running a government agency, a think tank, a media outlet or a major corporation, and don't have your own pet economist on the payroll, you're the exception."[1]

1 Justin Wolfers, "The Dismal Science: How Economists Came to Dominate the Conversation," The UpShot, *New York Times*, January 23, 2015, https://www.nytimes.com/2015/01/24/upshot/how-economists-came-to-dominate-the-conversation.html.

I first noticed this during a constitutional law seminar in law school, in which we discussed the abolition of slavery and its lingering effects on the politics of the American South. One student observed that "many researchers think that slavery actually depressed the advancement of the South's economy by making it more dependent on agriculture and less dynamic than the North." Another chimed in, echoing arguments historian Ed Baptist would make in his 2014 book, *The Half Has Never Been Told*: "Well, the northern economy actually depended on the slave economy's outputs, especially cotton, to provide the raw materials for its own economic advancement." And I, still in a bit of a libertarian phase, found myself arguing that the South's economic reliance on slave labor was necessarily inefficient because slaves weren't able to bargain fairly for wages and other benefits.

Now, of course, we all took the evil of the institution of slavery for granted, but the language of technocratic cost-benefit analysis was so ingrained that even a debate about chattel slavery took on the sanitized tone that is the hallmark of the dismal science. Even in law school, even talking about slavery, economics found a way of neutering our sense of basic justice. It is one thing to debate practicality and unintended consequences. It is another to allow that debate to crowd out your sense of right and wrong.

It is perhaps the biggest difference between the elites of our society and most of its population. Technocratic language has invaded every topic, and at a certain level, the way you speak about something warps the way you think about it.

Even something as fundamentally moral and human as the role of husband and wife could be infected by economics. Nobel Prize–winning economist Gary Becker authored a famous article, "Human

Capital, Effort, and the Sexual Division of Labor," seen by many as an economic response to increasingly cynical views of marriage in modern social and economic thought. In a good marriage, husband and wife will focus on different duties and excel at different tasks. Their marriage is less a sacramental union and more an economic partnership between laborers of different aptitudes. It's like a small business.

Stable, two-parent households are good because the children of those families earn more, are more likely to graduate from college, and cost less in net welfare benefits than those who come from broken homes. Economic logic saturates the thinking of our society's most powerful members.

This is such a thin and unsatisfying way to think about your life and the society you share with other people. "Human capital and the sexual division of labor" have their place, but what about love? And duty and honor and commitment? The depressed wages and higher welfare payments to broken homes are undoubtedly bad things. You know what's worse? The heartbreak of the parents and the misery of the children. Recall that my stepmother, a devout evangelical and committed Republican, once observed that though she voted Republican, she always felt they were the party of the rich. And something that happened in the 1990s, as Christian conservatives fused with the Republican Party, is that we were taken advantage of. Most Christians didn't care about lower taxes for global corporations or institutional investors. They may have even been actively hostile to those things. They accepted them as a necessary element of a diverse political coalition. Indeed, one of the subtexts of the Trump rebellion in the Republican Party in 2016 was that the business elites found out the working-class members of their party cared far more about factory jobs than abstract libertarian economics.

One of the reasons Donald Trump's first campaign took the country by storm is that he spoke in visceral, moral terms about basic fairness: America was getting "ripped off" by other nations stealing our industrial base; the United States needed to reform its health care system in a way that ensured no one "died in the streets." It's hysterical to look back at the think pieces written during the 2016 election—for example, in *National Review*, attacking Donald Trump for endorsing "protectionism" or "socialized medicine"—and realize that the very people who pretended to speak for Republican voters had no idea what Republican voters thought.

Oren Cass wrote a book a few years back, *The Once and Future Worker*, that made significant waves in economic policy circles, in part by attacking some of the critical assumptions of economists. In that book, Oren argues that "economic piety" has taken over American public life. In particular, he argues that an obsession with maximizing consumption has focused our policy, and indeed our entire culture, on a potentially harmful metric.

Oren's argument proceeds like this: One of the critical ways we measure well-being—perhaps *the* critical way—is by evaluating how much people consume. To say that someone lives in poverty or doesn't is fundamentally a measure of consumption: We quantify, in dollars, how much they're able to buy. And if their income is below a certain level, we say they're in poverty.

Oren traces how policymakers in the decades after World War II turned economic growth into a kind of obsession. We argued about how much to redistribute to poor people and how much to tax rich people, but our country broadly agreed that growth mattered most.

We even developed a metaphor—the economic pie—that captured both the importance of growth and the related question of how big a piece to give to each person.

Oren cleverly calls this view *economic piety*:

> The tenets of this "economic piety" were quickly embraced and remain widely accepted today. The phrase economic pie first appeared in the presidential lexicon in 1952. . . . John F. Kennedy used it when addressing the U.S. Chamber of Commerce. Presidents Lyndon Johnson, Gerald Ford, Ronald Reagan, George H.W. Bush, Bill Clinton, and Barack Obama used it too. The media and think tanks across the political spectrum bandy it about with ease.

The core thesis of Oren's book is that this way of thinking fails to account for people as anything besides consumers and thus undervalues other ways of measuring a good life. One obvious limitation is that our leaders have focused too little on how much our workers produce. Having the government write you a check for thirty thousand dollars a year may keep you from starving to death and it may help you afford health insurance, but it doesn't tell you anything about whether you're self-sufficient.

Usha and I once had dinner with a couple of the most successful technology executives in the country, each of them billionaires, when the topic of the universal basic income (UBI) came up. The idea of a UBI is that you supplement the existing welfare state with an automatic monthly payment for everyone, ensuring that every person in the country has a minimum standard of living. The UBI is a favorite policy intervention of Silicon Valley technologists who believe our country is no longer able to provide quality jobs to a lot of its citizens.

I pointed out that most major religions, as well as basic common sense, draw a distinction between earning a living for yourself and having it provided to you. A job isn't just a source of a wage; it also gives people something to do, allows them to feel accomplished, and provides community. Now, you can acknowledge (as I did earlier) that elites draw too much meaning from their jobs without ignoring the important role of self-sufficiency in how people find meaning. So I asked, "What would people do to replace the parts of their job that don't just enable consumption?"

One of the tech billionaires answered that people would draw their meaning—and I'm not making this up—from competitive video gaming. I was flabbergasted. Usha texted me from underneath the table: "These people are crazy, let's get out of here."

There's also the question of national self-sufficiency. It might be more efficient (though I'm skeptical) to have China manufacture all of our hospital gowns and masks. But as we learned during COVID, when a pandemic struck and the Chinese were unable to export goods, Americans had to cancel many necessary surgical procedures because our hospitals lacked the critical supplies to operate.

So much of the Trump administration's trade and economic policy is geared toward the promotion of this kind of self-sufficiency—both national and personal. The decline of the industrial economy over the 1990s and 2000s occurred at a time when national GDP growth was robust. For the previous generation's policymakers, it was apparently a trade-off worth accepting, despite a historic opioid epidemic and millions of workers forced to substitute good-paying factory jobs with part-time gigs. That a factory had replaced an

American worker with a Mexican one willing to work on the cheap was economically efficient.

You need not agree with the specific set of policies we've pursued to acknowledge that the old way of doing things had failed. We care about GDP in the Trump administration, but we also care about wages, and how many people are dying of drug overdoses, and whether our country can get the things it needs in times of international emergency. If that means the GDP is a fraction of a percent lower, then so be it.

This is hard for our technocrats because they struggle to put a value on anything that can't be specifically measured. And that meant for a long time we were ruled by numbers on a spreadsheet and the people who built those spreadsheets. Of course, we came to this state with the best of intentions. The concept of GDP, for instance, was popularized by economist John Maynard Keynes, as he was trying to quantify aggregate industrial capacity in World War II Britain. Measuring the poverty level—and aiming benefits at those beneath it—helped us prevent a lot of destitution. But we now live in a society almost blinded to considerations outside of the economic. This way of thinking is inherently opposed to the Christian way, which demands more focus on people.

Take, for instance, the time we spend with our children. Long before I ever held political office, it occurred to me that economic statistics often see kids as burdens despite the fact that they're the best part of my life. Domestic labor—that done by moms and dads—if unpaid, is uncounted in measures like GDP. When I leave work to spend time with my children, when I cook them dinner or argue with them about eating their carrots, I am engaged in economically unproductive work. No money changes hands, so it doesn't show up in our national figures. By contrast, if I left for dinner at 6 p.m. and returned to work until midnight while paying a total stranger to look after my kid, my contribution to GDP would be much higher.

Consider this fact from the perspective of families with a stay-at-home parent. Most Americans still report that they would prefer one parent to be at home with the children, at least when they're young. And a majority of women with small children wish to spend more time with their kids instead of at work. To be clear, most women want to pursue some work outside the home, but they prefer more flexibility and more time with their kids. Yet every one of these preferences is economically unproductive. Each time you choose family time instead of working longer hours, you are doing something directly at odds with the cult of growth.

The Working Families Tax Cuts signed into law in July 2025 included provisions that extended and boosted the Child Tax Credit and rewarded companies that provide paid leave to their employees. Many of these policies have been criticized by libertarian members of the Republican coalition. One piece in *The Wall Street Journal* argued that the Child Tax Credit is classic big-government thinking, and that it's equally defensible to provide a tax credit to parents of dogs as it is to parents of children.[2] Of course, I think children have a different role in society than dogs because I am blessed with both a heart and a brain.

I am especially sensitive to these issues around holiday time. Many members of my family work in retail, which is one of the

2 Adam O'Neal, "What Will Tax Reform Do for Puppies?," Opinion, *Wall Street Journal*, November 19, 2017, https://www.wsj.com/articles/what-will-tax-reform-do-for-puppies-1511071482?reflink=desktopwebshare_permalink.

few growing sectors of the economy in and around my southwestern Ohio hometown. And every year, in early November, I dread the logistics around Thanksgiving dinner. I say "dread" because it is rare that everyone can attend. Some of those pressures are reasonable—people have multiple family meals to attend, and they can't be in two places at the same time. But virtually every year, some accommodation is made not to the other side of the family or the realities of scheduling, but to the gods of GDP.

Black Friday is a really apt name for this.

It is always a sad spectacle: watching your own mother or niece or nephew apologize for making a living. We have grown numb to the absurd stories that greet us on Black Friday: the big-box store security worker killed by the Christmas hordes; the trampled pregnant woman; the thirty-two-year-old so desperate for a discounted Xbox that she pepper-sprayed her fellow shoppers. Some people laugh at them, but from the view of classical economics, they're doing something far more "productive" than reading a book or spending time with their children.

And layered on top of them are the hundreds of thousands of silent workers who leave Thanksgiving celebrations early (or miss them altogether) so they can fold clothes or unbox merchandise or stand guard at the entrance of a superstore like medieval knights.

A healthier society would recognize how gross it is to send sixteen-year-olds to work from 4 p.m. on Thanksgiving to 4 a.m. on Friday.

And it's not just Thanksgiving. One report in *The New York Times* told the story of a mother who worked more than fifteen years at Toys "R" Us, which she said often cut her hours or changed her shifts at the last minute.

"I was like: 'Wow, what am I going to do? How am I going to

feed my kids?'" she said. "I would go to food banks, churches to survive, and it was embarrassing but I had to do it."[3]

This problem will likely grow worse in the coming years. Right now, people are developing algorithms that make it easier to cut a worker's hours, or scale them up, in response to real-time events that affect the business. Imagine, for instance, working at a job and finding out that an application on your manager's phone has determined that, tomorrow, a combination of weather and traffic will mean fewer customers. So you get notified four hours before you were meant to arrive, after you've already arranged childcare, that your shift—and the wages you were counting on—has been canceled.

There's a growing body of literature that suggests people with unpredictable schedules are suffering in ways their wages don't measure. Their children have more behavioral issues and are more likely to suffer from emotional problems like anxiety and depression. But it's worth emphasizing, again, that these are considered tolerable externalities in producing the gross domestic whatever.

One of the benefits of labor unions is that they protect workers from this kind of tyranny of consumption. And while some of our critics on the left attack the administration for being insufficiently pro-labor, the most strident critics of our policy come from the right, where Republicans criticize us for being too accommodating to the labor lobby. I've supported blue laws—state laws that shut down businesses on certain days, like Thanksgiving—because these days are sacred and everyone ought to be able to participate in them equally. But we've got a long way to go. When

---

3 Claire Cain Miller, "How Unpredictable Work Hours Turn Families Upside Down," The UpShot, *New York Times*, October 16, 2019, https://www.nytimes.com/2019/10/16/upshot/unpredictable-job-hours.html.

Sean O'Brien, the head of the Teamsters Union, spoke during the 2024 Republican National Convention, some GOP donors complained that he sounded like a socialist. The president ignored these complaints. I thought Sean's arguments echoed a lot of the themes from traditional Christian social teaching.

Is it possible to take this critique too far? Of course, GDP is a useful metric. So are batting averages and pitching wins, but as Bill James has taught us, they don't explain the whole ball game.

* * *

One of the great blessings of my own life is that I was raised in a multigenerational household. Now, that's not to say I wasn't occasionally embarrassed by this, or that I didn't often wish I'd grown up in a traditional, stable nuclear family. But I benefited in an infinite number of ways from the constant companionship of grandparents, great-grandparents, aunts, uncles, cousins, and babies. For many of our holidays, there were four generations of family present.

My Mamaw famously potty trained me only after we ran out of diapers unexpectedly.

"JD, today we're going to pee and poop on the pot."

"No, Mamaw."

"JD, today we're going to pee and poop on the pot."

"No, Mamaw."

"JD, today you're going to p*** and s*** in that toilet, and don't argue with me."

"Yes, Mamaw."

When people ask me what I most admire about Appalachian people and culture, a few things come to mind. I sometimes talk about the sense of family loyalty and pride of place. I often say that my family cared far less about credentials and job accomplishments than about people and kin.

This attitude was far more Christian than anything I've encountered in the halls of power, and though I lost it for a while, the seeds planted by that family when I was a kid are undoubtedly a major part of my journey back to my faith. But at the top of the list, I note that in my family, we didn't warehouse our elderly. Mamaw spent a few months in a nursing home, and only then because she had had a major surgery and couldn't move. But though she was handicapped severely and could barely walk, she lived her last years in her own home, cared for by a combination of my aunt, my sister, my mom, and me. It was an odd arrangement, with a hospital bed in the living room, where she slept for her last few years. But it was home. My great-grandmother (her mother) also died in her home, surrounded by her friends and family singing Christian hymns. I am not aware of her spending a day in a nursing home, though she lived well past ninety.

Of course, some people simply must live in nursing homes. That is as true for Appalachians as it is for anyone else. But the sense of reverence for our elderly, that desperation to keep relatives out of corporate elder care, and the feeling of indebtedness—that no matter how sick or grumpy an old relative is, the proper thing to do is to visit them at their home with your children—is one of the things I most admire about my home.

But that model is disappearing for the simple reason that it's not economically efficient. Every hour that a relative spent caring for my grandmother instead of working in the labor force was a violation of the law of comparative advantage. Every minute of a family member's time spent tending to my great-grandmother was a dollar not spent paying someone else to do the job. This reduces GDP.

There is perhaps no area where our inability to distinguish economic from public good is more glaring than in how we think about modern technology. One of the largest companies in the world—and among the most productive—is Apple, which introduced the smartphone revolution to American life in 2007. Between the applications developed on the smartphones, the smartphones themselves, the data plans, and all the other secondary and tertiary inputs, about 7.6 trillion dollars in economic activity is tied directly to the smartphone, according to one 2025 estimate.[4] The smartphone is one of the most powerful drivers of economic growth in the world.

But all of these economic benefits come at a cost, and that cost is harder to measure though easy to see. It is now impossible to walk down a busy American street without bumping into someone stuck on their phone, dead to the world and to the personal space of the people around them. And more troublingly, American children are exposed at increasingly younger ages to these devices. Parents stare at their phones to read emails, children get sucked into social media, and the quality of our entire social fabric declines in the process. Ironically, my friends who work in Silicon Valley all prevent their own kids from spending too much time on devices. The true insiders know well that a little time on the phone is fine, but too much can be very destructive.

According to one study, simply having a smartphone within

4 GSMA, "The Mobile Economy 2026," accessed March 12, 2026, https://www.gsma.com/solutions-and-impact/connectivity-for-good/mobile-economy/.

reach decreases our attention span.[5] We're less able to focus and less interested in the people around us, purely through having one in the room. People of all ages show classic addiction responses to their smartphones—their brains experience a surge of dopamine in the reward centers that reinforces compulsive behavior. A study led by a physician at Cincinnati Children's Hospital Medical Center found that children who have too much screen time show actual structural changes in the brain: "The scientists looked at the children's brain wiring and found differences in the scans of those [with higher screen time scores]. In the parts of the brain related to language and literacy skills, their white matter integrity—associated with how quickly nerve impulses fire—was lower. . . . They also had lower expressive language skills, worse emergent literacy skills, and took longer naming objects."[6] Too much screen time makes children more impulsive and dumber.

Smartphones also radically increase children's access to illicit content online, from bullying to pornography. A kid with a supercomputer in their pocket can access virtually anything, from disgusting videos to the entreaties of pedophiles.

The ubiquity of social media, enabled by constant exposure thanks to smartphones, appears to be taking its toll, especially on teenagers. One report in *The Wall Street Journal* summarized the

5 Adrian F. War, Kristen Duke, Ayelet Gneezy, and Maarten W. Bos, "Brain Drain: The Mere Presence of One's Own Smartphone Reduces Available Cognitive Capacity," *Journal of the Association for Consumer Research* 2, no. 2 (2017): 140–54, https://www.journals.uchicago.edu/doi/full/10.1086/691462.

6 Kashmira Gander, "Children Who Use Screens Too Much Have Different Brain Structures, Scientists Suggest in 'Provocative' Study," *Newsweek*, November 4, 2019, https://www.newsweek.com/screen-time-damage-child-brain-development-language-skills-1469223.

depressing situation: "The glow of screens is unavoidable. Last year, the Pew Research Center reported that 95% of American teenagers have access to a smartphone. The nonprofit group Common Sense Media has found that contemporary teens spend six to nine hours a day online—and that 72% of teens felt manipulated by tech companies into remaining constantly connected."[7]

The numbers tell a depressing story of what all this exposure has done. From 2011 to 2016, the number of female freshmen in college reporting "overwhelming anxiety or panic attacks" shot from 31 percent to 62 percent. Since 2007, suicide among young girls has exploded, rising with widespread adoption of smartphones among kids.[8]

These effects are not incidental to the business model of smartphone companies or the applications that run on the phones. The entire smartphone and social media business model is predicated on the monetization of people's attention. Facebook sells ads, and it sells more ads for each "impression" they generate—meaning, each time a person actually looks at the ad. Applications, from games to hotel booking sites, generate more revenue for each additional minute a consumer spends using their program. Google scrapes more data—which it can either sell or use to further refine its product—for every search run on its platform. Netflix makes more money for every show you stream. Every single minute you spend talking to your spouse or playing with your children or volunteering for your church is a dollar lost for the information technology industry. They

---

7 Mary Pipher and Sara Pipher Gilliam, "The Lonely Burden of Today's Teenage Girls," *Wall Street Journal*, August 15, 2019, https://www.wsj.com/articles/the-lonely-burden-of-todays-teenage-girls-11565883328.

8 Pipher and Pipher Gilliam, "Lonely Burden."

have designed their hardware and applications for one purpose: to keep you engaged. And they've done so with frightening success.

And what do we call this brave new world and its metrics?

The attention economy.

While it hasn't generated many headlines, the Trump administration has taken several bold actions to try to limit the excesses. In K-12 schools on military bases—over which the federal government has direct control, unlike state education systems—we have completely banned smartphone use. Robert F. Kennedy Jr., the Secretary of Health and Human Services, began a massive new study on the effects of screens on kids. First Lady Melania Trump successfully lobbied for the TAKE IT DOWN Act, which targets bullying and revenge porn online.

The administration supports enhanced safety for children using social media and the internet more broadly. There are several competing proposals to achieve this; for example, as a senator, I cosponsored the Kids Online Safety Act, and there are a number of similar initiatives out there with parallel goals in mind. Because so much of the attention economy runs on harvesting people's private data, we've taken a number of steps to push back on that—in both court and legislatively.

A few years ago, Usha was traveling and I had some one-on-one time with my son. It was a busy time, and a text notification lit up my phone. Though it was early on a Saturday, and I didn't need to reply immediately, I couldn't stop looking at my phone—typing, then rereading the original message, then typing some more.

Ewan insisted that I put my phone away. He did that once, and I complied. (It would have been one thing if this was a matter of national security, but it wasn't.) But each time I took it back out—

almost compulsively—after that, he ran over, screeched, and batted it out of my hand. This happened a few times before I realized that Ewan knew instinctively what hadn't yet occurred to me: I was prioritizing my phone and my work over my own toddler. I asked him if he wanted to throw the phone away and he agreed: He tossed the phone across the room (it had a sturdy case), we laughed about it, and I replied to my text later.

My choice to pick up my phone over and over that morning was undoubtedly a failure of character. But my paternal sins are not purely a matter of individual character. Being a good father takes much more effort when we're constantly bombarded with stimuli that take our focus away from our children's needs. Limiting the reaches of the attention economy creates opportunities for moms and dads and kids to unplug and get away from their phones.

Predictably, we've faced withering attacks from some for showing insufficient respect to "the market," as if it violates some iron law of the economy to help people erect barriers between the digital economy and their very real personal lives. If a child wants to spend all day on social media as predators harvest their data and prey on them, some say that's a matter of personal choice. You don't need to agree with every policy solution we've pursued to recognize that our government doesn't (or shouldn't) worship these abstractions; we exist to serve human beings.

* * *

There is no group of people more inconvenient for our economic statisticians than children. As mentioned above, economic logic would argue that all the time you spend with your kids instead of paying someone else to raise them is a drag on GDP. But there are other ways in which children can make a promising economic picture look pretty bleak.

Consider two separate households, both with a mom and dad, one with just one child and the other with three. If both of those households earn sixty thousand dollars in annual income, economists will look at the first household as much better off. Why? Because the average consumption available to each member of the first household is twenty thousand, or sixty thousand dollars spread across three people. The consumption available to the second household is only twelve thousand dollars per member—sixty thousand spread across five people.

Scholar Scott Winship puts it thusly in a piece entitled "Shrinking Households Indicate Rising Living Standards," where he walks through the calculus that confronts many families: "With increasing wealth, families have substituted more 'stuff' for the children they would have had in the past. Greater wealth has also enabled more people to move out of their parents' home, delay or forego having to live with a spouse or partner, walk away from unfulfilling relationships, and live without roommates."[9]

One wonders how good it is to trade "stuff" for human relationships. In one sense, it's nice to live in a spacious apartment with plenty of room to yourself, but we obviously lose something when we sacrifice human contact in the process.

You might wonder whether economic logic actually enters most

9 Scott Winship, "Shrinking Households Indicate Rising Living Standards," Manhattan Institute for Policy Research, July 6, 2015, https://manhattan.institute/article/shrinking-households-indicate-rising-living-standards.

people's calculations. Do people really forgo having children for economic reasons? Well, not everyone, obviously, but as any good economist will tell you, people respond to incentives. And the incentives aren't exactly in favor of children.

A dystopian headline on CNBC pronounced: "Disconnecting to Spend Time with Your Kids Could Sabotage Your Career." The article discussed the "parenting penalty"—a well-known phenomenon where parents see a decline in both their job opportunities and their wages.

> "In a lot of workplaces, there is an expectation from employers that employees devote themselves fully to work," said [sociologist Kate] Weisshaar. "The expectation to work long hours, to be highly dedicated to work and to always be available can introduce challenges for parents, or any caregivers, who have other demands on their time besides work. So if employers are making promotion or hiring decisions based on these types of expectations and/or assumptions that parents can't or won't live up to expectations, then parents may be blocked from opportunities at work."[10]

The logic of prioritizing economic activity over family life affects all of us, even if we wish it didn't.

During the 2020 presidential campaign, Democratic candidate Kamala Harris proposed lengthening the school day for American children. The goal was to make the school day better map onto

10 Jordan Shapiro, "Disconnecting to Spend Time with Your Kids Could Sabotage Your Career," CNBC, May 11, 2019, https://www.cnbc.com/2019/05/10/disconnecting-to-spend-time-with-your-kids-could-sabotage-your-career.html.

the American workday, so that children would be at school for the entire time their parents worked.

This proposal undoubtedly came from a reasonable desire to make life easier for parents. But look how *Mother Jones*, one of the leading journals of the American Left, described Harris's proposal to ease the scheduling problem:

> That burden typically falls to women, a million of whom work less than full-time in order to keep up with caregiving responsibilities for elementary school–aged children. This hardship is particularly pronounced for low-income mothers and mothers of color, who are the most likely to have unpredictable or inflexible work schedules. Experts estimate the United States loses $55 billion in productivity each year thanks to the public school calendar.[11]

You can see here the tension between making life easier for families and maximizing GDP, and it leads Harris (and others) to make a fatal mistake. If the problem is that school schedules misalign with parental work schedules, why is the solution to force kids to spend a few extra hours at school or in after-school programs? Wouldn't it be better to enable parents of young kids to spend less time at work and more time with their kids? That's what Americans say they want but are unable to do. It's one of the reasons

11 Kara Voght, "The School Day Is Two Hours Shorter Than the Work Day. Kamala Harris Wants to Change That," *Mother Jones*, November 6, 2019, https://www.motherjones.com/politics/2019/11/the-school-day-is-two-hours-shorter-than-the-work-day-kamala-harris-wants-to-change-that/.

the Trump administration has promoted policies that give families more choice, rather than foisting a corporate-focused, one-size-fits-all model on people. This makes moral sense.

But not if you're trying to maximize GDP. If the goal is to promote economic activity, the interests of families will often take a back seat to the demands of businesses. A Christian approach to economics would demand something different: concern for GDP, yes, but only insofar as it promotes human flourishing. The economy is a means—an important one—to enable people to live good lives. The point at which we see the economy as the end in itself is the point at which we dehumanize ourselves. Unfortunately, the Christian antibodies to this kind of dehumanizing virus are substantially weaker.

* * *

In 2019 the state of Georgia caused a national firestorm when it enacted a "heartbeat bill"—legislation preventing abortion after the detection of a fetal heartbeat, which usually happens around six or seven weeks after conception. A few companies, joined by members of the Hollywood elite, threatened to boycott the state over the measure while it was being debated. Stacey Abrams—a once-and-future gubernatorial candidate and rising star in Democrat politics—amplified the attack. As she argued, the pro-life bill was bad for business.

Most advocates of abortion rights would concede that terminating a pregnancy is a tragedy. It's a little odd to formulate abortion rights as an affirmative good—and not even for the woman, but for corporations.

Yet if you think about it, Abrams's draconian formulation not only makes logical sense, but is central to a certain type of worldview. When she ran for governor in 2022, Abrams pointed to abortion as a solution to the sky-high inflation Americans were experiencing under the Biden administration: "Having children is why you're worried about your price for gas. It's why you're concerned about how much food costs. For women, this is not a reductive issue. You can't divorce being forced to carry an unwanted pregnancy from the economic realities of having a child." In a world where children are bad for business, it follows that abortions are good. The case for life—with all the obligations it implies—means less time at work. And when having babies is a drag on economic activity, the economic gods favor terminating pregnancies. And of course, it's not just the act of having children that we ought to be concerned about: It's spending time with them as well.

This type of logic exists across the political spectrum. In a piece for the libertarian Cato Institute, Vanessa Brown Calder makes an argument against mandatory paid parental leave benefits: "Unfortunately, a review of states and countries with government-mandated paid leave programs indicates they harm young women, whether they're available to fathers or not. This is because parental leave policies are associated with an increase in leave-taking and childbearing, which leads to lost labor or increased health care costs for companies."[12]

If you think about this argument for even a second, it's astonishing: Paid parental leave is bad for women, and the reason it's

12 Vanessa Brown Calder, "How Paid Family Leave Hurts Women," Cato Institute, May 30, 2017, https://www.cato.org/commentary/how-paid-family-leave-hurts-women.

bad for them is that it might lead to increased labor or health care costs for their employers. Never have I read a purer distillation of our worship at the altar of commerce. Yet if Calder is to be commended for a starkness that borders on sociopathy, much of the economic language around children and family comes to basically the same conclusion.

Given how destructive pregnancies, children, and policies that encourage either of them are, we might consider a more modest proposal:

If large household sizes mean smaller per-person consumption, we shouldn't just discourage birthing children, we need to do something about the ones that are already here. Politicians aim tax cuts and spending programs at people to give them more money to buy things and boost economic growth, but we may as well cut out the middleman. Let's just go around to every household and ship their youngest child to China.

Yes, the separation will inevitably cause some grief, but just imagine what we will do for per-capita income. Also, American parents, freed from the burden of raising this extra child, will be able to spend more time at work. Win-win!

* * *

The pressures to spend more time at work, pay someone else to raise your family, or forgo having children at all have led to a place with too few children. Across the Western world, every advanced economy now has fertility rates that are below replacement level. The only exception is Israel, a highly religious society that more than any other has rejected the cultural liberalism that has dominated the Western world. And for the first time in our history, women are telling pollsters that they're having fewer kids than they would like.[13] For virtually my entire life, economists have worried about overpopulation—from the strain on resources to the environmental consequences. Now, whenever a world leader walks into my office they talk to me about population decline. As a minister from one Asian country said to me, unsolicited: "I don't know why it's happening. Young people just no longer fall in love. And all of us have this problem, the disappearance of our people."

I don't think it's a mystery. All of our societies, despite their cultural differences at the surface, have followed the exact same path. Our young people may differ in some ways from those in Korea or Japan, but all of them are responding to the economic and cultural incentives: work more, consume more, achieve more. Suppress the biological urge to fall in love and have babies. Sacrifice family for your cubicle. We—across political movements and countries—have done this to ourselves. And it is no coincidence that we embraced this hypereconomic logic at the very moment our civilization moved away from Christianity.

As it happens, I don't even think this arrangement makes sense economically. While children may put a drag on the economic standards that are easiest to measure—like hours worked in a day—there's also evidence that societies with higher fertility rates are more dynamic. They take more risks, see more technological innovation

13 Wendy Wang and Brad Wilcox, "Women Want More Children Than They're Having. America Can Do More to Help," Institute for Family Studies, August 15, 2024, https://ifstudies.org/blog/women-want-more-children-than-theyre-having-america-can-do-more-to-help.

and increased productivity. It is no coincidence that the epicenter of the artificial intelligence revolution is the United States, still the youngest of the industrialized economies.

But if I'm being honest, I wouldn't change my mind even if an economist persuaded me that kids had nothing to do with dynamism or technological change. I'm uninterested in making people servants to the economy. The economy ought to be serving us.

Everything the naysayers offer about young kids is true. Children are undoubtedly exhausting. To be a parent of a young kid is to sleep too little and on some days to stumble through the world in a stupor. It is to lose your temper one minute and feel guilty about it the next. It is to sacrifice exercise, work, and healthy food when the demands of young tyrants (as all children are) must be met. There is even some evidence that having children (at least the first one) actually makes parents measurably unhappier in the short term.

But children are also a source of indescribable joy. I have sat with Usha and watched Ewan recite the varieties of pizza he knows, from the standard pepperoni and cheese to the made-up blueberry and sock. And in that silly moment, I have never felt closer to my wife, more united in purpose and pride.

Children foist upon us an understanding of the world that no book or experience can match. It was having my own son that gave me, for the first time, a new appreciation for my grandmother, mother, sister, and aunt. When I see news of a school shooting, or a child killed by some awful, rare, and incurable disease, it's always devastating, but my sense of empathy has increased tenfold ever since having kids of my own.

I have seen my close friends transformed by fatherhood. Men who were annoyed by screaming children on airplanes now have a little more compassion. Friends with daughters, terrified that their girls will one day encounter the worst of teenage male hormones, are thinking for the first time about how to promote virtue in both young men and women alike. Fathers are more attached to their wives, their families, and their communities. Others have written about the "heart expanding" effects of having children, and researchers have shown that fathers of daughters become more attuned to the feelings of both others and themselves. And as a father to my baby girl, I can tell you it's 100 percent true.

Yes, the economic benefits of children (at least over the long term) are real. But we ought to be able to say: We want more children in our society because children are profoundly good—the greatest value add we can create.

* * *

If you step away from the glory of economic statistics, so much of American life has gone wrong. An influx of prescription opioids became a flood of synthetic opioids, which has led to tens of thousands of deaths each year and a declining life expectancy among a substantial portion of our society. We have made great progress on reducing infant mortality, but we send our children into a world—even in the physical security of their own homes—that bombards them with images and influences that have left them isolated, depressed, and increasingly at risk of self-harm. We are more disconnected, lonely, and isolated, even in the midst of historic levels of material comfort.

All this economic abundance coexists with intense spiritual misery. We orient people toward a life of consumption. We tell them to find meaning in the home they buy, the money they earn, the prestige of their job. We bombard them with all manner of creature comforts, and add their consumption—price club mega-size junk—to our national GDP. We use that GDP as a yardstick for our broader society, which is why it's possible for false prophet economists to argue the American Dream is healthy even as suicide and addiction rates soar and the laughter of children fades from our streets.

A famous investor once told me, "In business or government, you often get what you measure."

And indeed we have. But what if we measured ourselves by a different yardstick? For, two thousand years ago, there came a man, all good and all powerful, who threw the money changers out of God's ancient temple and told us that possession would fail to satisfy the deepest yearnings of our heart.

God made us to work, yes. But to work to sustain our lives and to create beautiful and amazing things. An economy geared toward creation and dignity may very well produce more real prosperity than one geared toward finance and accumulation. This would undoubtedly be a more Christian economy. For too long, Christians have largely ignored the economic spheres of our social life and focused on the cultural.

And we have learned, perhaps the hard way, that they're not quite so separable.

CHAPTER 12

See You at the After-Party

One way my love for Usha manifests itself is with intense curiosity. From the moment we met, I've wanted to know the details of her upbringing, her political views, her favorite TV shows and movies. If she tells me she liked a book, I read it.

That's led me to read more than I otherwise would. Mostly classic English literature, especially Jane Austen. Usha had studied at Cambridge, in the UK, so I read her master's thesis about a printer active during England's seventeenth-century religious wars. Most of what Usha prompted me to read was entertaining, or at least interesting—she has good taste.

One night, she told me about a book she'd read by Joan Didion, called *The Year of Magical Thinking.*

"I'm really freaked out by death," she told me. "And I found it to be cathartic."

"Wow," I replied. "I'll pick it up from the library tomorrow."

I told her good night and that I loved her, and then I went to the online Oxford English Dictionary to look up *cathartic.*

ca·thar·tic
adjective

1. providing psychological relief through the open expression of strong emotions; causing *catharsis.*
"crying is a cathartic release"

The next day, I grabbed a copy from the library and read *The Year of Magical Thinking* almost entirely in one sitting. I can't think of another book that's had such an effect on me.

The book was beautifully written, a kind of elegy to Didion's late husband, John Gregory Dunne, who died suddenly as the couple sat down for dinner. It tells the story of the year she spent grieving her husband and coming to terms with illness, frailty, and death. Much of the book describes Didion's efforts to get her daughter, Quintana, the right medical care in the face of increasingly severe health crises. Usha explained that after Didion finished the book, her daughter died, too.

"Man," I said, failing to think of anything eloquent to say about such unspeakable tragedy. "What a crappy year for that woman."

"Yeah," Usha agreed. "I think that's part of the reason I found it cathartic. My life has been really easy. I haven't experienced real tragedy. Didion is so vivid she almost invites you to participate in it with her."

This exchange revealed a meaningful difference between Usha and me. I had experienced real tragedy while she hadn't, but that wasn't it. She was, in her own words, "freaked out" by death, and I simply wasn't. I had never feared death, whether as a believer or as a nonbeliever. At least not in an existential way.

Maybe I could pin this on religion, but the truth is that death did not scare me even during my atheist years, and I know many Christians who feel the opposite.

Didion's views mirrored Usha's. In considering her husband's death, her daughter's sickness, and what it all meant, Didion concludes:

> I think about swimming with him into the cave at Portuguese Bend, about the swell of clear water, the way it changed, the swiftness and power it gained as it narrowed through the rocks at the base of the point. The tide had to be just right. We had to be in the water at the very moment the tide was right. We could only have done this a half dozen times at most during the two years we lived there but it is what I remember. Each time we did it I was afraid of missing the swell, hanging back, timing it wrong. John never was. You had to feel the swell change. You had to go with the change. He told me that. No eye is on the sparrow but he did tell me that.

"No eye is on the sparrow" is an explicit rejection of the Book of Matthew, where the Gospels explain that God cares about even the smallest of His creatures. God's eye is on even the sparrow, Jesus tells His disciples.

To Didion, there is no divine providence to the world, no afterlife prepared. She has the memory of her husband and his love radiating through the ages, and that's enough for her. It is a beautiful thought, and I understood why it gave Usha comfort.

But it didn't give me comfort, even though I agreed—at the time—with Didion's basic conclusion.

I don't worry about what I will find on the other side of eternal sleep. Even as a child, I never feared hell. What I think Usha found cathartic is this idea that death is a burden not for the dead, but for the living. It is a weight to bear, a grief to feel, for those left behind. This is, of course, a labor of sorrow, but the sorrow of grieving death is much different from the sorrow of experiencing it.

When I reflected on Didion's book—and Usha's and my different reactions to it—in later years as a Catholic, I found myself stuck on a particularly odd part of my own theology. As a believer, I took the whole thing as true. I believed in hell. I may not have known what it looks like or feels like, but I didn't want to spend any time there. Christ offers us eternal life, a gift I accepted. But I was still not particularly worried about dying.

This wasn't just inconsistent with common sense. It was inconsistent with Christian doctrine.

In 1 Corinthians 15:32, Saint Paul asks rhetorically what purpose there is in virtue if there is no resurrection: "What advantageth it me, if the dead rise not? let us eat and drink; for to morrow we die." The message: In the absence of some heavenly reward, we ought to enjoy the moment as much as we can. In the song "Sunday Bloody Sunday," an impassioned anthem about the Troubles in Northern Ireland, U2—whose members are charismatic Protestants—borrows the line:

And today the millions cry;
We eat and drink while tomorrow they die.

The U2 song mocks the violent terrorists with this reinterpretation of the words of Saint Paul. If they took their duty seriously, all would lay down their arms and get to peacemaking.

The Act of Contrition, one of the oldest prayers in the Christian canon, echoes this theme:

> *O my God, I am heartily sorry for having offended Thee, and I detest all my sins, because I dread the loss of heaven and the pains of hell, but most of all because I offend Thee, my God, Who art all good and deserving of all my love.*

Usha, like Didion, dreaded neither "the loss of heaven" nor "the pains of hell" for the most logical of reasons: She simply didn't think they existed. I came to believe in both, but I still didn't find either particularly motivating.

* * *

John Calvin, the great Reformation theologian, argued that our destinies are decided by God before we're even born. From a Reformed perspective, this concept of "predestination" affirms a paradox: God is sovereign, but man also has free will. For my own part, the idea makes my head spin. But who knows—perhaps Calvin was on to something, and the concept of predestination helps to explain my own relatively untroubled perspective on the afterlife.

Many arguments in support of the Christian faith relate to people's fear of death. Pascal's wager, perhaps the single most famous argument for believing in God, goes like this: If you believe in God and you're wrong, you go to sleep after death and all you gave up was a little sinful behavior during your life; but if you don't believe in God and you're wrong, you burn in hell for eternity. So, the thinking goes, you might as well take the lower-risk bet, profess a faith in God, and live a decent life.

The fear of hell and death—and redemption from the same—is central to the Christian faith. Every Easter, Christians celebrate the resurrection of Jesus Christ from the dead. As 1 Peter 2:24 says, "Who his own self bare our sins in his own body on the tree, that we, being dead to sins, should live unto righteousness: by whose stripes ye were healed."

It is unsurprising, then, that so much of the argument for Christianity in popular culture rests on a kind of transaction: Believe this and you will be saved from suffering in this life or saved from hell or reunited with your loved ones after death.

I asked Father Henry, the man who baptized me, for his perspective.

"Is it possible for a Christian to believe in the concept of hell without being particularly afraid of it?"

He responded: "Hell is real, but it's also difficult to fathom. The more one cultivates a friendship with God, however imperfect, the more it seems unthinkable to choose separation from Him."

We spoke a bit about the Act of Contrition and how the prayer explicitly invokes the pains of hell.

"Remember, the prayer doesn't stop there," Father Henry reminded me. "We detest our sins, according to the prayer, '*most of all*, because I have offended Thee, Who art all good and deserving of all my love.'"

He continued: "Fear of hell is good enough to avoid presumption and a license to sin. But to stay there, psychologically or spiritually, is to remain stunted. It's totally inadequate in the grand scheme of things. God's goal isn't only to motivate us to fear punishment; it's also to enter into friendship with Him."

* * *

Another fear, far more powerful than the fear of death, hung over me.

Both Usha and I share a love of Great Britain—though she had previously lived there and, until I met her, I hadn't ever visited. On our first trip together across the pond, we rented a car. I had never driven on the left side of the road. Steering from what felt to me like the passenger's seat was somehow even more foreign than driving on the wrong side of the highway, and I nearly crashed in a roundabout a half mile from the airport. The rest of the trip was smooth sailing, until we transitioned from the highways of England to the backroads of Wales. Two cars going in opposite directions could pass each other with only a few inches to spare, and yet these sheep trucks came barreling down the road totally unworried about the prospect of a head-on collision with an American who had no idea what he was doing.

In Wales we visited Caernarfon, home to an extraordinarily old and beautiful castle. In 1969, Queen Elizabeth II crowned Charles Prince of Wales at Caernarfon Castle. Its massive exterior walls have survived largely unchanged from the original construction about seven centuries ago, when King Edward I made Caernarfon the administrative center for subjecting the Welsh to brutal Norman oppression.

The castle sits on a small peninsula that juts out into the River Seiont. We climbed to the top of the walls and looked down at the docked boats jostling in the water and at the medieval town below.

Our house in Cincinnati was built about 150 years ago, and people call it historic. At Yale, the oldest building on campus dates to the mid-eighteenth century. Tourists and students alike flock to Old Campus to gawk at it.

This castle, by contrast, was already hundreds of years old when English settlers first landed in the United States. For nearly a millennium, young men had climbed the castle walls and watched the sun reflected on the surrounding water. People sometimes talk about the size of the universe and how small they feel compared to the infinite stars many light-years away. I had never shared that feeling. But here, on the banks of a river I'd never heard of, in a castle we selected as a cool tourist stop, I felt for the first time something similar: the scale of time, and how little of the life of the world we'd ever see.

After we left Caernarfon, we stopped at a local pub. Usha was excited to introduce me to a "full English breakfast," though we were in Wales. It was pretty good, not that different from a Denny's Grand Slam—with the notable addition of mushrooms and something the Brits called "black pudding."

"What did you think?" she asked me.

"Pretty good. But I don't think I'm going to eat this weird thing oozing blood."

"No! About the castle. I knew you'd love it."

Usha did most of our travel planning. She did most of our life planning, as a matter of fact, even before we were married, and she knew me well.

"Blown away," I told her. "The coolest thing I've ever seen, and it's not particularly close."

We hopped in our car and headed to the next stop, the Welsh city of Conwy—which also had a very impressive castle. And for the next six days, we did what young people do on a vacation: We saw the sights, we slept in, and we ate and drank too much. Every day reinforced my feeling of being a hiccup in the vast scale of time. In Oxford, we strolled in courtyards nearly a millennium old. We drank beer in pubs that were older than the Declaration of Independence. We read plaques on cottages dating from the fifteenth century.

We guessed at the ages of churches. Usha had a better eye for the age of buildings than I did. But we were both often off by hundreds of years. We started a practice that has continued through our marriage: to go to the places other tourists don't. To get off the beaten path, not to photograph a landmark or to say we'd seen something, but to understand what living in a foreign place feels like.

Back in Wales, a couple of utility workers near a downed power line had stopped us as we walked from a pub.

"We've never seen you two around here. Where are you from?"

"We're Americans, just taking a walk."

"Are you on holiday?"

"Yes."

"Not sure why you'd want to visit this place!"

Hilariously, the utility workers were dedicated conservatives who'd read some of the articles I'd written in *National Review*. They were Englishmen living in the Welsh countryside who read

American conservative periodicals. *The world is a strange place*, I thought.

"I think about five people read those articles. Amazing that four of them are standing right here."

"Who's the fifth?"

"My mother!"

The gentlemen gave us some food recommendations and wished us well. Not far from them, we found an ancient church with a graveyard. The headstones in its cemetery were almost unreadable. We caught a few of the dates—most of the stones were centuries old.

"All graves eventually go unvisited," a friend once quipped. And here on a cloudy summer day in the British countryside, I felt there was great wisdom in that fundamentally depressing observation. All of these graves were now unvisited. Each body that lay lifeless underground was now forgotten—their names no longer even readable.

The church had hardly fared better than the grave sites. It was locked up and empty, though it was clearly well maintained. The internet told me the church still offered regular services on Sunday, though I learned that the Church of England's membership was declining. As its older attendees passed away, fewer young people seemed interested in what the Church had to offer.

Dread came over me. Perhaps this church would meet the same fate as the headstones nearby.

"Do you ever feel," I asked Usha, "a sense of dread when you see these beautiful places that have fallen into disrepair? I look at this church. It's simple. It's not some grand cathedral. It probably barely fit one hundred and fifty people in its prime. But it's a beautiful building. And there was a time when it was alive and vibrant. Now it isn't. That really bothers me. I can't quite explain why."

"'Dread' is too strong," she said. "But I do understand the sadness."

* * *

At some point in the past, this church was filled with the voices and cries of children. Of parents shushing them. Of grandparents during a baptism laying their hands on the heads of the next generation. Of people looking at its beautiful stained glass windows and high steeple and thinking, as I did, that though this building was built by the hands of man, it called us to the divine.

This church had consecrated countless marriages, celebrating the start of new families. It had served as a community center, where Christians long since forgotten had helped feed and clothe their neighbors in times of struggle. Its pastors had counseled people in sickness and death, and had buried them outside in its beautiful cemetery. And now the church was crumbling, its cemetery abandoned. How long would its current congregation even last?

Not long if you believe the statistics. According to *The Guardian*, crumbling churches are the UK's "biggest heritage challenge." From 2013, when I gazed up at that church's ancient steeple, to today, about 3,500 churches have been closed in the United Kingdom.[1] The congregations housed in these beautiful buildings—and in many cases, the buildings themselves—are simply disappearing.

1 Harriet Sherwood, "Crumbling Churches are 'UK's Biggest Heritage Challenge,'" *Guardian*, January 24, 2024, https://www.theguardian.com/world/2024/jan/24/thousands-churches-risk-closure-uk-heritage.

And it was here that I discovered something like the fear of death: not of my own physical death, or of the spiritual death of hell, but of civilizational death. Of laying your head on a pillow, taking your last breath, and not knowing whether what comes after you will be as beautiful and wonderful as what came before.

I dread inheriting these beautiful buildings, the stories and the joy that happened inside of them, and then letting their memory slip into nothing. Allowing their foundations to crumble. Witnessing some gaudy, disgusting shopping mall be built on top of them—only for that, too, to fall into disrepair. I dread leaving my kids a world where people no longer visit the graves of their ancestors.

When I was a kid, we learned of the great deeds of our civilization's forebears. We learned of the men who stormed the beaches at Normandy and saved the world from fascism. We learned of Robert E. Lee and Stonewall Jackson, strategically brilliant Confederate generals of the Civil War, tragic in their heroism, who put their virtues to use for the wrong cause. We learned of their counterparts on the Union side, who fought for the right cause and did so valiantly. And we knew that schoolchildren elsewhere learned a slightly different history of the same war, a history unique to their geographies and the roles those places played in the conflict. We learned this was part of the complicated diversity of the United States—that a child in Georgia understood the deeds of General Sherman differently than did a child in Ohio.

And we all agreed that it was tragic for brother to have raised arms against brother, that the brutality of their battle was regrettable, but that they were brave and good men, that the United States had endured, and that the war's cost in blood had secured the eradication of slavery. We read letters by the men who paid that price—letters to sweethearts they'd never embrace again, letters to parents they'd never see again. We took, as Abraham Lincoln said, "increased devotion to that cause for which they gave the last full measure of devotion."

We learned that when General Lee brought his starving army to surrender to General Grant at Appomattox, General Grant treated his vanquished foe with kindness and respect. Grant gave Lee's army food, and in that act of grace and charity the seeds of national reconciliation were sown. Whether our great-great-great-grandfathers fought for Grant's or Lee's army, we learned that their actions that day had made it possible for us to be part of a United States of America. We learned of their faith, of the service each man rendered in the years after the war, and of what it all meant for our shared national project. We learned that it is one thing to vanquish an enemy and another to humiliate him. Grant was right to win; he was also right to show charity in victory.

We learned of all that came before that war. We learned of Christopher Columbus conquering the oceans and Lewis and Clark opening up a new continent to exploration. We learned of the slaves who were brought over and how they helped build the country with their bare hands. How they were mistreated and struggled but came to prevail at the end of the long road to freedom. We learned of the English pilgrims who began permanent settlements in the New World. We learned of the Indians who found themselves in frequent conflict with the new settlers, but who carved out their own chapter of the American story. We learned of the Christian missionaries who brought the Gospel to a new continent, and of Martin Luther King Jr.'s moral courage to demand that the United States live up to "the true meaning of its creed." We learned of the Founding Fathers, who first drafted that creed, who disagreed about its precise meaning but fought together as countrymen to gain independence from the tyranny of the most powerful empire in the world. We learned of the wilderness and the bounty of the United States, its limitless natural resources, and the pioneers who turned those natural resources into the modern inventions that rocketed men to the moon and allowed us to communicate with people thousands of miles away at the touch of a button.

We learned that all of us took part in this story. That all of us knew someone who had fought in an important war, or laid a brick in a beautiful home, or mopped the floors of the NASA facility that first sent a man to the moon. It was our story, and though some played a major role and others were mere supporting characters, all of us should be proud of it. The ambitious among us dreamed of one day becoming leading characters ourselves. The less ambitious felt content that we lived in the kind of place where a good job and a nice family life were available to everyone.

As in any story, there were imperfections and narrative shortcuts. Our collective memory was faulty. Our native sons and daughters were marched off, massacred, and lied to, and our accounts of what happened in the past were biased. But what we learned was a mostly true and entirely useful story, something that gave us both roots and a sense of potential. It was the glue that connected us to ancestors long dead and children we hadn't yet had.

Toward the end of her life, I interviewed Mamaw for a school project. I was amazed at how much the story of World War II—which ended when she was twelve—figured into her own understanding of her life. She spoke of her brother and father, sent to the Pacific to fight the Japanese. Her relief that the war ended before my grandfather was old enough to fight. Her regard for the men and women who united—the men at the front lines, the women in the factories—to defeat the Nazi war machine. She wasn't a general or even a soldier, but the sense of her pride in that moment, the purpose it gave her, was palpable. Even all those years later; even though most of the generation that fought World War II was dead.

Mamaw felt that some connective glue bonded generations past and present and that these moments in history were important components of that glue. These memories created communion between our ancestors and our descendants. It's one of the reasons I became so enraged by the Bush administration's response to 9/11. They marshaled that reserve of patriotic goodwill to sell a series of disastrous conflicts. And as destructive as the war in Iraq was, it always bothered me more that it was sold to the American people by tapping into the very best of us.

When they told us this was our generation's fight, just as Germany and Japan were Mamaw's fight, when they told us Saddam Hussein was the Hitler of the new century, and that we had this last opportunity to stop him, they were misusing the story that gave Mamaw's life meaning. That story is a precious thing, and leaders owe a sacred obligation to use it carefully.

And if my own mortality and hell's torments are never something I've been particularly afraid of, I am very much afraid of losing this story. Of losing the glue that connects me to my grandmother, the generations that came before her, and the generations that will thrive—or not—long after I'm buried.

* * *

When I first made some money, I reached out to an eighty-year-old cousin to buy the family cemetery in Eastern Kentucky. I spoke about this cemetery—probably about a half acre—in my acceptance speech at the 2024 Republican National Convention. Even as vice president, I try to visit at least once a year. It's a beautiful part of the country, my favorite part in many ways, and I still have relatives there whom I love to see.

But I also visit because I find it oddly comforting to know that I'll be buried among my ancestors. I walk in that ancient plot of land and speak to people long dead, some of them gone before my grandmother was even born. I've visited that cemetery before every major life decision, from proposing to Usha to running for the Senate. I listen to the birds chirp and watch the grasshoppers dance from grave to grave, and I remember that I used to chase the ancestors of those grasshoppers in these very mountains, when the people now buried were alive and breathing and watching over me.

I talk to my grandparents and my great-grandparents, like patron saints of the episodes and emotions we all experience in the course of life. I talk to Mamaw when I need strength or focus and to Papaw when I need wisdom. I talk to Mamaw's mother, Mamaw Blanton, when I need kindness or empathy and to her father, Papaw Blaine, whom I never met, when I need toughness.

I bought the cemetery for selfless reasons. I wanted to preserve this outdoor temple of the dead for my family and the sake of those buried. But I bought it for selfish reasons, too: for the moments of quiet reflection I find only in this place, unique in all the world. I bought it so that when I am buried, my children will have a place to visit and speak to their ancestors.

I took Usha there before we married, thinking about *The Year of Magical Thinking* and her own reflections on death. I didn't expect a particular reaction, but I had to show it to her. I joked that if we ever got married, she didn't have to worry about a burial plot. She laughed and told me she'd prefer cremation to a hole in the ground in Eastern Kentucky.

"Fine." I laughed in return as I pointed to a plot right next to Mamaw and Papaw. "I'll toss the ashes in here with me."

If Usha's fear of death was more personal, mine was more collective. I'm terrified, not of dying or being buried, but of occupying a grave that my children never visit. I fear the emptiness of a beautiful church, and the possibility that it will never be as vibrant or alive as it once was.

* * *

My big fear isn't death but that we inherited a great civilization and are slowly letting it fall into disrepair. I may never meet my ancestors in the next life, but if I do, I don't want them to tell me that they built magnificent buildings and we let them crumble, that they drafted beautiful works of literature and we spit out clichés on social media, that they went to the moon with slide rules but we couldn't get back even with the aid of the supercomputers that they also built.

I explained this fear to a priest. Does God really care about our civilization? Our works of art? Our beautiful buildings?

He explained that a core tenet of Christian political philosophy—going back to Saint Augustine in *The City of God*—is that political or temporal success doesn't necessarily follow Christian virtue.

Sometimes God rewards the pagans and sometimes He punishes them. Sometimes God rewards the Christians and sometimes He doesn't. Some of what the pagan Romans built still stands, but much was destroyed. The same is true for the Christian Romans. God works in mysterious ways, and we don't always understand His plan.

"But," the priest explained, "a lot of this civilizational inheritance still stands, and it stands as a testament to God. It is an instrument. When you look at a beautiful church, you don't just feel nostalgia; you feel a sense of duty to build on that legacy. That is God using these instruments." His words were truer for me than he realized. It was, after all, a beautiful cathedral that helped call me back to faith.

"One of the wounds of sin is the veil of death, which violently separates us. Faith in Christ involves trust that His victory over death will be true for us, too. That the chains of communion will continue to bind us even after death."

In America we often use the phrase *may he rest in peace* after the death of someone we care about. This comes from a common prayer at Christian funerals: "eternal rest grant unto him, O lord." In the Eastern Christian tradition—think Greek or Russian Orthodox—they use the phrase *memory eternal.* It comes from the thief who hung next to Christ on the cross, who asks Jesus, "Remember me when thou comest into thy kingdom." So it's primarily a prayer to God—a request that God remember the dead eternally.

But I like to think of it as a command to the living, to remember what the dead loved and did and said. In my hardest moments, I remember the things my grandmother said to me when I was a little boy. And I say those things to my kids and hope they'll remember them long after I'm dead. Memory eternal is the promise that when you speak to the dead, they say something back, even if only as a vapor from the past.

And memory eternal is the promise that something about you will live on, even if only as vapors passed from one generation to another.

The philosopher Ernest Becker argued that the fear of death motivates much of human civilization. Knowing that we'll die, we try to achieve some sort of symbolic immortality to give meaning to what is, inevitably, a short-term project on this earth. I always found this idea a little absurd, at least as applied to myself. It's hard to imagine a nonexistent fear motivating my decisions.

But perhaps a fear of death comes in many forms. For most of us, it's a recognition that our physical bodies will die. For others, it's a serious case of FOMO—a fear of missing out; not death itself, but the knowledge that the party will inevitably go on without us. And for someone like me, it's a sense of despair over the prospect of leaving things worse off than we found them—a death, not of an individual, but of the civilization that gave an individual's life meaning.

Memory eternal is the antidote to all of this. Whether you're worried about yourself or your civilization, it addresses the despair that so many people feel. It ensures that the communion we seek in life runs not only among those living today but also across the generations that came before us and those yet to come. Some may say that this is too instrumental a view of religion. But if a set of beliefs is going to work, it must be both true and relevant: A truth that doesn't speak to people is like a seed sown in the desert.

* * *

According to Christian teaching, Simon Peter the Apostle went to Rome after Christ ascended into heaven and began his process of evangelizing what was then the center of the Western world. Christians in the first century faced extraordinary persecution in Rome. It's not an exaggeration to say that Christianity's journey to become the largest religion in the world started in Rome with Peter. Though it took centuries, Christianity would become the official religion of the Roman Empire, and through that empire it would spread across the globe.

The story goes something like this: Emperor Constantine, three centuries after the death of Christ, found himself presiding over an empire racked by increasing religious strife. The Christian religion, birthed in a small outpost of the empire, was picking up adherents. But its followers posed a political problem, so the political authorities persecuted Christians, sometimes aggressively.

During one of Constantine's battles, a bright cross appeared in the sky, with the words *In hoc signo vinces*—"By this sign, you shall conquer."

Constantine won the battle, ended the persecution of Christians, and began constructing some of the great churches of Rome—including Saint Peter's Basilica, the seat of the Pope. And history marched on from there.

But if you go back another few hundred years, you'd be forgiven for thinking this fledgling religion would disappear like so many cults of the ancient world. Simon Peter—a revered figure among all Christians but considered the first Pope by Catholics—didn't have an emperor on his side. He encountered great persecution. Many of his followers were put to death.

In fact, Christ said this would happen. In the Book of Luke, Christ explicitly tells His apostles that they will be harassed, tormented, even killed in His name. In Sean McDowell's exhaustive analysis *The Fate of the Apostles*, he argues that most apostles suffered an unknown fate—history simply didn't record well what happened to them. But five of Christ's original twelve apostles likely died as martyrs, killed because they refused to say they had made it all up. There's your model for belief—to die for the simple truth that Jesus Christ came back to life after He had been crucified and killed.

Simon *Peter*, first among Christ's apostles—the rock (*petra*) upon which He would build His church—may have suffered the grisliest death. Three hundred years before Constantine would build a church to the religion Peter brought to Rome, Peter was crucified just like his master. By some accounts, he asked to be crucified upside down. Most researchers (secular or otherwise) agree that Peter was martyred in Rome, likely around AD 66, at the hands of Emperor Nero.

Different Christian denominations ascribe varying levels of reverence to Peter. Some think he was merely an important early Christian leader. Others—in particular, Catholics—see him as the first head of a unified Christian Church. But I find his story especially reassuring, however you understand Peter's role in the early Church, despite his particularly violent end.

The lesson of Peter is that, yes, a particular belief can cause real pain or suffering. Yes, it can even get you killed. But there's a continuity across the generations. There is work done in this life, seeds planted whose fruit death conceals.

You can imagine Peter, crucified upside down on a hill in Rome called Vaticanus, suffering terribly, looking out with his dying breath at the greatest and most powerful empire in the history of the world. By every objective measure, the political power of Rome had triumphed over the spiritual power of the Gospel. If Peter could see any of his followers, he knew he was leaving them to a life of persecution and struggle. There was no obvious triumph in Peter's life, no temporal victory.

The very thing I fear is the thing that Simon Peter—fisherman from Galilee turned evangelist in Rome—experienced: death without triumph. Death knowing that your friends will be worse off, at least in the short term. Death without any certainty that your earthly labors will bear fruit.

And in this fear, my own vanity convicts me. For the story of Peter is not of a cult leader who died and left a fledgling church. It is the story of a man who, if you believe as we do, saw his friend and teacher crucified and then literally raised from the dead. It is the story of a man who saw God Himself manifested in the flesh. It is the story of a man drowning at sea, rescued by the son of God walking on water. And it is the story of a man who came into a heavenly reward after death. To focus on his earthly punishment is to ignore the lesson of his life, and the faith that gave it purpose.

If I am at risk of ignoring the rewards of heaven, I also ignore one of the more temporal implications of Christian civilization: that toil doesn't always lead to instant gratification. Many of the Christian leaders who fought for the abolition of chattel slavery never saw their work rewarded. Many of the Christian leaders who worked to feed hungry children held children as they starved to death. The first apostle was tortured to death, possibly nailed to a cross upside down, in a foreign city surrounded by the most powerful and hostile empire in the world.

One of the most important lessons of the Gospel for Christians is that God works mysteriously—frustratingly, even—on His time, not ours. We are called to action, yes, but we are also called to humility about the consequence of that action.

I first visited Rome nearly two thousand years after Simon Peter's death, about seventeen hundred years after Constantine first saw His sign. Not long after Constantine made Christianity the religion of the empire that had murdered Peter, he sent Roman soldiers to the site of Christ's death and resurrection to save as much of the history as possible. If you ever visit the site of Christ's crucifixion in the old city in Jerusalem, you will stand inside a church started by the Roman Emperor Constantine.

And in the square where Peter was put to death, you will find brilliant grand columns of travertine stretching several football fields in length, forming the boundaries of what we call Saint Peter's Square.

The second time I visited Rome was to celebrate the inauguration of Pope Leo XIV. Two thousand years after Peter was put to death, a man whom billions understand to be the 266th successor of Peter celebrated his inaugural Mass. The Roman Empire had fallen centuries earlier, but the Church founded by Jesus Christ was still going strong.

As I stood there in Rome, looking out at the hundreds of thousands gathered to celebrate this occasion, the historical irony—maybe it was even a catharsis—washed over me.

I wondered if Simon, the Jewish fisherman, ever thought to himself that the empire that saw the death of his Lord (and later him) would disappear, but the church that Peter—Christ's rock of the ages—had started in Rome would endure.

And while the political establishment of the Roman Empire long ago disintegrated, the churches built over the millennia were still standing and inspiring the faithful. The Gospel preached precariously in the early days of the Church was now the foundation of faith for over 2.5 billion Christians. It took some time, and many of the men and women who worked hardest for the Church saw it only at its worst moments, from its persecutions to its moral failings. But the Gospel endured, nonetheless.

Here in Rome it was obvious:

Caesar was dead.

Christ still lived.

EPILOGUE

By Their Fruits

A friend once told me that "optimism"—a sort of blind faith that things will be better in the future—is misguided, and that it's much better to be hopeful. Hope is the antidote to despair and one of the fundamental Christian virtues. To believe in God and His only begotten son is to have hope.

There is much in my life that gives me hope for the future. While undoubtedly imperfect, our country remains the most dynamic in the world—with innovations on the horizon that will allow us to cure diseases and reach the stars. My family is healthy and happy, and I can't help but see the beauty in the world through my children's eyes. When I published *Hillbilly Elegy* in 2016, I thought my mom would never meet her future grandchildren. Today, she is eleven years sober and our three kids love her dearly.

One of the great Christian lessons in my life is the power of redemption. The resentment I once felt toward my mother has faded away, replaced by admiration for her humor and patience with my own kids. Their birth gave Mom and me a second chance. "Life is good" has taken on a new meaning for me, as I have seen new human life heal old hurts and build new bridges.

It is perhaps because I've seen the power of new life that I worry so much about the declining population of the Western world. In every advanced economy save Israel—the tiny Jewish state—native-born population numbers are falling. This includes the Christian (or formerly Christian) countries of Europe and the Asian Tigers.

The reasons for this decline are complicated, but the best explanation ties to religiosity and secularism: The more religious a country it is, the better it fares with family formation. This is why Israel alone is exempt from this trend and why fertility is much higher in the United States than the rest of the Western world—we're far less secular than Europe. Still, here, as in multiple Western countries, more people are dying than being born. Our abandonment of Christian culture has coincided with an apparent decline in our collective will to live.

In private, world leaders raise this issue often. Whatever country they're from and regardless of their politics, they are aware this is a problem. Many countries have tried to reverse the trend with generous subsidies or other social programs. And each nation worries about it for different reasons. One German leader told me it would be hard to increase their military power because they simply didn't have enough young people to recruit. Others have anxiously observed that their pension programs are going bankrupt and their economies lack dynamism because of their shrinking labor forces.

These are all valid concerns, but the absence of babies worries me for more fundamental reasons. My children gave my mother and me a second chance. My cousins are some of my closest friends. How many friendships will never blossom, and how many families will never heal, because we have deprived ourselves of children?

I loved Japan when I visited a couple of years ago, but how will it flourish or even exist after another century of population decline?

And of course, babies are downstream of romantic love. A society without children is a society without that, too.

As a teenager, I admired (and I still do) James Dobson, the conservative Christian radio broadcaster. In the 1990s, Dobson often discussed the dangerous rise of pornographic culture. Social conservatives predicted at the time that the decline of sexual morality would lead to a world of sexual anarchy and promiscuity.

Yet, instead of promiscuity, we got a generation of young people who are lonely and isolated. Studies have shown that young adults in 2025 date and have sex less than any generation alive today.[1] Whatever the faults of the hookup culture of late-2000s Ohio State, at least young people were meeting and falling in love with one another. We replaced that culture with dating apps that don't produce much dating.

Between my speaking events and working with young staffers, I talk to a lot of young people. Their descriptions of modern dating sound like scenes from a postapocalyptic movie. The lucky ones find themselves in "situationships" that have little chance of progressing to anything more serious. The unlucky ones are lonely and frustrated.

Sometimes a young person will ask me—well, more often Usha, really—to set them up with someone, and we'll say, "We can try. What are you looking for?"

---

1 Institute for Family Studies, "Adults Are Having Less Sex Than Ever, with Gen Z Seeing the Steepest Decline: Study," September 11, 2025, https://ifstudies.org/in-the-news/adults-are-having-less-sex-than-ever-with-gen-z-seeing-the-steepest-decline-study.

"Honestly," they'll tell us. "What you guys have."

And this breaks my heart because, as lucky as I've been in life and love, I'm not alone—most of my friends in our generation found genuine happiness. The next generation sees our success as so unusual that it borders on a fluke.

A few friends at Turning Point USA—the youth political organization—held a focus group to better understand the pitfalls of modern love for its Gen Z members. Turning Point's membership leans politically conservative, but the panel confirmed what the data tell us: Many young people have exited the dating market altogether. Young women and men are frustrated by how few of their peers want to find love.

One young woman noted how social media has degraded social skills. "I think a lot of relationships between guys and girls can even be somewhat awkward," she said. "Especially the first time meeting somebody, because the majority of our communication is done online now." Another young man put it more depressingly: "You're just sending photos back and forth on Snapchat. You're not really communicating."

When I read through the full report from this focus group, I was struck by how these young people misperceived one another. The men talked about how none of the women wanted to get married or have kids, even though that's what the women said they wanted. The women talked about how none of the men wanted to get married or have kids, even though that's what the men said they wanted.

And yet, the survey revealed one bright spot. Not the dating apps, which everyone agreed produced either loneliness or situationships. But, as one young man with a girlfriend said, "Where people actually do end up in a serious relationship, they're meeting through friends or through church." The technology that promised to connect these young people has failed them, but the most ancient social technology of them all—the congregation—is bringing them together.

* * *

Much has been made about rising racism in modern America. In 2021, Gallup found that race relations had reached their lowest level in a decade.[2] On the left, people worry about a rising tide of white supremacism. On the right, people worry about rising anti-white rhetoric or anti-Semitism on college campuses.

From the intermarriage of the Spanish and native populations in Mexico to the American melting pot of the nineteenth century to the Civil Rights Movement, Christianity has long brought people together. And yet, as our leaders have ushered in an unprecedented increase in demographic diversity through immigration, they have simultaneously discarded the most powerful force for cultural cohesion: Christianity. It is hardly any surprise that the fruits of their labor are rising racial conflict and gender division. Secularism has produced social strife despite its promises of enlightenment.

Now, you might be thinking: *But our country has always had religious freedom and rejected the idea of a state religion. Are you saying you have to be a Christian to be an American?*

Not at all. As I said in a speech in late 2025:

2 Gallup, "Race Relations," accessed March 12, 2026, https://news.gallup.com/poll/1687/race-relations.aspx.

> I'm not saying you have to be a Christian to be an American. I'm saying something simpler and truer: Christianity is America's creed, the shared moral language from the Revolution to the Civil War and beyond.
>
> Across that history, our country's major debates have always centered on how we could best, as a people, please God. That creed motivated our understanding of natural law and rights, our sense of duty to one's neighbor, the conviction that the strong must protect the weak, and the belief in individual conscience.
>
> Even our famously American idea of religious liberty is a Christian concept. Because we're all creatures of God, we must respect each individual's pathway to that God.

To put it more simply: I'm not demanding that you become a Christian, though I'd welcome it. I'm proposing that we have now run an experiment of replacing a Christian culture with something else for decades. And the fruit of that experiment includes rising racial strife, a gender gap among our young people, falling rates of love and partnership, and a society with a declining population.

I want to be clear on something: I'm not criticizing just the political left. Each of us, in our own weird ways, is guilty of casting aside the Christian inheritance of our civilization. Republicans are far too willing to worship the market and assume that free commercial transactions inevitably lead to good. Democrats are far too willing to idolize the self and assume that everything done in the name of self-discovery is good.

We know what can go wrong here: Business leaders move factories away from honest workers in Michigan to sweatshops in Asia in the name of market forces. And moms and dads walk out on their families in the name of self-discovery.

We ought to stop worshiping such false idols and get back to worshiping God.

Ironically, one of Christianity's greatest fruits is that it produces societies that are strong enough to tolerate remarkable debate and dissent. It's not a surprise that virtually all of the modern theories of government arose in Christian societies.

I have a friend who describes himself as a Nietzschean—a follower of the German philosopher Friedrich Nietzsche. He is openly scornful of my Christianity, calling it a slave religion. I laugh when he tells me that Christianity is how weak institutions keep strong people down and that if I ever want to realize my full potential, I'll need to discard my faith.

He has many other ideas that you might consider offensive, and on at least some of them, I'd agree with you. There was a time when I would have found him less a curiosity and more a danger. But my Christian faith anchors me enough that I mostly just find him interesting. And I feel the same way about my libertarian friends or when I come across an academic with a Marxist critique of society.

In *Sentimental Education*, Gustave Flaubert describes early nineteenth-century Paris as a bustling place, as much for its ideas as its commerce. Young men and women would debate monarchism versus republicanism, the ideas of the Church set against the ideas of Charles Fourier. For any person yearning for an intellectually rich life, a nearly 100 percent Catholic society from two centuries ago is far more interesting than a secular college campus in 2026.

How did we end up here? We replaced real diversity of thought with superficial diversity. Show up to a college campus protest today and you'll likely see people who present as alternative: people with pink or purple hair, unusual piercings and tattoos, or different pronouns.

Yet the ideas in their heads will differ little from the conversations in the corporate boardrooms of Apple or McKinsey. Their inch-deep diversity conceals a conformism so intense that they refuse to befriend people who think differently from them.

I wonder if this groupthink explains why previous American generations saw much higher economic growth than we have today. People who fear dissenting ideas will fundamentally fear the future. Luckily, there remain in our country enough true intellectual mavericks to get us to Mars and beyond. Our Christian culture is weakened, but far from gone.

* * *

The past few years of my life have been defined by one triumph—my election as Vice President of the United States—and two tragedies, one an act of God and the other of man.

When I was still a senator, I got a call from my dad telling me he was having some trouble swallowing and was undergoing a battery of tests. Dad was not the type of person to complain about medical problems, so I knew it was serious. A week later, my half brother, Cory, told me that our father had stage 4 esophageal cancer and—if the doctors were right—had only weeks to live.

My return to faith had given Dad and me a common language again, but even as adults, our relationship felt like a work in progress. Whatever had led him to give me up for adoption when I was six, I had never thought it was cruelty. But those years of separation had still left their mark. As did the fact that I had chosen to take my maternal grandfather's last name—Vance—rather than my actual dad's. There had always been a gulf between us, though it had shrunk over time.

Nothing bridged that divide more than the arrival of my own kids, who loved their Papaw (and Mamaw, as they called my stepmother). We spent time together over holidays and whenever else we could spare it. My dad accompanied me on long walks through Cincinnati and Washington, DC, and made fun of me for picking up our dog's poop—something he had never done in the rural settings he called home. We talked about Jesus, and marriage, and family, and Ohio State football. My relationships with my mom and dad taught me that genuine healing is possible, that hurt and pain need not define any one person, or two people, or their connection to one another.

For my dad and me, at least, cancer would cut that relationship short.

Dad was certain throughout his illness that God would heal him. He rejected chemo because he knew it would make him sick, and he printed Bible verses about God's healing powers to reassure me that he would be around for years to come. He attended faith healing seminars at his church. When his illness took a particularly dark turn, I sat by his bedside as we listened to beautiful Pentecostal worship music. Before I left his side, I gave him a long hug and told him that I loved him. He asked my stepmother why I seemed to be saying "goodbye."

"Doesn't JD know," Dad asked, "that God will heal me?"

It was one of his last lucid days on this earth.

God did not heal him.

He died a few days later.

In truth, I was angry that we never had much closure. We never had the sort of conversation we might have had, had we known it would be our last. He maintained he would be healed until he could no longer keep it up.

"I hope that when I go," I told Usha, "I am not in denial about it. I want to be able to say goodbye."

* * *

I became Vice President of the United States not long after my dad's death, and about eight months into the term, I finished a meeting and looked at my phone. My text messages were lighting up in group chats that included Charlie Kirk, the conservative media star and Turning Point USA founder.

"Praying for you CK," read one.

"Hang in there Charlie, we love you buddy."

I walked out of my office, and my staff looked like they had seen a ghost.

"Charlie was shot," my chief of staff, Jacob, told me. "It doesn't look good."

Charlie was perhaps my best friend and closest confidant in the world of politics. He was one of the few people I talked to about the stresses the national campaign placed on our family. He stood in the front row during my 2024 Republican National Convention speech—the biggest moment of my life in the public eye—smiling and cheering the whole way. Because he was incapable of envy, he was everyone's biggest cheerleader.

Politics is a dirty business sometimes, one where you have to make compromises and shape the public narrative in order to achieve the best possible—rather than the perfect—outcome. Charlie served as my sounding board and strategic partner. He called me in the summer of 2025 to talk about two things he was seeing among young conservatives that really worried him. The first was that they were very angry about Israeli influence in American politics. The second was that some were going from legitimate disagreement with the Israeli government to anti-Semitism.

"Young people think we allow Israel too much influence over our foreign policy, and they're concerned about it. But for some, that concern is turning to anger, and even Jew hatred."

Charlie was unusually perceptive. He saw that heated foreign policy disagreements, filtered through the internet, could bleed into ethnic hatred, and he worried about it. And while Charlie loved Israel, he agreed with a lot of his young fans that the Israeli government was not always aligned with the interests of the United States. He knew the situation was delicate and complicated, and he treated it with genuine care, appealing to the better angels in all of us. He did so in his conversations with the president and me, but also in the ways he engaged his massive following. Charlie worked directly with young activists on how to prevent their views on this political issue from feeding bigotry. And he did the same on so many issues, from family policy to immigration. I selfishly thought in that moment that I didn't know what I'd do without his guiding voice.

Of course, I hoped above all that he would survive for his wife and kids. I hoped he would survive because it was unjust to deprive a young man of so much life. And for the hour or so after he was shot, I thought he might. We prayed that God would save him. But God saw it differently. He didn't answer my prayers in the way I thought best.

Usha and I flew the next day to Utah to escort his body back to Arizona. It was the least I could do. His parents and sister were in shock, and his wife, Erika, was utterly devastated. I had never seen a person so heavy with grief. It is one thing to lose an elderly parent. This was something else.

Erika alternated between sobbing so much she couldn't speak and sharing beloved memories about Charlie. In moments like this, I feel the need to say something profound or comforting. But there was nothing to say, so I listened.

Erika's thoughts kept returning to her kids. Charlie had been a devoted and loving father, and it crushed her to think that their children—then aged one and three—would have few, if any, personal memories of him.

I realized that in such moments, everything worldly we value fades to nothing. Erika didn't care that her husband was politically influential or had the president's ear. She cared about her babies and the fact that an assassin had stolen Charlie from them—so many memories and moments with their father robbed from them forever.

"He never yelled at me. Never cussed at me. Never lost his temper with me or the kids," she said. And in the impromptu eulogy of her deceased husband, Erika convicted me, though I'm sure she didn't know it. Had I ever yelled or lost my temper with the kids? Indeed.

I found myself wondering what my wife and kids would say

about me if an assassin took my life. Mostly good things, I thought. But none of them will care that I was the vice president.

Charlie was a person of profound faith. After his death, public commentators debated whether he, a lifelong evangelical, was on the verge of converting to Catholicism. He had certainly appreciated some things about Catholicism. He called himself the most Catholic evangelical in the world, and he admired the Catholic Church's ancient traditions and respect for Mary. In one public radio broadcast, he said that too many Christians had lost sight of the importance of the Mother of God.

"Some Catholics come too close to worshiping her," he once told me. "But she is undoubtedly the most important human being to ever live"—he didn't count Christ as purely human—"and we ought not to ignore her."

But Charlie loved much about the American evangelical church. It's hardly a coincidence that his memorial service felt as much like an old-fashioned American revival as it did a funeral. My guess is that he would ultimately never have become Catholic, but who knows? The Lord cut his journey short.

Charlie taught me to love all parts of our Christian communion. I take from Charlie a certain charity about the body of Christ—the Church, defined very broadly. I am proud of my denomination, and I follow its (very strict!) rules as well as I can. When I fail, I go to confession and get back on the proverbial horse.

But if Charlie was right, and I think he was, there are things we Catholics can learn from Protestants, and vice versa.

That has to be true. Otherwise, why would God have allowed His Church to scatter and divide like this?

We Christians are only able to argue about grace and good

works, the veneration of saints, and the legitimacy of ecclesiastical authority because God gave us brains, and part of how we come to know Him is by figuring it out together.

After Charlie's assassination, his political opponents surfaced clips of him making inflammatory comments on this or that topic. Some even went so far as to celebrate his death or suggest he'd had it coming. But most people, even those with wildly different political views, remembered a man who would rather debate ideas than commit violence against his opponents. And they recognized that Charlie, barely thirty years old when he was killed, was still learning and evolving, as we all do over the course of our lives.

For every clip of Charlie as an ideological pugilist, there were a dozen of him patiently discussing an issue, or encouraging his fans to let a nervous kid speak, or offering to pray with someone he disagreed with. Charlie contained multitudes, and I took some satisfaction from the eulogies noticing that fact. At his best, he shined as an amazing example of Christian charity. At his worst, he was a sinner, like all of us.

One silver lining of Charlie's death is that it forced me to look at my father's passing in a new light. Dad and I never said goodbye, it's true, but I never said goodbye to Charlie either. Life and death don't always tie up together in a neat bow.

I came to see my dad's strength—how even as his health declined, he never complained. He was, in the final weeks of his life, effectively starving to death, unable to eat even a bite of food. Yet he would offer his grandchildren ice cream and donuts and everything else he desperately wanted for himself but couldn't have. God may not have healed my father's earthly body, but He did give him a divine patience to endure this final burden. Who was I to judge my dad's confidence that God would heal him? It gave him comfort and the strength to live his final months on this earth fully.

In the months after Charlie's death, I often picked up the phone to call him. I always hung up quickly, realizing before the first ring that my friend would not answer.

In Psalm 73, Asaph pleads with God, wondering why good men suffer while the wicked prosper. It is a tale as old as time: Bad things happen, and fate seems to mock us as a good man dies of cancer or is shot in the neck not even a month after his daughter celebrates her third birthday. And as all this tragedy unfolds, we are somehow meant to believe that an all-powerful God loves us and still allows this crap to happen.

To even utter it sounds so absurd.

And yet I do believe it. I believe it because the Church has endured through chaos and fracture for two thousand years. I believe it because I have seen faith transform the lives of people from every class and station. I believe it because I have knelt at the site of Jesus Christ's crucifixion and felt the presence of God.

As Christians, we are all, together, part of the same Church. Those who suffered and those who prospered. Those who voted for me and those who didn't. The living and the dead. My grandmother and my father, though they disliked each other. Charlie Kirk and Pope Francis, despite their different views. Saint Augustine and Father Henry. Me and my son.

I believe in that communion of saints, and I believe that although God sometimes rewards the wicked and punishes the good for reasons we can't possibly understand, He also casts upon us little rays of light even in the darkest moments.

And so it was for me. As my wife held Charlie Kirk's widow on the first day of her terrible sorrow, Erika told Usha between sobs that she regretted having only two kids with Charlie.

For years I had asked Usha to have another baby, and for years she had told me she was done—especially now that public service had elevated us into the national spotlight.

But something changed for Usha, and not long after we buried my friend, she became pregnant with our fourth child, a boy.

One life was stolen from us, but another was given.

I don't know why God does things like this. But I am grateful to Him that there will soon be another source of joy in our lives. Another person added to the communion of our family and hopefully to that of the Church. Another person to whom I will sing, "Jesus loves me, this I know." Another beautiful soul to wonder at, and fall in love with, God's beautiful creation.

As our son grows, the world will continue to spin round and round. I pray to God that I will be a good father. And that our son will one day in turn be a good father. And that after I'm gone, our son and I will be blessed with generations to follow.

Because *life is good.*

Our human story will oscillate between tragedy and comedy, while God's love and creation will inspire, confuse, and at times anger us.

But through all of that, I'm certain God's Church will endure, because Jesus Christ and His truths endure. And we will all get our chance to make our mark on His Church before we enjoy the rewards of heaven—and communion with Him.

Amen.

ACKNOWLEDGMENTS

I decided to write this book back in 2017, and have written off and on pretty much since then. Because of that, there are many people who helped make it possible. (And for anyone I accidentally left out, I am sorry!)

Jacob Reses, now my chief of staff at the Office of the Vice President, and Amalia Halikias, provided invaluable research and editorial feedback, especially early in the writing process.

Chris Buskirk and Pascal-Emmanuel Gobry read early drafts and helped refine the thesis. Jonathan Jao (my former editor) and Dorian Karchmar (my agent) gave valuable feedback. Sean Desmond, my editor at Harper, gave the book a breath of fresh air (and new life) and had great patience as the book was delayed by national campaigns and then by national governance.

Father Henry Stephan and Andrew Walker provided extremely helpful commentary on some of the book's theological arguments—implicit and explicit—and helped me crystallize my own thoughts.

James Hitchcock proved an invaluable editor, working through multiple drafts and refining various concepts, especially down the stretch.

I am grateful to all of them.

But I am most grateful to Usha, whose patience and skill as an editor made the book possible at first, and then better over time. There is at least a little irony in the fact that my non-Christian wife helped lead me back to my own Christian faith, and then made it possible for me to discuss the journey on paper. The Lord works in mysterious ways, indeed.

ABOUT THE AUTHOR

JD Vance currently serves as the Vice President of the United States. He is also the author of the bestselling memoir *Hillbilly Elegy* and a former senator from Ohio. A US Marine Corps veteran of the Iraq War, Vance later worked in venture capital, investing in and advising companies focused on economic growth in the Midwest. He lives with his wife, Usha, and their children.